POLICE UNLIMITED

CLARENDON STUDIES IN CRIMINOLOGY

Published under the auspices of the Institute of Criminology, University of Cambridge; the Mannheim Centre, London School of Economics; and the Centre for Criminology, University of Oxford.

RECENT TITLES IN THIS SERIES:

Personalizing the State: The Anthropology of Law, Politics and Welfare at the UK's Margins
Koch

Common Enemies: Crime, Policy, and Politics in Australia–Indonesia Relations
McKenzie

Embodying Punishment: Emotions, Identities, and Lived Experiences in Women's Prisons
Chamberlen

Professionalizing the Police: The Unfulfilled Promise of Police Training
Fielding

Getting Out: Early Release in England and Wales, 1960–1995
Guiney

Sentencing Policy and Social Justice
Henham

Cold Case Reviews: DNA, Detective Work and Unsolved Major Crimes
Allsop

Police Unlimited

Policing, Migrants, and the Values of Bureaucracy

PAUL MUTSAERS

OXFORD
UNIVERSITY PRESS

OXFORD
UNIVERSITY PRESS

Great Clarendon Street, Oxford, OX2 6DP,
United Kingdom

Oxford University Press is a department of the University of Oxford.
It furthers the University's objective of excellence in research, scholarship,
and education by publishing worldwide. Oxford is a registered trade mark of
Oxford University Press in the UK and in certain other countries

First Edition published in 2019

Impression: 1

Published in the United States of America by Oxford University Press
198 Madison Avenue, New York, NY 10016, United States of America

British Library Cataloguing in Publication Data

Data available

Library of Congress Control Number: 2018962988

ISBN 978–0–19–878850–8

Printed and bound by
CPI Group (UK) Ltd, Croydon, CR0 4YY

For Marleen, Maarten, and Midas

General Editors' Introduction

The *Clarendon Studies in Criminology* series aims to provide a forum for outstanding theoretical and empirical work in all aspects of criminology and criminal justice, broadly understood. The Editors welcome submissions from established scholars, as well as excellent PhD work. The Series was inaugurated in 1994, with Roger Hood as its first General Editor, following discussions between Oxford University Press and Oxford's Centre for Criminological Research. It is edited under the auspices of three centres: the Institute of Criminology at the University of Cambridge, the Mannheim Centre for Criminology at the London School of Economics, and the Centre for Criminological Research at the University of Oxford. Each supplies members of the Editorial Board and, in turn, the Series Editor or Editors.

Police Unlimited: Policing, Migrants, and the Values of Bureaucracy offers a compelling account of the Dutch police force and its relationship to ethno-racial profiling practices. Based on long-term ethnographic and multi-sited fieldwork with various police teams across the Netherlands, much of the book explores a paradox at the heart of Dutch policing: at a time when the Dutch police force has become more concerned than ever to combat ethno-racial profiling, racial tensions both within the work force and with regards to street policing, remain strong. Paul Mutsaers argues that this paradox can only be grasped by moving away from dominant views of the police force as either an all-embracing system or alternatively as an assemblage of idiosyncratic individuals. Rather, the focus has to be placed on dominant 'frames' (social rules or guiding principles) that give direction to individual officers' actions, sometimes against their own intentions. The most dominant frame operating in the contemporary police force, Mutsaers tells us, is a 'psychologising discourse' that reduces ethno-racial tensions to problems of individual cognition and behaviour and hence constructs them as private issues that are then excluded from public debate or interest. Paul Mutsaers weaves his ethnographic observations into a theoretically sophisticated analysis in clever and convincing fashion. The case studies provided illustrate the complex social and political processes that are conducive towards ethno-racial profiling both within the police force and in relation to migrants. These include popular media and political discourses that demonise ethnic minorities, the wide discretionary powers given to police officers in their daily policing, and management styles that devolve responsibilities onto individuals in tense situations.

This work will undoubtedly appeal to academic researchers with an interest in policing, migration, and law and society, and it will also be of interest to social anthropologists. Indeed, the book exemplifies the riches that can be gained in taking a multi-disciplinary approach to matters. We also think that the book will appeal to police practitioners and to members of the public concerned about policing, police and minority ethnic group relations, and policing and migration. As Editors, we commend the author for making significant contribution to the field of criminology and to our understanding of the complexities of policing in a political and racialized context. We are very pleased to welcome *Police Unlimited: Policing, Migrants, and the Values of Bureaucracy to the Clarendon Studies in Criminology* series.

Loraine Gelsthorpe and Kyle Treiber
Institute of Criminology, University of Cambridge
January, 2019

Acknowledgements

My all-time favourite author, C. Wright Mills, wrote more than half a century ago that neither love nor hatred of work is inherent in man. For some it is a mere source of livelihood, for others a significant part of inner life, an exuberant expression of self. Both perspectives put a serious toll on the worker. The first category wants to restrict labour time, but often can't. The second always tends to lengthen the working day, but shouldn't. There is really only one person who has been able to prevent me from definitely falling into the second category and that is my wife, Marleen. Thank you for being the intensely human woman of acute intelligence, immense generosity, with a delightful sense of play and humour that you are. It was you who taught me the art of separation that keeps the academy, that greedy institution, out of our family life. Two beautiful sons, Maarten and Midas, remind us every day of the pure happiness that comes from it. I also thank our parents, Franka, Jos, Mariet, and Jacques, for always being there for us and for helping us navigate the intricate worlds of work and private life.

Many people have contributed something to shaping what has emerged between these covers. First and foremost, I would like to thank the many officers of the Dutch police for tolerating my presence for so long. Our conversations have been numerous and fruitful. I hope that this book repays some of my debts. Special gratitude goes to Senior Constable Murat Kiral, whose friendship I deeply value. Financial support for research was provided by the Police Academy of The Netherlands and I especially thank Roel Holvast and Peter van Os for their generosity. Tanya Pretorius at Fontys University helped me greatly to cross the t's and dot the i's.

At the Tilburg School of Humanities, I owe my gratitude to Odile Heynders, Jan Blommaert, Sjaak Kroon, Arie de Ruijter, Ad Backus, Piia Varis, Tom van Nuenen, Massimiliano Spotti, Fons van de Vijver, Karin Berkhout, Carine Zebedee, Erna van Ballegoy, Herman Beck, Jenny-Louise Van der Aa, and Willem Drees for their continuous support, also in more difficult times. I am particularly grateful to my former supervisor, Hans Siebers, whose intelligence and sharp wit led to numerous fruitful conversations that sparked my interest in the two main issues addressed in this book and for which I have built on his work: the migrant-hostility and psy-frames which are the two major sources of ethnic conflict and exclusion at the Dutch police.

Draft portions of the manuscript were presented at the European Group of Organization Studies Conference (2009 in Amsterdam), the International Critical Management Studies Conference (2009 in Warwick and 2011 in Naples), the Equality and Opportunity International Conference (2009 in Istanbul), the Australian Research Council's Centre of Excellence in Policing and Security International Conference (2010 in Canberra), the Criminal Justice Cooperation Conference (2010 in Canberra), the Annual Ethnography Symposium (2012 in Liverpool and 2013 in Amsterdam), the Joint Spring Conference of the American Ethnological Society and Association for Political and Legal Anthropology (2013 in Chicago), the Annual Meeting of the American Anthropological Association, the AAA (2014 in Washington DC), and, most recently, the Danish Institute for International Studies and the Danish Institute Against Torture Joint Workshop (2017 in Copenhagen).

Draft versions of this manuscript kept changing throughout all these years, and in the process, I have had the privilege of meeting many scholars who in one way or another helped me to bring this project to a conclusion. At the University of Oxford, Centre for Criminology, Mary Bosworth, Ana Aliverti, Ines Hasselberg, Andriani Fili, and Alpa Parmar, as well as all the other members of the Border Criminologies group deserve special mention. Our fenced world is in dire need of public border studies initiatives such as yours. An equally important public initiative is Anthropoliteia, a group blog on policing and security from an anthropological perspective. The anthropology of police would not be what it is today without Anthropoliteia and its general editor, Kevin Karpiak (Department of Sociology, Anthropology & Criminology at Eastern Michigan University). Thank you, Kevin, for including me in the blog, AAA panel discussions, journal publications, and book projects. One of these panel discussions—Critical Potentialities of the Anthropology of Policing: Accounts of Police, Power and Politics on Public Display—took place at the AAA annual meeting in Washington DC (2014) and I thank the participants for their great contributions: Eilat Maoz (University of Chicago), Craig William Schuetze (University of California, Santa Cruz), Michelle Stewart (University of Regina), and Simanti Dasgupta (University of Dayton). Most of all, I thank Beatrice Jauregui (University of Toronto) for being an excellent chair. Your anthropological work on police in India has been an inspiration for years.

Academic work can be both tedious and competitive, requiring a great deal of discipline to carry on the work. At times, encouragement is needed. I thank John van Maanen (MIT Sloan School of Management) for his timely intervention at the Annual Ethnography Symposium in Amsterdam (2013). John, you may not know it, but your support came at the exact right moment. I also thank Peter Albrecht (Danish Institute for International Studies) and Maya Christensen (Danish Institute Against Torture) for organizing an inspiring workshop on urban policing. This workshop confirmed it: the similarities between policing in the Global North and South are no longer to be denied. Last but not least, I thank Jennie Simpson for years of friendship and collegiality. Your public and applied anthropological work on criminal justice and mental health in the United States has helped me to stay close to the ground. Moreover, your reports from Washington DC on the radical turn in politics have kept me away from the popular desire to believe in a 'comfortable cleavage' between the Global North and South.

Finally, I wish to thank various editorial teams. I am grateful to the editorial teams of the British Journal of Criminology, Critique of Anthropology and Anthropology of Work Review for having secured such excellent reviews and for giving permission to reprint (parts of) my articles in this book. The editorial team of the Clarendon Series of Criminology of Oxford University Press has been very patient with me and has given me all the time I needed. Here we have a group of people who appreciate slow science. Thank you for everything, especially for the two excellent reviews, which have been crucial in advancing the arguments in this book.

All of you have given valuable input to this book, but I take responsibility for its contents entirely upon myself. The final product is my problem.

Paul Mutsaers

Contents

1

Introduction: The Anthropology of Police

> 'It's just that we are scared as hell when we encounter police!'[1]

After more than an hour of timid talk and table staring, it was finally said. Having gently pressed the group of Somali-Dutch women to tell him why they never volunteer crime-related information or stand up as witnesses, John, a community officer in Tilburg, was finally told that the Somali community considers the police a threat.[2] That day, the twenty women who were present in the community centre murmured in consent when one of them told their beat constable that the police was thought of as a security *risk*, not a security *provider*. Upon hearing this, John was somewhat puzzled at first. For many years, police talk in the department had been permeated with cultural stereotypes of minority groups such as the women in John's presence. In the same community centre where John had organized his meeting—together with other local authorities and a welfare organization—to talk about this vexing issue of legal alienation, he also attended a police training on what the Dutch police call 'multicultural craftsmanship'. During that two-day training it struck me that the legal alienation of Dutch Somalis (and other people from that region) was casually explained as a problem of their culture. Being told about the popular distinction between cultural collectivism and individualism, most of the ninety-something uniformed police officers that formed the police team I was observing then accepted the explanation that Somalis tend to retreat to their communities

[1] Somali-Dutch woman in Tilburg, The Netherlands, 2012

[2] Tilburg is an average-sized Dutch city on the border with Belgium and the hometown of the present author.

whenever difficulties (e.g. crime) occur. Insularity simply defined their place within the polity and this was explained in terms of cultural essentialism, not, for instance, in terms of state legitimacy, socio-legal order, or police–minority group relations.

'So, why are you afraid of us?' asked John, while fully aware of the fact that he was not included in the shared definition of 'us'. John was one of the exceptions, which may have to do with his own ethnic minority background, tracing back to Vietnam and Indonesia, or with the fact that he is the embodiment of good police ethics, the sort of officer who gives the public confidence in law enforcement as a neutral force.

In hindsight, as I encouraged him to think actively about it, he could formulate an answer to his own question. As we cycled back to the police station after the meeting was closed, John reminisced about his first days in the district. One of the first instructions he received was never to approach a group of Somali men alone. Although few of them have criminal careers, most officers were firmly of the view that these men are not to be trusted and that there is always the risk that they might suddenly lose their tempers and direct that anger towards the police. The fact that John is not exactly the prototypical police officer may account for his different view about risk and danger. While exchanging our thoughts, John came to the realization that the problem at hand had little to do with the Somali culture as a *group trait*, but with risk profiling by police as a cultural *process*, that is, a norm-based classification process, in this case regarding danger, deviancy, and delinquency. Reminding me of Douglas' work on the anthropology of risk, he ruminated about risk and danger as ideas that are always culturally conditioned and become prominent in the public's mind according to the strength of particular social concerns (Douglas 1992; Douglas and Wildavsky 1983). We talked at length about these public concerns and social criticisms—such as the negative representations of the Somali community in the local media or the deployment of political connections by local vigilantes to have Somalis banished from public places—and connected these to the ways police officers are biased towards highlighting certain risks and downplaying others, often to the detriment of already marginal migrant groups. Encouraged by an actuarial justice apparatus that is designed to scan risks and prevent crime, such profiling behaviour is rarely without consequences and serves as a good explanation for the migrant-hostile policing lamented by the Somali-Dutch women in the community centre.

Clearly proud of the fact that he was not going to give in so easily to this sort of stereotypical risk profiling, John told me about his first day in the district: 'Of course, I immediately joined these Somali men in the park and we had a nice conversation. Maybe it was because of my colour, but they really liked me and we had a good time.'

It is not inconceivable, however, that this was part of the problem the women were facing: the unpredictability of police behaviour. Some officers were friendly, others followed them like hawks. Most officers were aware of the law, but some acted beyond it, making it a habit to banish homeless Somalis to the borders of the district—so-called dumping, or police-initiated transjurisdictional transport of troublesome persons (King and Dunn 2006). Most officers acted in accordance with their own private caprice, which turned police behaviour into something erratic, volatile, and irregular. This made it very hard for the women to build up trust in the organization. 'For instance,' said one of the women, 'when we come to the station to report a crime, we don't trust that our anonymity is protected.'

'But the personal details of an informant never appear in a police file,' John tried to explain in vain, while mentioning a new police report system called Anonymous Crime Reporting (*Meld Misdaad Anoniem*) that had recently come into operation.

'That may very well be the policy, but how do we know that it actually happens?' Then another woman chimed in: 'You must take into account that ninety percent of the participants here in the room come from war-torn Somalia, where reporting a crime to the police would almost certainly mean that you're the next victim', depending, it was later explained to me, on the tribal backgrounds of victim, witness, and officer.

All I could think about, as the anthropologist at the table, was why the imported fear of this kind of tribal policing had not disappeared from view in The Netherlands, where most of the women had been living now for ten or twenty years. Afterwards, I heard from one of my key informants at the municipality, who worked with the Somali community and who was also from Somalia, that people are so afraid of police that they not only avoid them but often turn to informal mechanisms to deal with their problems as well. This made sense, as anthropologists have long emphasized that the criminal law and its institutions are the most coercive of social control mechanisms available to people (Geertz 1983; Malinowski 1926; Rosen 2006), but it also troubled me. Taking lessons from legal anthropology and sociology (e.g. Hertogh 2014; Merry 2010), we know that when people in a particular community no longer define themselves by the law or relate to the world through legal categories and discourses (legal *consciousness*) and refuse to turn to the law for help (legal *mobilization*), the law is eventually going to be isolated from the community it is supposed to regulate (legal *alienation*). Anthropologists around the globe have found that when the law and its public institutions are experienced as irrelevant or inequitable, people start to cobble together their own security solutions, giving rise to all sorts of 'citizen', 'statephobic' or 'self-help' security initiatives (e.g. Denyer Willis 2015). Such an undermining of state sovereignty has already been observed across the Global South and there is no reason whatsoever to assume that this development is contained by the boundaries of countries notorious for their weak legal systems and cultures, or so I will argue in this book. The same underlying mechanisms are at play in the Global North.[3]

Conflicted Contours of Policing

Security issues are a growing public concern that is dominant in politics, policy, and media (Maguire et al. 2014; Mutsaers 2016a). They appear globally and daily in media images of threats, conflicts, chaos, and disorder. This brings to our attention something we often tend to forget: that police are virtually everywhere. Police are so commonplace across the globe that it has been rightfully said that they have reached the status of a 'global form',

[3] I agree with Thomas Hylland Eriksen that the world map is much more colourful than the monochrome surfaces produced by a planet divided into the Global North and Global South. Moreover, the Global South can be 'employed in a postnational sense to address spaces and peoples negatively impacted by contemporary capitalist globalization' (*Oxford Bibliographies* 2017: n.p.). In this definition the Global South and North are de-territorialized geographies as there are 'Souths in the geographic North and Norths in the geographic South'. When talking about the north–south divide in this book, however, I do not address the negative effects on people as much as the modes of governance in different parts of the world. Here we see that modes of policing typical in many postcolonial societies are making their appearance in the Global North as well.

a term coined by Ong and Collier (2005) 'to refer to a diverse group of phenomena with a distinctive capacity for decontextualization and recontextualization, abstractability and movement, across diverse social and cultural situations and spheres of life' (Garriott 2013, 2). Police forces come in various forms and it has been frequently noted that they are symbiotic with a wide variety of political regimes, but they qualify precisely as a global form because they share a core function that defines the modern state: maintaining order by force (Bittner 1970).

Furthermore, today's world is increasingly marked by the idea that police are a prerequisite for social order (Comaroff 2013; Garriott 2013); that without them all hell would break loose. This goes beyond the fact that police are generally recognized as the strong arm of the state, the troops of law and order. It is perhaps even more important that the public perception of police is 'part and parcel of the way [people] regard the whole political and social order and its institutional framework' (Smith 2007, 34). As the 'immediate face of government' (Manning 2010), the police represent the state, the law, and the social order the state protects. After Durkheim, many criminologists and legal scholars have argued that law enforcement, criminal justice, and criminal punishment are the most significant expression of the state, the glue that holds society together (Albrecht 2007). Durkheim was one of the first to recognize this integrative function of the law and its institutions. In *The Division of Labor in Society* ([1893]1997), Durkheim stated that law reproduces the main forms of social solidarity in society. This idea resonated in the first studies in the field of legal anthropology, that distinct intellectual specialty that emerged in the 1920s with Malinowski's *Crime and Custom in Savage Society*, which emphasized that law and society co-evolve and that the idea of a lawless society is in fact oxymoronic (Donovan 2008; Malinowski 1926). If we accept that law and society co-evolve, that they are mutually constitutive, we must also accept Durkheim's insistence that 'we should not say that an act offends the common consciousness because it is criminal, but that it is criminal because it offends that consciousness. We do not condemn it because it is a crime, but it is a crime because we condemn it' (Donovan 2008, 49). As such, crime must be understood not as a natural fact but as a social one insofar as it needs to be explained by the sociality through which it is given meaning and by the legal structure in which such meaning is inscribed and encoded. Thus, when criminal justice agents act against crime, they feel backed up by the dialectics of law and society. Durkheim mainly wrote about the integrative function of punishment, but present-day criminologists have also pointed at the role of policing in preserving social bonds. Harkin (2015), for instance, was awarded by the British Society of Criminology for substantiating the claim that the police too reflect social attitudes and stoke activity in the collective consciousness, constructing social bonds and reinforcing solidarity.

However, while legal anthropologists long ago suggested that the 'legitimate use of physical coercion by a socially authorized agent' (i.e. policing) gives the law its teeth and as such is the *sine qua non* of law in any society (Hoebel 1954, 26), decades of police scholarship have shown that police and law are in fact distinct modalities of power (Martin 2007). Martin argued that the 'ideal of their integration remains one of the unresolved dilemmas of modern governance' and that the task of the anthropologist—especially, I like to add, in light of our understanding of police as a global form (Ong and Collier 2005)—is to 'reveal and clarify culturally distinctive aspects of how the intrinsic tensions between legal order and police practice are managed in [particular times and places]' (2007, 671–2).

Police scholars have demonstrated repeatedly that officers do not merely apply legal maxims as ministerial agents of the state (Bittner 1970). They deviate from and subvert the law when they draw on their professional culture, political beliefs, prejudices, and personal interests while they are at work (Zedner 2004). They carry with them a stock of knowledge about social types that are (re)constructed in the processes of law enforcement and maintenance of order (Cicourel 1968), as epitomized by the vignette that opened this chapter. When roaming in a district, containing a demonstration, responding to an emergency call, mediating a conflict, investigating a homicide, or policing a riot, the police are actually (re)producing social hierarchies in the settings in which they operate. 'Escapees', 'bogus migrants', 'incorrigibles', 'chronic offenders', 'troublesome youth', 'gang members', and other labels meant to categorize social classes are often very sticky and rarely stay without consequences in the context of policing. Police work can be of great value to the lives of people and is often appreciated, but it can also delimit people's lives and opportunities. For some people, law enforcement is a last resort they gratefully accept in emergency situations, for others it may exact high costs in terms of stigmatization, humiliation, even brutality (Fassin 2013a). In the words of Comaroff:

> [C]ops are regarded, ambivalently, as both a positive presence, a 'prerequisite of social order' and a popular nightmare, a dark, often excessively violent force that undermines that very order, blurring the line between those who administer the law and those who evade, erode and exploit it. (Comaroff 2013, xii)

In other words, compared with a Durkheimian consensus model of law enforcement, a conflict model that takes law enforcement as a focal point of conflict and struggle in modern societies may be equally, perhaps even more, valid—especially in plural, multicultural, multi-faith societies (Zedner 2004). This conflict model seems to be supported by current events around the world since we are living in a century in which we can open any page in the atlas and find instances of public outcry and protest against the police almost anywhere around the world (Mutsaers and Van Nuenen 2018). Scanning some of the major events of the twenty-first century, we can confirm that police are often a main problematic portfolio for contemporary governments because they loom large in public debates and are the focus of many protests and uprisings. These anti-police protests, very much like the police themselves, appear to have reached the status of a global form, especially because protestors are often plugged into globalized circuits of communication. The deaths of African-American citizens, widely covered in the world's media, might be recalled, with the police shooting of Michael Brown in 2014 perhaps one of the most memorable. His body was left on public display for hours after Officer Wilson had pulled the trigger in Ferguson, Missouri, triggering a nationwide uproar that lasted for months. The United States is not the only place where public protests against police violence have occurred recently. In The Hague, for example, the streets were engulfed with protestors grieving the death of the Aruban Mitch Henriquez, who died of asphyxiation after he was held in a chokehold by five police officers (see Chapter 2). Numerous other cases of public outcry have led to protest movements in France, the United Kingdom, Turkey, Venezuela, Brazil, Uganda, Ukraine, and Hong Kong, during the Arab Spring and #Occupy movement—all of which either began with or were closely related to police violence (Mutsaers 2019; Mutsaers et al.

2015). Increasingly, police tend to emphasize rather than dissolve existing lines of division in society (based on class, race, ethnicity, gender, sexuality, etc.), and in the process, widen the gap between legal order and police practice. Taking these moments exhibiting tense relations between police and public into account when analysing police legitimacy, and the social acceptance and credibility of police more generally, it is obvious 'that an undiluted Durkheimian view [is] grossly inadequate' (Smith 2007, 39).

The potential for a comparative analysis of these 'conflicted contours of policing' (Denyer Willis 2016) has been greatly increased by the recent work of a variety of scholars that can be loosely grouped together under the rubric 'the anthropology of police' (Karpiak and Garriott 2018; Karpiak 2016a, 2016b; Mutsaers et al. 2015). In contrast to other disciplines in which global comparisons are often made possible only after an initial phase of ethnocentrism has passed (the Anglo-Saxon bias in classic police studies is exemplary), anthropology typically starts from the outset by breaking through the discrete frame of the nation-state, accounting for social variations in the world as well as for similarities between social systems and human relationships (Eriksen 1995). The same holds true for police anthropologists. Although it must be acknowledged that anthropology is a latecomer in the study of police, it has only taken a few short years to cover quite a bit of the earth's surface, including countries such as France (Fassin 2013a), South Africa (Comaroff and Comaroff 2004; Hornberger 2004, 2011, 2013; Owen and Cooper-Knock 2014; Steinberg 2012), India (Jauregui 2013, 2014, 2016), Taiwan (Martin 2007, 2013a, 2013b), Brazil (Caldeira 2002; Denyer Willis 2015; Robb Larkins 2013, 2015; Scheper-Hughes 2006; Penglase 2013), Portugal (Zoettl 2017), the United States (Karandinos et al. 2014), Nigeria (Owen and Cooper-Knock 2014), Niger (Göpfert 2016), and The Netherlands (Çankaya 2011, 2012; Mutsaers 2014a, 2014b, 2016b).

By and large, these studies seem to corroborate one of the first general statements made by anthropologists on police and other agents of criminal justice: they often cause disorder instead of order (Comaroff and Comaroff 2006a, 2006b, 2007). This, I believe, has to do with the two aforementioned and interrelated factors: the police are often socially divisive, and their activities frequently take place in the 'zones of ambiguity between the presence and absence of law' (Comaroff and Comaroff 2006b, 5). For instance, in her work on the Uttar Pradesh (UP) police in northern India, Jauregui (2016) reports on the sectarian violence committed by Hindu police officers against a Muslim youth who was illegally detained and severely beaten in the name of public order (the officers on duty were on high alert for riots between Muslims and Hindus, riots that may have been triggered by ethnoreligious police violence in the first place). More generally, she states that UP officers often display 'vicious hyper-empowerment' in a variety of forms, such as illegally detaining and torturing suspects, engaging in brutal attacks on peaceful protestors, extrajudicial killing, and discriminating against members of minority groups. Across the Indian Ocean to the south-west, anthropologists studying police in South Africa, for example, have written about the informal privatization of public policing by means of an extreme form of community policing, leading to an intimate but violent relationship between police and particular segments of the public (Hornberger 2011, 2013; Owen and Cooper-Knock 2014; Steinberg 2012). Across the South Atlantic in Brazil, we find anthropological accounts of an even more brutal relationship between police and the people. In his work on police and organized crime in São Paulo, Denyer Willis (2015) writes about a 'killing consensus' that turns the policing of favela crime into a joint effort involving both police and organized crime groups, who share a common enemy: 'a "disposable" population that [the state] allow[s] to be preyed on under an acknowledged definition and common denomination of deservedness' (2015, 12). Such a raw form of illegal class policing, exacerbated by a porous culture of law, is hardly more visible anywhere else in the world (see also Robb Larkins 2013).

All these examples are drawn from post-colonial contexts. In that respect, Comaroff and Comaroff (2006a) raise a legitimate question in their editorial preface to *Law and Disorder in the Postcolony*: are post-colonial countries haunted more than countries in the Global North by the dialectics of law and disorder? It appears indeed to be the case that these dialectics are inflated in the Global South, where most of the weakest legal cultures can be found, but, they argue, there is no 'comfortable cleavage' between the Global North and Global South: 'many of the great historical tsunamis of the twenty-first century appear to be breaking first on their shores—or, if not first, then in their most palpable, most hyperextended form—thence to reverberate around the Northern

Hemispheric cosmopoles' (Comaroff and Comaroff 2006a, ix). The question thus arises: is the world at large looking ever more 'post-colonial'? While critics may dismiss this reversed telos-of-modernity thesis—which deviates from traditional models of modernization and progress that take 'the North' as a model for 'the South'—as worst case-scenario thinking, I believe it is precisely the power of anthropology to study police as a global form and actually do something with the comparisons that follow from such research. I will argue in this book that many of the developments in the field of policing in the South—where police legitimacy is often far from unequivocal—can be read as a sign of what is to come to the rest of the world.

First indications of the proliferating problem of lawlessness and deep-seated discriminatory policing in the northern hemisphere have already been brought to our attention. In France, where police are regularly targeted in large-scale protests, Fassin conducted his acclaimed study of a Parisian anti-crime brigade and its relationship with under-privileged minority youth. In his book *Enforcing Order* (2013a) he concludes that the security actor in question causes insecurity and disorder:

> Not only … has it been established that patrol work as it is typically practiced is generally ineffectual, but also it has been demonstrated that, even in its aggressive form, such as the anticrime squads, the marginal benefits of reduction in crime are cancelled out by the perverse effects of the resentment generated and the disorder provoked: exasperated and alarmed by the brutality of law enforcement operations that often aggravate problems they were supposed to resolve, residents no longer have confidence in public institutions, which they see not as serving them but, on the contrary, as contributing to their stigmatization. (Fassin 2013a, 221–2)

In a contribution to *The Anthropology of Security*, Fassin (2014) coins the notion of 'petty states of exception' to interpret his ethnographic data: temporally, geographically, and juridically limited forms of lack of respect for the rule of law, which occurs when police officers insult, illegally detain, injure, stop and frisk, or otherwise harass youths from ethnic minorities, in complete disregard of their own public role. Similar forms of 'police punishment' (Harkin 2015) have been observed by Zoettl (2017) in his work on police officers in Portugal and their extrajudicial punishment of youth offenders (often regarded as 'non-citizens'). Although such accounts of illegal and discriminatory policing are increasing, both in range and depth, they are not new. As early as 1998, Choongh proposed his social disciplinary model of policing, which, in contrast to legal models of policing, does not aim at legal adjudication but at direct social control through the identification and summary punishment of classes of people who in various ways reject prevailing norms.

What *is* new, however, is that such police practices have prompted anthropologists and scholars in adjacent fields to explore their alienating effects. As indicated by the vignette at the beginning of this chapter, many people no longer feel that the police are willing or able to solve *their* problems. For those people, police are indeed a security risk instead of a security provider, which corrodes their 'idea of police' (Júnior and Muniz 2006): the expectation that the police will intervene whenever called, or, more generally, 'a measure of overall public faith that the state police force will reliably resolve all exigent crises' (Martin 2007, 674). When the idea of police is strong, people will find it unnecessary to make other arrangements; when it is weak, the credibility of the police force decreases and people will come up with their own security initiatives.

The rise of so-called citizen, statephobic, or 'self-help' security has become something of an academic growth area for anthropologists working on policing and security issues. Here again, the most visible, spectacular, and horrifying manifestations of such alternative security forms can be found in the Global South. In their introduction to *Law and Disorder in the Postcolony,* Comaroff and Comaroff (2006b, 9) write that in many post-colonies, 'the reach of the state is uneven and the landscape is a palimpsest of contested sovereignties, codes, and jurisdictions—a complex choreography of police and paramilitaries, private and community enforcement, gangs and vigilantes, highwaymen and outlaw armies'. Introducing a book that includes work on death squads in Brazil (Scheper-Hughes), communal violence in Indonesia (Spyer), witchcraft and the limits of the law in Cameroon and South Africa (Geschiere), and the 'ethics of illegality' in the Chad Basin as an alternative framework to the law (Roitman), this citation does not seem far off the mark. When police legitimacy—and through it, state legitimacy—is dispersed and contested and the state is no longer sovereign (cf. Geertz 2004), law and disorder indeed best describes reality. Unfortunately, this is a reality that many people in the post-colonial world wake up to daily.

The development of so-called parallel or horizontal sovereignties cannot, of course, be attributed solely to failing police forces and concomitant security voids, but neither can this relationship be ignored. Goldstein (2003, 2010) draws a direct connection between the rise of vigilantes in marginal Bolivian communities and some of the population's dissatisfaction with the state and its policing and justice systems. He describes how citizens enact their own private strategies for 'making security': the poor by lynching criminal suspects, the rich by employing private security firms. In a similar vein, Gore and Pratten (2003) explain the rise of separatist ethnic youth militia in Nigeria as a (particularly violent) response to a predatory state that secures its income by means of extraction (of bribes) rather than taxation (see also Pratten 2008 and Smith 2004). We come across similar accounts with respect to Mexico (Johnson 2007), Brazil (Da Silva and Cano 2007), and South Africa (Comaroff and Comaroff 2007) in *Legitimacy and Criminal Justice*. As stated earlier, these 'security actors' are often characterized by their antagonistic relationships with police, but such antagonism is not reported in all places at all times. In *The Killing Consensus*, Denyer Willis (2015) offers the novel conclusion that police and organized crime groups in São Paulo are not necessarily antagonistic. While these criminal groups can be seen as non-state security actors who have their own tribunals and pseudo-juridical processes, they also share a common enemy with the police. Sometimes, the police are little more than cogs in the machinery of organized crime. Similar conclusions are drawn by Jaffe (2013, 2015) in her work on 'the hybrid state' and in particular on the outsourcing of sovereignty by the Jamaican state to local dons in order to govern the unruly segments of Kingston Town.[4]

It should be emphasized that no comfortable cleavage or significant difference exists between the Global North and South when it comes to these alternative security initiatives. In the North,

[4] By 'sovereignty' I am following Comaroff and Comaroff: '[T]he more or less effective claim on the part of any agent, community, cadre, or collectivity to exercise autonomous, exclusive control over the lives, deaths, and conditions of existence of those who fall within a given purview, and to extend over them the jurisdiction of some kind of law' (Comaroff and Comaroff 2006b, 35).

centralization of authority in the state has a longer history—and 'a single, vertically integrated sovereignty may still hold sway'—but particularly in inner cities, 'policing has as little purchase as it does in any postcolonial context' (Comaroff and Comaroff 2006b, 40). It is increasingly clear that the same problems plague the North and South. In Goffman's (2014) ethnography of the pervasive policing of a neighbourhood in Philadelphia, for instance, we read that residents think of the police as an occupying force. She describes her (mainly ethnic minority) informants as members of a 'fugitive community' constantly on the run from police. Because police–community relations are fraught with tension, and allegations of racial profiling are commonplace, people have such a weak idea of the police that they take care of their own protection, beyond the boundaries of the law. To these people, the police symbolize an oppressive white authority.[5] In unexpected places, such as The Netherlands, particular communities are increasingly alienated from the state and its legal institutions (so-called *rechtsvervreemding*: see Hertogh 2011; Ministerie van Veiligheid en Justitie 2016; Mutsaers 2016c; Zouridis 2016). This legal alienation manifests in the form of withdrawal (avoiding police, both in service and adversarial contexts), protest (the aforementioned street protests in The Hague offer an example), crime (specifically subversive crime, designed to question state authority), or self-help security (such as in the case of Dutch Somalis cited earlier).

The police are worthy of our continued attention and they need to be held up to scrutiny continually. After all, when police continue to make categorical distinctions between classes of people (based on race, ethnicity, class, etc.), act outside the boundaries of the law, and make large sections of society feel they are either overpoliced or underprotected, it should not come as a surprise that populations who take the brunt of such policing become alienated form the legal authorities and seek protection elsewhere. As stated earlier, police are so ubiquitous that they have been taken for granted as a prerequisite of social order, but in reality,

[5] Another example taken from Philadelphia is the study of Karandinos and his associates (2014) on the moral economy of violence in a Puerto Rican neighbourhood. The authors interpret the ubiquitous gang violence as 'solidarity exchanges of assistive violence dynamized by kinship and gender obligations … operating within a moral logic framed by economic scarcity and hostile state relations' (Karandinos et al. 2014, 1).

criminal law only sits at the most coercive end of a continuum of institutions of social order (Zedner 2004). When the legitimacy of the criminal justice system becomes weak, communities *will* seek alternative mechanisms for maintaining social order (Smith 2007).

Again, the rise of these alternative social control mechanisms following the gross failure of police forces (and criminal justice systems more generally) to serve and protect has become an academic growth area. However, our understanding of why and how exactly police forces are failing is very limited. To be sure, there is a burgeoning descriptive literature on, for instance, police discrimination (e.g. Bonnet and Caillault 2015; De Koning 2017; Fassin 2013a; Gowricharn and Çankaya 2015) but the problem is precisely that it is mainly descriptive. As an anthropologist, I value work that is suffused with precise and protracted descriptions of small facts and the circumstances in which they take place which force theory to stay close to the ground (cf. Geertz 1973). I am also convinced that, in order to be able to formulate a theory at all, these descriptions need to be drawn into a comparative analysis. Put differently, different police ethnographies need to be brought into contact for the sake of ethnological knowledge production that ultimately serves to develop and sustain a police *anthropology*.

For newcomers to the field of police studies, this is a grand ambition and anthropologists still have a lot of work to do before we can genuinely speak of an 'anthropology of police' (although there is no harm in using the phrase to describe a burgeoning subdiscipline). This is one reason why the present book is necessarily limited in ambition and focus: there simply is not much to compare, yet. Still, I think that the currently available police ethnographies contain so many valuable insights and are so rich in detail that an upscaling of the analysis is justified. With respect to a second reason, it must be admitted that my police project (2008–2013) was originally intended as a case study of police discrimination in The Netherlands. As my project ran parallel with the ascendancy of police anthropology at large, comparative work could only be done later, after the ethnographic work had already been concluded. As a consequence, I could not benefit from the creative interplay of 'fieldwork', 'headwork', and 'textwork' (Van Maanen 1988, 2010), at least not with respect to anthropological work on the police. Occasionally, the reader may consider the comparative analysis to be of an 'add-on' nature. I hope this will be interpreted as a start-up problem of the sub-discipline rather than as an individual shortcoming of the present author.

State Externality versus Proximity

As an introduction to the empirical parts of this book, I will use the remainder of this chapter to discuss what I consider to be the main problem of present-day policing: the unmediated proximity between police and policed. This is a problem that is closely related to the perennially relevant question: wherein lie the outer bounds of police power?

How police relate to the people they police is a matter that has long concerned scholars of law enforcement, especially because this relationship tells us something about dynamics between state and society more generally. As I have written above, as the front-line organization of the state, the police are a crucial factor in how people experience state authority at large. Epp and colleagues (2014) astutely observed, for instance, that no form of government control comes close to the police practice of stop and search, at least not in the United States, where they conducted their study on police stops and their power to define race and citizenship. For such a form of government control to be legitimate, people must believe that the decisions made and rules enacted by police authorities are 'right' or 'proper' and ought to be followed (Tyler 2006). Police legitimacy, in turn, is a prerequisite for state sovereignty, as we saw in the previous section.

In Western liberal democracies, police authority has typically been legitimized and structured by a form of social organization we have come to know as legal bureaucracy. Ideal-typically, legal bureaucracies are 'rational and impersonal, beholden to clearly codified rules and free of politics' (Jauregui 2016, 11). They are founded on a conception of the state as an 'externality', that is, 'a kind of distinct ... sphere of human actors and action that is, if not fully enclosed, then largely divorced from "the people"' (Jauregui 2016, 11). This sort of formalized distance between state officials and citizens has been deemed necessary to keep both popular and sovereign power in check. Police officers and other state officials are supposed to steer clear of popular justice and state politics and are expected to operate without regard to person. The master analyst of bureaucracy, Weber (1978) himself, was very clear about this matter:

Not only any sort of 'popular justice'—which usually does not ask for reasons and norms—but also any intensive influence on the administration by so-called 'public opinion'—that is, concerted action born of irrational 'sentiments' and usually staged or directed by party bosses or the press—thwarts the rational course of justice. (Weber 1978, 980)

Legal bureaucracies gain legitimacy because they (strive to) guarantee procedural justice and fairness—they transform state officials into politically neutral agents. This transformation is made possible by an institutionalized capacity to separate different spheres of social activity, spheres that are differentiated for the sake of pluralism, equality, and liberty (Walzer 1983, 1984). This 'art of separation' (Walzer 1984) builds a world of walls, with each wall protecting another sphere and creating another liberty. It is not 'an illusory or fantastic enterprise [but] a morally and politically necessary adaptation to the complexities of modern life' (Walzer 1984, 319). It guarantees that a person's success in one setting is not convertible into another, to ensure for instance that financial power cannot buy political clout or ethnic loyalties cannot influence police behaviour. It separates religion from state affairs. It prevents the police from invading private homes. It keeps official governance and unofficial power relations from becoming entwined (Jauregui 2016). In short, it protects individual freedom through institutional integrity.

Bureaucracy is an indispensable tool in the art of separation. It stands at the social foundation of modernity as it teaches humans to operate in non-inclusive terms as role agents rather than as private persons. In the words of Kallinikos (2004):

[T]he historical background of the social relations out of which bureaucracy emerged suggests some important qualifications. Rule-bound behaviour was fashioned to accommodate the functioning of modern organizations whose operations could no longer be anchored in the normative certainty of *Gemeinschaft*. Being active on a spatial and temporal scale that extended far beyond the limited world of pre-modern communities, modern organizations needed both the legitimacy and new principles for controlling their operations. The construction of formal role systems for regulating human behaviour in organizations emerged as a historical innovation, essential in sustaining the egalitarian ethos of modern society. Formal role systems provide transparent motives and legible behaviour, on the basis of which one can decide whether citizens are treated equally and the employees of the organization protected from any abuse of arbitrary exercise of power. (Kallinikos 2004, 17)

It was this historical innovation that led to a distinctive anthropology, a distinctive contemplation of modern mankind; one that centres on what Gellner (1994) called the modular person. The modular person is able to segment social life into separate and relatively independent spheres and to 'repress those aspects of their character that do not bear on the execution of organizational roles' (Gellner 1994; Kallinikos 2003, 606). When applied to the context of criminal justice, we understand that modular agents of the law make sure that social forces (e.g. public sentiments) are mitigated by legal practices and institutions. They never come out raw; public sentiments cannot be accepted uncritically by legal institutions. So, whenever public sentiment demands a closer surveillance of 'risky' individuals despite their clean rap sheets, the modular agent steps in by brushing aside all private considerations and sentiments and emphasizes the importance of the 'bureau' as a unit of governance. Repeat offenders who have been punished are rehabilitated in society, and modular judges are not sensitive to the punitive gap caused by the mismatch of their judicial decisions and the ruling popular punitivism of the time. Ethnic minorities are treated equally in all cases.

In practice, this modularity is hard to maintain at all times and in all cases as a perfect bureaucratic organization is almost impossible to achieve. Ethnographic studies of bureaucratic practice have revealed the enormous amount of work necessary to operationalize bureaucracy in actual events (Martin 2007). Bureaucracy as a Weberian ideal type is always more idealized than typical, that is, more the object of aspiration than an accomplished fact. This holds true in particular for police organizations, where, considering their mandate and monopoly on violence, it is perhaps most needed. This paradox has been clearly formulated by Stinchcombe (1980):

> Perhaps nowhere is [the] potential conflict between individual decision-makers and the principles of bureaucracy better illustrated than in police departments. Few other agencies demand such procedural regularity while at the same time requiring such autonomous self-direction from its lowest-level ranks. By virtue of the awesome nature of the police mandate, the complex situations to which they must respond, and the very ambivalence of their role in society, the administration of law enforcement would appear to necessitate a unique organizational approach. (Stinchcombe (1980, 5)

In police organizations, discretion increases as one moves *down* the hierarchy (Wilson 1968). In contrast to lower ranks in other large-scale public organizations, rank-and-file officers have wide discretion over the dispensation of benefits or the allocation of public sanctions, a discretion which is practically unreviewable (Lipsky 2010). The uniqueness that Stinchcombe referred to thus has to do with the paradoxical combination of discretion and obedience, operational freedom and regulation—a combination that is still best captured by Lipsky's concept of street-level bureaucrats (2010).

This, however, is not what I consider to be the main problem of present-day policing. Discretionary policing is a constant, because the supply and demand sides of manpower are almost never balanced when it comes to policing. Zooming in at the extremes of a sliding scale, this can either mean that officers have to condone most law-breaking due to a lack of time and select some cases which they deem most important, or that they have to sit through eventless shifts characterized by inactivity and boredom, responding to every minor infraction with a spectacular display of force (this underreported dimension of discretionary policing—caused by boredom rather than heavy caseloads—has been described very well by Fassin 2013a). In both instances, officers are likely to be influenced by other things than the legal bureaucracy. Put differently, they will also intervene on the basis of prejudice (see the earlier references to police discrimination). In theoretical terms, such acts are examples of non-modularity, breaches of the principle of state externality.

However, they would be precisely that: breaches of a norm. They would offend the bureaucracy but leave it intact. Non-modular fish would swim in a sea of modularity, characterized by formalized distance (rather than informal contacts), public roles (rather than private personalities), and protocols and regulations (rather than prejudices and gut feelings). This focus on individuals' norm violations is best explained by a human failure model of police misconduct that is centred on 'rotten apples' (Punch 2003). When officers abuse their discretionary powers (to elevate their own status, to extract money, goods or services, to teach particular groups about their 'place in society', or for whatever reason), they are considered deviant or abnormal. However, this model can only be used to explain police discrimination or other forms of police behaviour that are opposed to the legal bureaucracy if that legal bureaucracy is indeed the norm—if modularity and state externality are foundational to the police organization in question. The fact that this is often *not* the case is what I consider to be the main problem of present-day policing.

In the Global South, where bureaucracies were often not elaborate to begin with (Comaroff and Comaroff 2007), we often see that policing *tout court* 'works via political performances, particularistic relationships and populist conceptions of justice, rather than by following legal codes or rules of equality and fairness' (Jauregui 2013, 547). While such forms of policing come in different guises, they all have something in common: the substitution of state externality by the opposite notion of 'state proximity'. Such proximity leads to a close and intimate rather than distant and formalized relationship between police and the policed. Sometimes such intimate relationships develop in a positive atmosphere of community orientation and service, but they can also take the form of intrusive and pervasive policing. In any case, different social spheres (such as the private and the public) are conflated, which means that the art of separation as a protection mechanism becomes dysfunctional.

A more positive account of such intimate relationships can be found in the work of Martin (2007) on police in Taiwan. Martin concludes from his ethnography of neighbourhood police that state authority, originating from the rule of law, cannot always be imposed on the 'dense fabric of particularistic relationships that constitute the substantive order of local life' (2007, 694). As Taiwanese patrolmen are held personally responsible for maintaining order in their area of watch (and penalized when they fail), they need to strike a 'reasonable balance' between law and sentiment that takes public opinion and particularistic relationships into account and does not always take the law as the last word. These 'sentimental' and 'particularistic' relationships define 'a space of intimacy explicitly insulated from the formalized distances of public interaction' (2007, 689), and most of the time, Martin saw that patrolmen were basically preoccupied with 'repairing' and 'harmonizing' (*xietiao*) social relationships in order to maintain the peace. It is perhaps not entirely a coincidence (because he refers to Martin's work) that Göpfert (2016) also uses the term 'repair' to describe the activities of the gendarmes in Niger (who use the word *gyara*). Göpfert describes various cases of under-enforcement in which his informants pursue out-of-court settlements to solve disputes and conflicts, often by using community pressure.

Although such intimate relationships between police and the policed carry the potential to solve issues without raining down the full weight of the law on people's heads, they also have a darker side. They stretch the outer limits of police power. The most explicitly formulated critique in this respect can be found in Hornberger's work on community policing in South Africa (2004, 2011, 2013). As a true anthropologist, Hornberger is skilled in *Verfremdung:* making the familiar strange, looking at things quizzically, thinking along unfamiliar lines. She interrogates conventional wisdom on community policing, which is generally hailed as a promising and legitimacy boosting police strategy because it keeps police close to the people. Hornberger, however, describes what happens when they come too close: a privatization of public police. She is not referring to the replacement of public police by private police, a longstanding concern for police scholars (e.g. Bayley and Shearing 1996; Shearing and Stenning 1983), but to privatization *within* public police organizations and to the demise of the police's institutional integrity more generally. These developments, which all have to do with the (partial) replacement of legal authority (of the institution) by personal authority (of the individual officer), lead to 'your police, my police' situations in which those who are (violently) overpoliced by some officers turn to different officers to demand punitive police action against others in the community. 'This intimate proximity allows for the activity of policing to be influenced by popular desires for a personal relationship with a forceful state' Hornberger (2013, 599). These relationships can be activated by people for the purpose of immediate justice, tangible punishment, and instant protection. They blur the line between vigilantism and policing (see also the work of Buur 2006, Hansen 2006, and Owen and Cooper-Knock 2014, for similar remarks on 'police vigilantism' in South Africa). In these cases, the idea of police depends on personal access to the police, resulting in what Martin (2013a) calls 'particularistic legitimacy', a form of legitimacy that is reproduced through personal relationships and positional power (rather than procedural justice, equality before the law, and other ostensibly universal principles).

In addition to these examples of people's private access to police, others can be found of police access to people's private lives. Arguably, this is an even more serious problem since police and the policed are part of a system of ranked groups, which means that inequality typically constitutes their relationship.[6] One of the most engrossing accounts in this respect is, again, Goffman's *On the Run* (2014), in which she writes about the struggles between police and the policed for control over the streets and homes of Philadelphia. Goffman talks about a 'surveillance state' that 'criminalize[s] entire blocks, and transform[s] the very associations that should stabilize young lives—family, girlfriends, jobs—into liabilities, as the police use such relationships to track down suspects, demand information and threaten consequences' (Goffman 2014, back cover). The book is full of stories about how police surveil funerals of killed gang members because that is where they expect to encounter targeted suspects, or stories about relatives of (often black) suspects who are intimidated by officers and forced to cooperate with them. It is important to realize that Goffman does not point to the defects of character of police officers to understand police racism and violence (which would square with the 'rotten apple' model of human failure). This is not a matter of unlawful discretionary policing; the real problem consists of the tasks that officers are assigned (Jencks 2014). In other words, the problem should not be sought in the blind spot of bureaucracy (the invisibility of 'street cops'), but in the fact that it is shaking at its very core. The real problem here is the impotence or unwillingness of 'management cops' to honour the legal bureaucracy and its principles of state externality and modularity.[7]

Finally, I would like to argue that the notion of 'state proximity' in the context of policing does not only refer to police invasion of private space, to pervasive surveillance, or to 'your police, my police' situations. Modularity and the art of separation also refer to a distance that is not literal or relational but symbolic in kind. The police uniform ought to be a symbol of neutrality. State externality of police officers demands that they operate without prejudice to the individual, that is, without regard to

[6] Becker once wrote, tongue in cheek, that 'no one proposes that addicts should make and enforce laws for policemen' (1967, 241). What's more, those subjected to police intervention are usually also denied the luxury of what Scott (1990) called 'negative reciprocity', that is, trading a slap for a slap or an insult for an insult (leaving aside some exceptions; see Jauregui 2013b on the 'provisional authority' of police officers in India).

[7] The difference between 'street cops' and 'management cops' is borrowed from Reuss-Ianni (1983).

class, ethnicity, race, religion, etc. The fact that race and poverty continue to be criminalized around the globe once again points to the fact that state proximity remains a significant problem (e.g. Aas 2011; Andersson 2014; Body-Gendrot 2010; Harcourt 2007; Robb Larkins 2013; Rosas 2012; Sausdal 2018; Wacquant 2009; Zedner 2004). The best work that I have come across in this respect is Harcourt's book, *Against Prediction* (2007). Harcourt discusses actuarial methods in the US criminal justice system. These methods are known in the vernacular as 'risk-profiling', but Harcourt gives a more precise definition:

> [S]tatistical methods [that use] large datasets of criminal offending rates in order to determine the different levels of offending associated with a group or with one or more group traits, and on the basis of those correlations, to predict the past, present or future criminal behavior of a particular person and to administer a criminal justice outcome for that individual. (Harcourt 2007, 16)

We know from anthropological theory (Douglas 1992; Douglas and Wildavsky 1983) that risk-profiling is a norm-based classification process; an everyday, one could say, *cultural* activity in which people draw on the environment to make sense of the world and have it operate on the basis of selected norms that, in the case of criminal justice, concern classifications of deviancy and delinquency. As we saw in the vignette at the opening of this chapter, a focus on such everyday risk-profiling can help us understand discrimination in the sphere of discretionary policing. However, the main difference between everyday risk-profiling and actuarial methods is that the latter turn group categories into a systemic feature of the criminal justice process. So, in the case of racial profiling, it is no longer the individual officer that—willingly or unwillingly, consciously or subconsciously—applies race categories when scanning the streets for risks and dangers, but the police system that analyses criminal offending rates in the jurisdiction to discover racial disparities, which are subsequently used to allocate police resources. This is not a matter of discretion but design.

The problems with racial profiling and other actuarial methods are myriad. For example, Harcourt draws our attention to the so-called ratchet or multiplier effect, which he describes as a disproportionality that grows over time. 'The disproportionality in question is between the makeup of the offending population and the makeup of the carceral population—that is, the population that has criminal justice contacts such as arrest, conviction, fine, probation, imprisonment, parole or other supervision' (Harcourt 2007, 147). The ratchet effect occurs when incarceration rates are subsequently used to boost racial profiling further, which in turn will increase the racial disproportionality in incarceration rates, which is then used to further legitimate racial profiling, and so on and so forth. Prediction tools like racial profiling eventually 'aggravate the difficulties that profiled persons already have obtaining work, education and a better quality of life—thus perpetuating the pattern of criminal behavior' (Harcourt 2007, back cover).

Structure of the Book

The risks of state proximity are manifold, and yet law enforcement agencies have been carrying out numerous anti-bureaucracy reforms roughly since the 1980s. These reforms square with a more general 'bureaucracy bashing', which has been abundantly reported in the academic literature (e.g. Du Gay 2005; Höpfl 2006; Kallinikos 2007; Maravelias 2007; Siebers 2009a). To understand the heated discussions between those who advocate for and those who reject the role of bureaucracy in police agencies, it is helpful to briefly look into the academic discussion that revolves around Bauman's conception of 'the bureau' and Weber's conception of it (see Du Gay 1999). For Bauman, bureaucracy leads to hyper-rationalism, appalling impersonalization, and the destruction of moral personality (he articulated these ideas in his celebrated *Modernity and the Holocaust*, 1989). What Bauman describes as the dehumanization of the objects of bureaucratic operation has also been described in anthropology by Herzfeld (1992) who referred to it as the 'social production of indifference'. Understood as such, bureaucracy lies at the roots of indifference and the obliteration of individual responsibility. It is seen as the social evil of our time; the evil of impersonality, alienation, and coldness (cf. Sennett 1974). What Westley (1953) saw as a vice—the personalization of state power—is actually a virtue from this perspective, as it allows individual officials to exercise a capacity for moral action (Du Gay 1999).

Bauman locates the essence of moral relationships in the sphere of direct contact and proximity. As Du Gay states, it does not come as a surprise therefore that he regards the separation and division that is so characteristic of bureaucracy as crucial elements in the 'silencing of morality'. Bauman claims to follow Weber in this respect, yet Du Gay convincingly argues that Bauman's stance is the very antithesis of Weber's. He posits that Weber regards the bureaucratic separation of the private person and the public office as essential to the formalistic impersonality that is necessary to institute blindness to social standing. The division between person and office is exactly what is considered the most elementary and socially innovative characteristic of the bureaucratic foundation (Kallinikos 2004). It is *the* source of democratic equalization, because office holders who have learned to comport themselves in a manner befitting the vocation of office holding can operate without regard to person (Du Gay 1999). So, instead of regarding bureaucracy as an institution that degrades human dignity and perpetuates social inequality, it has to be understood as an effort to create 'responsible, accountable governance by ensuring that discretion is not abused, that due process is the norm not the exception, and that undue risks are not taken that undermined the integrity of the political system' (Du Gay 2005, 4; Kallinikos 2004).

The problem is an old one for police organizations, as is clear from Wilson's decades' old remarks:

> For some purposes or to some people, the problem with the police is that they don't follow the rules. They question when they shouldn't, search when they mustn't, arrest when they have no grounds. The remedy, therefore, is to bureaucratize, or 'judicialize,' the police: make them subject to more and more explicit rules, have these rules reviewed by the courts or by other nonpolice agencies, and reduce their discretion wherever possible ... Other persons, and in different circumstances ... want the police officer to perform as a 'professional' who has a service function ... Training and supervision, this argument goes, should encourage the patrolman to take a broad view of his role, exercise initiative and independence, appreciate the discretion he necessarily possesses, and learn his beat and work with the people on it. (Wilson 1968, 281–2)

In The Netherlands, where I conducted my police ethnography, decisions to de-bureaucratize the police were made long ago and were underpinned by the argument that the gap between the public expectations of how police behave and actual police practice had grown too large. By 1977—and this turned the Dutch police into pioneers—it was felt that a new paradigm had to be developed if a crisis of police legitimacy was to be averted. The

Project Group on Organizational Structures published the report *A Changing Police* (Heijink et al. 1977), in which it was argued that the much-criticized traditional bureaucratic police system had to be replaced by something new (cf. Van der Vijver and Zoomer 2004). The traditional system was considered too bureaucratic and insufficiently embedded in society. In order to improve police legitimacy, the police had to start operating 'closer to the public' and adopting a 'client-centred orientation' to increase the 'level of satisfaction'.

These efforts to bring the police closer to the people and to improve the police image culminated in a frontal 'attack on bureaucracy', as it was first called by a former Dutch Minister of Security and Justice, Ivo Opstelten, during a security conference in 2010. This attack on bureaucracy became an important campaign for the new right-wing coalition at that time, which led to the largest reorganization of the Dutch police in recent history: the amalgamation of twenty-six police forces into one National Police (NP). A substantial part of the plan of attack on bureaucracy concentrated on what Kallinikos (2004) called 'secondary' or 'derivative' aspects of bureaucracy: regulations, rules, and red tape (Opstelten 2012). According to the minister, police officers and citizens alike were getting tired of the 'paper punching madness' and the 'burden of registration', so he called for the elimination of unnecessary regimentation and argued that bureaucratic control could be limited by means of centralization. This, he said, would bring the police closer to the people simply because executive personnel would have more time to spend on the streets.

In the process, however, the 'primary' or 'constitutive' aspects of bureaucracy (Kallinikos 2004) also came under attack. Among these, I include all the aforementioned aspects that are intended to secure state externality and modularity: role divisions, a restricted police mandate, operations without regard to the individual, clear separation of private and public spheres, etc. The minister intended to liberate police professionals by encouraging independent judgment and wider discretion as well as job enlargement rather than restricted roles. 'Craftsmanship' was his magic word. In the White Paper, *Minder regels, meer op straat* (freely translated as 'Less rules, more street presence'), the minister pleaded to 'do justice to the craftsmanship of officers and detectives ... to give them more latitude to make decisions to take local circumstance into account' (Opstelten 2012). Shortly thereafter,

Dutch police scholars saw an expansion of preventive powers and a great deal of discretionary authority (Van der Leun and Van der Woude 2011).

The use of 'craftsmanship' is an interesting choice of words. Craftsmanship is commonly understood as 'an enduring, basic human impulse, the desire to do a job well for its own sake' (Sennett 2008, 9). Accordingly, the craftsman is someone representing 'the special human condition of being engaged' (Sennett 2008, 20). As such, (s)he can be seen as the polar opposite of the bureaucrat, who works in the spirit of formalistic impersonality (Weber 1978). The notion of craftsmanship was already popular in police discourse when I started my fieldwork in 2008, so the minister had selected a term that resonated well. A different but related term that I heard a lot was 'authenticity'. Against all the expectations that I had at the outset of my fieldwork, I noticed that canteen conversations but also leadership trainings, job interviews, and other human resource-related business were saturated by talk about authenticity, personality, personal development, identity, and other 'soft skill' matters (Urciuoli 2008). As one human resource manager said during an interview:

> Police leaders must be themselves, that is, authentic ... In a job interview you are primarily looking for the true self of a person. And you know what ... an answer is not right or wrong—I mean substantively. No, it's about how you come to it. This means that you look for who someone really is. (see Chapter 4, interview with Human Resource Officer in 2011)

In an employers' statement published by the national human resource division of the Dutch police, it was stated along the same line that:

> the police organization pursues diversity and this requires a variety and authenticity of leadership in the police organization ... Leaders coach and impassion employees in order to let them excel in the things they are good at; this gives employees a chance to act in accordance with their own views ... Leaders must be capable of touching upon the authenticity of employees. (Werkgeversvisie Politie 2008, 77–8)

Such views and definitions align with the idea of craftsmanship. After all, the craftsman is 'free to control his own working action ... There is no split of work and play, of work and culture. The craftsman's way of livelihood determines and infuses his entire mode of living' (Mills 1951, 220). The craftsman is indivisible, a totality, an organic whole: (s)he is 'non-modular' (Gellner 1994). As I mentioned earlier, this non-modularity was the normal human condition in pre-modern times, but it now seems to have made a comeback and reappears in the form of authenticity, intimacy, subjectivity, and identity in the workplace. These features thrive in the 'post-bureaucratic organization', where personal and organizational lives are meshed (Tucker 1999) and where bureaucracy has been (at least partly) replaced by 'biocracy': a form of labour control 'whereby bios or life itself becomes an essential human resource to be exploited' (Fleming 2014a, 26). Biocracy encourages the 'whole person' in the workplace and can be seen as a holistic type of power that extends the otherwise finite register of work (Fleming 2014a, 2014b). As I will discuss in this book, such a type of power can turn an organizational like the police into a 'greedy institution' (Coser 1974) that tends to become unlimited when it comes to the private dimensions of police *and* the policed.

In the three empirical chapters that follow this introduction, I intend to add some flesh to the bones of the conceptual structure introduced in this chapter with concepts such as state externality/proximity, bureaucracy/biocracy, and modularity/non-modularity. As an anthropologist I grow uncomfortable when I get too far away from the 'immediacies of social life'—to borrow from Geertz (1973)—so I will do my very best to shed a clear light on the ethnographic data that helped my thinking about these concepts in the first place.

These data come from a police study that I carried out in The Netherlands between 2008 and 2013, first as a junior researcher at the university and later as an employee of the Police Academy of the Netherlands, which hired me between 2011 and 2015 to undertake a PhD study on police discrimination. Initially, I was predominantly interested in discrimination *within* police departments; that is, in inter-ethnic labour relations (see Chapter 4). Shortly before my project started, a former police commissioner and then director of the National Expertise Centre Diversity (LECD) of the Police Academy had stated in the media that minority police officers suffered from 'institutional discrimination'.[8]

[8] It was due to the support of the LECD director that my project began in the first place. Contact was established by a colleague, Hans Siebers, who met the director in October 2007. They decided to initiate a line of research to understand this 'institutional discrimination' of police officers with a migration background.

This was a bold and brave statement, which opened up a new discourse in the media. Suddenly, ethnic minority officers appeared on television and in the papers to share their experiences about discrimination, which in many cases had cost them their jobs.

However, as I started interviewing officers and joining them 'on the beat' (which I did for about twelve months; see the Appendix for some notes on methodology), I began to notice that police discrimination 'out there' on the streets was a problem as well, and that it was related to the same factor that also caused police discrimination within the force: the celebration of post-bureaucracy (or biocracy) as a better, more humane form of social organization. The post-bureaucratic organization applauded individual expression, professional freedom, authenticity, craftsmanship, discretionary policing, community involvement, the opening up of organizational boundaries; all things that in one way or the other could be linked to police discrimination. Remembering my anthropological training in *Verfremdung*, or estrangement, I tried to step outside the 'grounded political commitments' (Karpiak 2016b) that were everywhere and that targeted bureaucracy as an evil force. Eriksen argued in his book, *Engaging Anthropology* (2006, 38), that an engaged anthropologist, very much like a *parrēsiast*, has to speak 'against received wisdoms and representations that are dominant in a way that entails a certain personal risk' (these risks are discussed in Chapter 5). This is what I tried to do. It was not always easy, however, because it often conflicted with another standard in anthropology: always to appreciate local knowledge and local voices. Not that I did not consider them, but often only a handful of people dared to venture into unknown territory and had the will, strength, and audacity to question tightly held presuppositions about bureaucracy and its associated principles of state externality and modularity. I hope that I have found a good balance in this book, one that does justice to both central and peripheral forms of local knowledge.

In Chapter 2, I discuss various cases of police discrimination (or more specifically: migrant-hostile policing). Despite persistent efforts of senior police managers to reduce police discrimination to a problem of deviant individuals (the 'rotten apple' approach), the cases can be better understood through the lens of a 'rotten

They approached me with a research assignment to conduct fieldwork along the lines already established, which started in the spring of 2008.

orchard' approach (Punch 2003). In fact, I strongly agree with Punch that the metaphor of rotten apples is often 'part of the rationalization process that beleaguered institutions engage in when defending themselves. What usually cannot be admitted is that deviance had become *systemic*—in some way encouraged, and perhaps even protected, by certain elements in the system' (Punch 2003, 172). In most cases, however, when police discrimination is recognized and discussed as a supra-individual or systemic problem, we find general references to police culture, especially to some dominant traits such as masculinity or group loyalty (Loftus 2009). In Chapter 2, I want to go beyond such police culture-as-trait analyses. If police culture is going to be used as a heuristic to understand, perhaps even explain, discrimination, it should be looked at not (or not only) as a set of shared traits but as 'historically persistent'—but, we should add, not necessarily stable—'patterns of meaningful organization' (Martin 2016, 463). Keeping in mind the current anti-bureaucracy reforms discussed earlier, we are facing a history in the making that leads to a non-modular constitution of present-day policing in The Netherlands. This, I believe, is the root cause of police discrimination.[9]

The non-modularity in Chapter 2 mainly refers to the lack of separation between the organization and its individual members, that is, between roles and personalities, (public) institutions and (private) individuals. In Chapter 3, I turn away from this 'biocratic governance' and draw attention to the fading division between the Dutch police organization and its organizational environment. With the celebrated demise of bureaucracy as well as the 'phoenix-like emergence of the "post-bureaucratic or network organization"' (Coupland and Reed 2004, 5), the bureaucratic delineation of public institutions, separating them from their organizational environment, has increasingly been under attack as well. To meet the demands of an ever more articulate public, as well as those that arise with new and complex security problems, police organizations worldwide have accepted the need for strategic partnerships and networks (see Diphoorn and Grassiani 2016 for a recently published overview of 'pluralized policing', 'security assemblages', and the like). That police power is now often divided across a multiplicity of organizations and institutions is now a

[9] For a rehabilitation of bureaucratic principles as a tool against ethnic exclusion in the Dutch police, see also Siebers (2009c).

social fact (Karpiak 2016b). The expanded notion of police power urges us to look beyond the police organization proper if we wish to understand police discrimination. In Chapter 3, I mainly focus on a local security network in the south of The Netherlands, specifically on their pervasive policing of 'illegal' immigrants.[10]

In Chapter 4, I move away from policework on the street to consider some internal affairs that concern discrimination.[11] In a way, this chapter refocuses on biocratic governance, but this time not with the intention of studying its effects but instead considering its modes of operation. A number of ethnographic cases are discussed that help us understand how biocracy—the inclusion of the 'whole person' in the workplace—works as a holistic type of power that makes it almost impossible for officers with a migration background to combat discrimination. More specifically, I will concentrate on diversity management, personal development plans, and other psychological instruments as forms of 'identity control' that stretch the outer bounds of labour control.

Chapter 5, the concluding chapter, is used to synergize the previous chapters as well as to add something new to them. Both functions are captured by the title *Reclaiming the Public in Policing*. On the one hand, I will argue that the empirical and conceptual work in this book points to a corrosion of the public character of policing, which is saddling us with law enforcement agencies that find it more and more difficult to exclude politics, particularism, and populism from their operations. It is imperative, therefore, that we 'unthink' bureaucracy as the social evil of our time and revalue the public contours of policing.

A second way of reclaiming the 'public' in policing—this time not defined as a particular quality of police but as an active and engaged citizenry that is involved in public debates on police—has to do with the role of police scholars outside the academy. I advocate a 'public anthropology of police' (Mutsaers 2015a; Mutsaers et al. 2015) that urges anthropologists to give their police ethnographies extra-academic appeal and make them accessible to a broader public. Throughout my project, I felt it was my duty to

[10] This chapter is a slightly reworked edition of an article published in *The British Journal of Criminology* (Mutsaers 2014a). Reprinted by permission.

[11] This chapter is a combination and revision of two articles published in *Critique of Anthropology* (Mutsaers 2016b) and *Anthropology of Work Review* (Mutsaers 2014b). Both reprinted by permission.

go public with my ethnographic findings, because I believe that the public value of police ethnography is a democratic one, in the sense that, when cast as a public act, it can bring the police under scrutiny by an assemblage of actors and institutions inhabiting a broad swathe of political, ethical and epistemological positions (Mutsaers et al. 2015). From this perspective, police ethnographies can fulfil a democratic function by prompting informed discussions on policing that involve politicians, policy-makers, legislators, police officials, and non-governmental institutions, as well as an active and engaged citizenry, re-established in its responsibility to participate in public debates on police (Fassin 2013a, 2013b). In Chapter 5, I focus on the 'public afterlife' (Abu-Lughod 2016; Fassin 2015) of my police ethnography and discuss how my work was received and discussed by various publics and counter-publics. As we will see, the police responses to my study are in fact an enrichment of it, as they give us deeper insights in how the police react to *their* counter-publics.

2

Migrant-Hostile Policing

Case 1: an arrest gone wrong

His mouth agape and his breathing barely detectable, the Aruban Mitch Henriquez was lying on the ground with his hands cuffed behind his back and his eyes shut, surrounded by several Dutch police officers. Like many of the fatal encounters of African-Americans with police in the United States, this arrest-gone-wrong was captured on video with a smartphone, directly uploaded on the web, and thrown into the public spotlight. In contrast to the video that captured the police beating of Rodney King in Los Angeles, 1991, this recording can easily be retrieved with a few keystrokes. When replayed, one can hear the familiar background voices expressing indignation and outrage from people who were present at this site of police violence. I say *familiar* because the upsurge of 'hashtag activism' against the police (Bonilla and Rosa 2015) has offered such voices a prominent place on social media platforms.

Henriquez, father of three, had travelled to The Netherlands for a family visit, coming from Aruba—one of the four constituent countries that form the Kingdom of the Netherlands. On 27 June 2015, he was at a summer concert in The Hague. There he made the mistake of underestimating the power of 'denied negative reciprocity' (Scott 1990), which characterizes hierarchical relations of the kind that exist between police and the policed: do not trade a slap for a slap, an insult for an insult, or a bad joke for a bad joke. In the company of several police officers, Henriquez had half-jokingly touched his crotch while shouting that he had a gun in his pocket. According to some bystanders, this was a joke, as in a Caribbean context 'gun' can refer to impressive male genitals.

During my fieldwork I had discovered that Dutch police officers can be very good at maintain joking relationships with members of the public. In anthropology, the joking relationship is known as a 'relation between two persons in which one is by custom permitted, and in some instances required, to tease or make fun of the other, who in turn is required to take no offence' (Radcliffe-Brown 1940, 195). The relationship is one of 'permitted disrespect', characterized by friendliness and antagonism at the same time, which can be symmetrical (two persons make fun of each other) or asymmetrical (A teases B but B refrains from joking back). While Henriquez's joking act could be interpreted as a hidden form of protest, reminiscent of Scott's descriptions of the mocking and vengeful scripts used by subordinates to ridicule their superiors (Scott 1990), he was immediately confronted with the asymmetry of the relationship. After he had shouted that he had a gun, the officers present responded and took him into custody. They later declared that Henriquez had resisted arrest—the proverbial trading of a slap for a slap. He had traded twice, once with a joke, the second time with uncooperative behaviour during the arrest, and paid for it with his life. Results from the autopsy indicated that he died of asphyxiation after being held in a chokehold and being crushed by five officers who sat on his body. The National Department of Criminal Investigation ruled out the possibility that he was carrying a gun, nor had he ingested a lethal dose of drugs or alcohol, as the toxicology report pointed out. His death was a chokehold death, a thorn in the side of the authorities, considering the controversy surrounding the use of the technique. Chokeholds are not part of the rules of engagement and not taught at the police academy, yet they are routinely used in discretionary policing.

The death of Henriquez wrought havoc on the streets of The Hague. Protestors occupied a neighbourhood, the notorious *Schilderswijk*, known for its history of police discrimination, to voice their dissent. It was the careless way in which the case was perceived to be handled that made people fly into rage and pour torrents of scorn on the Dutch criminal justice system and the police in particular. At first, the Public Prosecution Service, informed by the five officers involved, had stated in a press release that Henriquez had collapsed in a police vehicle on his way to the police station, but the video proved otherwise. It showed that Henriquez was already unconscious when he was surrounded by the five officers in question. Instead of following emergency protocol prescribing resuscitation, they dragged him into a police vehicle. Prompted by what they could view on the Internet, people started to invoke online images of Eric Garner, who died from a chokehold performed by New York Police Department officers, and Freddie Gray, who was forced into a police van by the Baltimore police despite having sustained a spinal cord injury. Evidence available online forced a correction from the Dutch, who were forced to admit that Henriquez was already dying immediately after the chokehold was performed. The recording of the event by a mobile device reversed the 'hierarchy of credibility' (Becker 1967), which usually allocates the right to police members to define a situation, to tell others what 'really' happened.

Case 2: an arrest that never took place

A statue of Alois Senefelder (1771), the Prague-born inventor of lithography, rises above the entrance of what used to be the Senefelder printing office, at the Admiraal de Ruijterweg in Amsterdam-West, built in 1910 and declared a city monument. The ground level of the building is now a supermarket. I first set foot in this building in 2012 when I was on patrol with a constable and a senior constable of the Amsterdam police.

An April shower had forced us into the car. We were cruising along the main street that cuts the rest of the city from its centre in a western direction. While cruising, we discussed a particular aspect of police business: blood feuds in Turkish families. Both my companions had a Turkish background and had developed interesting perspectives on this issue. Conversations and reminiscences fill much of a police officer's time, especially during uneventful car patrols like this one. This particular moment gave us the opportunity to have a long discussion on the central topic of my ethnographic study: police and migrants. Just when we really started to engage on the topic, however, we were interrupted by a message received from the area control room. A shoplifter was caught red-handed in the supermarket by a private security guard.

The senior officer (I call him Kerem) flexed his shoulders and threw the car into gear. Within minutes, the Senefelder building was in sight and Kerem slammed on the brakes. The vehicle screeched to a stop. He and his junior colleague, Serhat, rushed inside in expectation of some serious action, but within seconds their adrenaline had dissipated. The shoplifter turned out to be a man whose major problem was homelessness, not lawlessness: a man who had been caught for 'the usual behaviours born of street life' (Scheper-Hughes 2006, 159). What is more, he had not even passed by the shop counter, or so it seemed. According to the law, he had not yet stolen anything, or so it seemed. The security guard had challenged the man because he saw that he was hiding canned food under his jacket.

I noticed that the patrolmen realized that opportunities for 'real' police action are few and far between, a familiar realization, and for a moment they were unsure of what to do next. Eventually, they decided to take the man to a more private part of the building in order to have a conversation with him. It turned out that the man did not speak Dutch; he was an immigrant from Morocco who had lived illegally in Spain for most of his life. To make things even more complicated, the security guard spoke in broken Dutch and had difficulties explaining, in unambiguous language, what had happened (did the suspect pass the shop counter or not?). Disheartened by the lack of action, confused by the 'superdiversity' of the linguistic situation (Blommaert 2013a), and moved by the suspect who beseeched them to release him, the officers decided to drop the matter and leave. Prescriptions of police conduct are not carved in stone; adjustments can always be made if needed, or desired. In this case, it meant that a man was not drawn into the criminal justice system and simply disappeared back into anonymity.

Case 3: a populist arrest

On 5 November 2016, a columnist for *NRC Handelsblad*, a respected newspaper in The Netherlands, published a critical column about a tweet that was sent out a couple of days earlier by a juvenile officer of the Rotterdam police (Van Veelen 2016). The officer in question had tweeted about his 'catch' of three juveniles (aged ten, twelve, and sixteen) and attached a mugshot that showed the three youths with hoodies on, facing against the wall.[1] The juveniles were charged with bicycle theft. The entire

[1] The tweet, in full, read: 'Gisteren zijn een 10, 12 en 16 jarige uit rdam aangehouden tz fietsendiefstal. #middeldijkerplein #Barendrecht'. This is

situation is reminiscent of what Choongh (1998, 30, emphasis original), quoting Garfinkel, wrote: 'The power to arrest and detain "*suspects*" at the police station allows each officer to extract the submissiveness which he feels is his due, for the police station is an ideal location at which to subject recalcitrant member of the policed community to a status degradation ceremony.' However, this time, the officers in question decided to make the degradation ceremony available to the public via social media. In addition, this time, it was not the decision of one cowboy but of an entire police communication department. Another newspaper (*Algemeen Dagblad*) conducted a public opinion poll which found that 80 per cent of the 13,000 people who had been surveyed did not find the photo problematic. Some were even displeased by its anonymity: 'You still don't get to see anything'; 'They need to be publicly disgraced and have their hands chopped off'.

In other words, there seemed to be a moral consensus regarding the conduct of the tweeting officer. This was justice without trial (Skolnick 1966), undisturbed by the rule-bound nature of the criminal process. On his Twitter account the juvenile officer argued that 'the public needs to know that juveniles commit bicycle theft too'. This statement was later repeated by the National Police in a press release which stated that the police organization considered the photo harmless: it was simply intended to inform people about the developments in their neighbourhood and the tweet was considered the most expedient way of informing the public about the rise of bicycle theft in the district. The head of the communication department of the Rotterdam police added: 'Several colleagues of that particular police team had looked at the photo before it was published. I think there is nothing wrong with it ... We want the public to become aware of bicycle theft ... As an organization we have become much more transparent over the years.'

The Non-Modular Constitution of Present-Day Policing

Decisions that are made by rank-and-file police officers are low profile and therefore very hard to review, especially when it is decided not to invoke the law (Goldstein 1960)—such as in the

translated in English: 'Yesterday, a 10, 12, and 16 year old from Rotterdam were arrested for bicycle theft. #middeldijkerplein [which is a place in Barendrecht] #Barendrecht [which is a place in the Netherlands close to Rotterdam]'.

second case cited in this chapter. In this case, we saw that a man was set free; a man who may or may not have been culpable of the petty crime of which the private security guard had accused him. One of the functions of police is to 'negotiate demands' (Huey 2007) and in this case the patrolmen acceded to the wishes of the suspect, who begged to be released. Independent of time or place, police discretion remains an important cause of the 'varieties of police behaviour' (Wilson 1968) and thus of discriminatory enforcement. The variability may depend on efforts to make police interventions more visible—for instance by citizens (as in the first case) or the police themselves (as in third)—and the ubiquity of camera phones and online file-sharing has certainly augmented the visibility of executive police (Brown 2016). Yet, a certain amount of freedom will always be conferred on police officers who must make decisions *in situ*. As Bittner wrote: 'Policemen are inevitably involved in activities that cannot be fully brought under the rule of law' (in Martin 2018).

That discretion is an important feature of policing has been abundantly reported in the academic literature and does not need repeating here. What I will attempt to show, however, is that discretionary policing does not equal idiosyncratic policing. Police officers always work with 'background expectancies' (Cicourel 1968) or 'frames' (Goffman 1974) when they are on the job. A frame is

> a particularly tangible metaphor for what other sociologists have tried to invoke with words like 'background', 'setting', 'context', or a phrase like 'in terms of'. These all attempt to convey that what goes on in interaction is governed by usually unstated rules or principles more or less implicitly set by the character of some larger, though perhaps invisible, entity (for example, 'the definition of the situation') 'within' which the interaction occurs. (Berger 1985, xii–xiv)

One obvious frame that guides officers in their work is the law itself. Criminal law sits at the most coercive end of a continuum of institutions of social order (Zedner 2004) and can be distinguished from more informal forms of social control such as kinship, education, religion, or culture more generally. Admittedly, some anthropologists have taken law as one aspect of culture alongside others—the 'force of organized society to regulate individual and group conduct to prevent, redress or punish deviations from prescribed social norms' (Hoebel 1954, 4). From this 'law-as-culture' perspective it is interesting to look at how cultural aspects are given 'authoritative recognition' (Rosen 2006) in law and how 'webs of signification' (Geertz 1973) are spun in law and legal processes. Although it offers an intriguing take on the matter, this perspective begs coverage in a different book.

Here, I take the law and the concomitant bureaucratic structuration of policing as an official sphere of social activity that can be distinguished from other, unofficial spheres (e.g. cultural, family, or religious life). I will argue that this modularity, this separation of spheres, is a precondition for a neutral police force that treats people equally and without regard to the individual. In opposition to this modularity, the Dutch police favour the ubiquitous 'psy-frame' that becomes operative through particular human resource practices, styles of supervision, conditions of work, structures of incentives, and organizational policies (see especially Chapter 4). The institutionalization of this psy-frame makes the inclusion of non-official aspects of police work not a matter of discretion but design. The foregrounding of people's psychology, and their inner life more generally, must be seen as an organizational strategy to humanize police officers, to prevent them from hiding behind scripts, roles, and routines. The psy-frame constitutes the 'come-as-you-are' ideology that I described in the Introduction as fundamental to the post-bureaucratic organization that operates as a 'biocracy' (Fleming 2014a, 2014b). While the psy-frame has, of course, not altogether replaced legalistic and bureaucratic frames, it has risen to a level that ought to concern us.

Anthropologists of the police have recently paid attention to this idea of 'humanizing' the force. Reflecting on earlier ruminations on it, Karpiak and Garriott (Karpiak and Garriott 2018) raise the important question: what would such an act of humanization look like? And what responsibility do we, as anthropologists of the police, have in this respect? This second questions refers to anthropologists' representations of the police in their writings. In her contribution to the same volume, Verdery reflects on this vexing issue by discussing how different publics responded to her attempts to humanize the Romanian communist secret police, the Securitate, which she had studied (and which had studied her!) for many years (Verdery 2018). Some people considered these humanizing attempts misleading, even downright immoral, accusing her of ignoring the pain and sorrow caused by the Securitate. This example makes clear how important it is for anthropologists of the police to think seriously about their representations (see also Chapter 5 of the present book).

Karpiak and Garriott's first question—what would an act of humanization look like?—not only refers to how police are represented by scholars but also to how police represent themselves. What happens when police are 'humanized', such as in The Netherlands, and what does such humanization mean? Cabot, in her work on the Greek police, hits the mark when she states that 'police are often seen to be dangerous and corrupt for how prejudice, political interests, and "lawlessness" are assumed to shape their actions' (Cabot 2018, 216). Numerous cases will be discussed in this and following chapters to show the effects of such 'humanization', or sphere conflation, but let us begin with a short analysis of the three cases already discussed.

Case 3 is perhaps the most obvious example of humanization or sphere conflation as a deliberate and organized act. To acknowledge this, it is important to realize that the tweet cited was posted after careful planning and consensus formation. Moreover, according to the latest statistics, the Dutch police now have an organized 'tweeting force' of more than 1,800 officers. Together they form a mass medium, and a very special one indeed. Considering the need for the police in abnormal situations, police tweets are likely to display people in their most vulnerable, embarrassing, disgraceful, painful, or outrageous moments. Police posts may display or describe pain, anger, shame, and defeat. While anonymity and privacy should limit the content and tenor of police tweets and other online police media activity, the public nature of any posting ought to be borne in mind. The uploading of the mugshot of the three juveniles will undoubtedly have had its social effects in the private spheres of kinship and friendship. Online posting of any content—a photo, a tweeted response to any given situation—has the potential to exacerbate reactions to that situation, by the subjects, their family, friends, and the wider public. Publicity and visibility matter, as they are very much likely to increase the amount of shame experienced by the suspects and their circle of intimates.

Police tweets expand the potential of informalized action and increase soft power of police to warn people and make them more vigilant. Online posting via tweets and other social media can be extremely helpful as a means by which police can exert soft power. However, exercising this power can have unforeseen and unwanted effects. Owen and Cooper-Knock (2014, 12), in their work on police in Nigeria and South Africa, coin the term 'police vigilantism' to make the point that 'police can behave in ways that mimic non-state actors who are termed "vigilantes".' Evidently, police vigilantism is a special variation because it merges legal authority with informal action that does not necessarily facilitate criminal justice work. Many police tweets are not intended to play any role in criminal investigations but ought instead to be understood as part of public relations. They can inform the public about past—and sometimes ongoing—police actions in order to make people more familiar with police work and to bring the police closer to the people. As such, they are an expedient way of countering the state externality and impersonality that the Dutch police has been trying to get rid of since the 1970s.

But such involvement and engagement comes at a price: a false anchoring in the normative certainty of *Gemeinschaft* that privileges some groups at the expense of others. In this light, a police tweet can be understood as a public text that is 'composed in the language of the law [but] intersect[s] with the fabric of particularistic "*sentimental feelings*" that define the political textures of local community life' (Martin 2007, 684, emphasis original). One must be careful not to generalize here. The moral consensus that appears from the opinion poll mentioned earlier is strikingly at odds with the realities of power imbalance, inequality, and class hostility that characterize modern society, that is, the *Gesellschaft* (Zedner 2004). Considering the juveniles' appearances (the hoodies, their obvious ethnicity), this particular tweet is likely to count as one of many factors that complicated the already troubled relations between the police and individuals from ethnic minorities and reinforces rather than dissolves existing divisions in society. It is not hard to imagine that the tweet will make people more vigilant in very particular ways, that is, making people aware of those at the margins of society. This vigilantism squares well with dominant Dutch police discourses on migrant juveniles as the 'enemy within' (Bonnet and Caillault 2015).

Compared to Case 3, the decisions of Officers Kerem and Serhat led to a very different outcome. In contrast to the degradation ceremony that took place in Rotterdam, the privacy of the suspect in Amsterdam was respected; he was brought to a more private part of the building. Rather than inflicting extrajudicial punishment on the suspect through public shaming and deprivation of dignity that the youths were made to endure in Case 3—one aspect of 'police punishment' (Harkin 2015)—the officers respected the suspect's dignity. They complied with the 'watchman style' (Wilson 1968) that officers adopt to keep the peace. Watchmen gauge the seriousness of the reported offence based on its immediate consequences. When the offence is mild and the consequences negligible, the (suspected) lawbreaking may be condoned. Back in the car, Serhat said that he pitied the man suspected of shoplifting only moments earlier. He considered him a poor creature who had experienced a lot of bad luck in life. In his short career as a police novice, he had seen many homeless people like the present suspect and held little hope that their life chances would improve.

When we arrived at the station, I took some time to jot down the events of the day in my notebook. While doing so I remembered a book chapter written by Roitman (2006) that I had read a few weeks earlier. Roitman had written about road banditry in the Chad Basin and developed a theory centred on what she called the 'ethics of illegality'. This theory states that given the context in which people live, they etch out a space of ethics that cannot always be understood with reference to a fixed and external code of morality (such as, for instance, the criminal law). People develop an ethical reasoning that helps them live with particular actions that are criminalized by the authorities. Simply put, poverty can force people to circumvent the law. Without calling it this, Kerem and Serhat had appropriated an ethics of illegality, a clear example of an act of humanization.

At first glance, they seem to articulate a completely different world view than the officers in Rotterdam. Whereas the tweeting officer deems the official course of criminal justice insufficient to protect the public and punish the suspect, Kerem and Serhat's case seems to posit that social justice ought to be seen as a prerequisite of criminal justice. However, these officers also have something in common with the tweeting cop: a deviation from a strict and formal enforcement of criminal law, which Wilson would capture in his notion of 'legalistic style'. They walk on the same quicksand because they, too, police with regard to the individual. The Twitter disgrace was condemned by human rights organizations and legal experts, but the same reaction might well have occurred in response to the humanitarian reasoning of Kerem and Serhat, albeit from the opposite point of view, if it had been known to the public. If they had been accompanied by a native Dutch police officer, accusations of favouritism may have easily followed ('you're helping out a fellow Muslim', an accusation that often takes place irrespective of the actual religious background of the parties involved).

In fact, as we will see in more depth in the next part of this chapter, such accusations attacking the integrity of the police took place during my fieldwork. A native Dutch police officer told me during an interview in 2009 that she began to distrust a Turkish-Dutch colleague during an interrogation of a Turkish-Dutch suspect. Her colleague greeted the suspect in Turkish and started to translate all questions. The female officer confessed during the interview (with me) that this made her suspicious: 'I was like "hey, wait a minute. What lies behind all this talk? Are you the colleague that I think you are? How incorruptible are you?"'

The Turkish-Dutch officer in question stated in a separate interview that he was caught off guard by his colleague's reaction. After all, colleagues sought his language skills all the time and the station chief even applauded his translation work. Most people simply considered it much more efficient to use him rather than bringing in an official and expensive translator. Remarkably, another station chief (in the same city) had the audacity to ask me some years later to pay special attention to the integrity of Turkish-Dutch officers in particular. I ignored him (cf. Gowricharn and Çankaya, 2015, for other work on distrust with respect to the integrity of minority officers in The Netherlands).

The only serious case regarding an attack on an individual's integrity that I came across occurred in the context of the killing of Henriquez (Case 1) and it involved the highest-ranking officer in the country: the former Chief of the National Police, Gerard Bouman. As vehicles were set ablaze and the streets of The Hague were crowded with protestors, he promised the five officers responsible for the tragedy that they would keep their jobs and ignored the decision of the prosecutor to suspend them without pay. Making promises that were not his to make and that could interfere with the course of justice, he reinforced a view of the police that gave cause to the protests in the first place; that police work is shot through with hostility towards migrant that allows officers to victimize migrants with impunity. Replacing role-based distance and separation from subordinate officers with personal affinity towards them, the chief of police preserved a form of solidarity that the director of the Dutch division of Amnesty International called 'perplexing' and 'unacceptable' (Reub 2016).

Case 1 is crucial to our understanding of the non-modular constitution of policing and its implications. Not only does it show that defensive solidarity and group loyalty are integral and *enduring* features of rank-and-file police culture (cf. Loftus 2009, 2010), it also shows that they feature prominently at the highest echelons of the organization. It can be argued that there is a homology between the physical threat to the street cops in The Hague ('I have a gun') and the code of silence on the one hand, and the social threat of the protests that questioned police legitimacy, faced by the paternalistic chief of police on the other hand. The need, keenly felt, to protect each other, if necessary at the expense of protocol and procedural justice, must have increased still further when some protestors caused their protest to become very personal, holding up banners depicting individual officers with photographs and hateful captions. The desire to seek protection of and among in-group members is a very human reaction in threatening situations, but that is not the point here (although I am particularly interested in such a 'humanization' for reasons outlined earlier). Personalization and the wrongful use of discretion are not exclusive to the realm of rank-and-file policing; the highest-ranking officer in uniform sets the example. Non-modularity, that is, the lack of capacity or desire to separate official from unofficial spheres, trickles down from the top to the bottom.

'As visible symbols of state authority', argues Loftus (2009, 117), 'the police are prone to become socially isolated from the outside world.' Consistent with other police scholarship (including Loftus' work), I too encountered officers who felt alienated from the public. The sometimes-violent protests in The Hague, for instance, caused great indignation among local police and national leaders alike. Political and police leaders blew 'political life' into Henriquez's dead body (Verdery 1999). Politicians of the Dutch Law & Order party (the VVD neoliberals), for example, cleverly used the protests to advance their own political agenda. The Prime Minister (from the VVD) depicted the protestors as mentally deranged: he refused to talk to 'retards'. The mayor of The Hague (also a VVD neoliberal) attributed the protests to a combination of tropical weather and the Ramadan. People were hot and hungry, which made them do all kinds of weird things.

Eventually, hundreds of protestors were arrested for defying a ban on public assembly that was quickly enacted.

Similarly, police officers in The Hague and elsewhere throughout the country expressed their disbelief and outrage on social media regarding what they saw as the disproportionate violence of the protests that, to be fair, sometimes verged on rioting. As such, they effectively turned the argument into one that worked in both directions; after all, things had started with disproportionate police violence in the first place. Throughout my fieldwork, I encountered police officers who used derogatory terms to describe (particular segments of) the public and who quickly lost their tempers in case of disobedient behaviour or minor public order incidents. As Loftus (2009) observed, alienation and isolation lead to a strong sense of togetherness, 'insiderism', and group loyalty among police, which in turn further sets them apart from the public.

It is important to acknowledge that the closed nature of police organizations does not necessarily stem from its bureaucratic structure, as is often suggested. On closer inspection, the examples discussed here seem to point in the opposite direction. Contrary to the anti-bureaucratic thought that guides current police reforms—that is, bureaucratic impersonality and overregulation are responsible for 'unresponsiveness', a loss of liberty, and the mutual alienation of police and the public—they show that a breach of protocol, untruthful statements, lack of transparency, prejudging the outcome of events or the guilt of individuals, personal power, and an improper stamping of authority are the actual culprits. Things would probably not have spun out of control if the prescribed bureaucratic capabilities and comportments had been firmly in place. Personal liberty, rights, and freedom are, as the Henriquez case exemplifies, dependent on—instead of antithetical to—bureaucracy and the rule of law (Du Gay 2005). These achievements and their social effect—peaceful coexistence—are a direct result of the separation of private and public conduct. The art of separation (Walzer 1984) was clearly forgotten when the personal considerations of the five officers in question prevailed and when the chief of police asserted his personal authority.

The Ubiquity of Migrant-Hostile Policing

At two o'clock in the morning of 9 January 2013, I am with Harry during a final shift, which starts late in the afternoon and lasts until the early hours in the morning. At this unearthly hour, we have parked the car on a parking lot to keep an eye on a few shops across the streets, which had recently been burgled. If it had not been the end of a busy night, this would have been a good moment to consider the sacrifices officers continually make during long stretches of uneventful shifts, waiting for the occasional moment of thrill and excitement. However, it had been a busy night in which my companions set up two traffic controls at two different locations, among other tasks.

Earlier that day, I headed to an idyllic village nearby with six officers. The village, Hilvarenbeek, had recently become the new area of watch of one of my companion's, who had recently been promoted to community officer. In the car on our way there, Harry murmured sarcastically: 'We go there because everybody has a right to his portion of police service', being under the impression, like everybody else in the patrol unit, that nothing requiring police presence ever happens in that particular village. 'We go there because Halil needs to show his face and make a good impression on the residents as their new community officer.' (Ironically, a week later two calls came in at the station from people complaining that an *allochtoon*—the Dutch word used to denote non-Western minorities—was spying on them. It turned out to be Halil, who was working in plain clothes.)

Around 7 p.m., we arrived at the location (a gas station) the officers deemed suitable for the traffic control and they started preparing the setting. About thirty minutes later, I found myself with a flashing light in my hand, directing drivers to the parking space in the gas station, where the traffic control took place. One officer on a motorcycle was responsible for the 'road block' (their term), one was watching over the police cars and four were manning the control, which involved checking people's driver's license and insurance papers as well as performing an alcohol check on drivers (where officers suspect excessive drinking).

While directing the traffic—a task that I took very seriously—I chatted to Mehmet, a Turkish-Dutch senior constable. He decided that there was no point in beating about the bush and said 'I don't know what we are doing here. This is really not our *target group*' (my emphasis).

That this was how they all felt became clear from the lenience with which the officers treated drivers during the control. Only once did the officer on the motorcycle engage in a high-speed pursuit, chasing a driver who tried to avoid the road block. Otherwise, it was a quiet evening and nothing of note really happened. Not a single citation was issued despite the fact that several people were found not to be in possession of either their driver's license or car insurance papers and despite the fact that these were not the kind of circumstances that compel selective enforcement (it was a quiet road, the officers had plenty of time to stop any car they chose). One man was even allowed to call his wife and ask her to bring his driver's license to him. To general laughter, one officer asked to see her license too. After an hour or so, the traffic control was over.

We drove to an unmanned police station nearby, where we drank a cup of coffee we had no time to consume. The operator at the precinct station forwarded an emergency call that had come in from the asylum seekers' centre at the outskirts of an adjacent town. A quarrel had developed into a threatening fight between two groups. As the unit nearest the scene we were dispatched. Driving over one hundred miles an hour, we rushed to the centre, where we arrived fifteen minutes later. Miraculously—and to the disappointment of my company—there were already many police officers in attendance. We left without having to intervene.

Later that night another traffic control took place, this time in the officers' own neighbourhood (Stokhasselt-Noord), the multi-ethnic quarter of the city of Tilburg where the police station is located. The sociological distance between the population of this neighbourhood and the population in Hilvarenbeek is considerable, measured by annual income and ethnic background. 'While statistics can never adequately describe a community', I agree with Reuss-Ianni (1983, 34), 'they can at least set proportions.' According to the Central Bureau of Statistics in The Netherlands, people in Hilvarenbeek earn on average €30,200 a year, whereas in Stokhasselt-Noord the average is €21,300 (the overall Dutch average is €29,800; all figures are for 2010). In Hilvarenbeek, 22 per cent of the working population earns a high salary (more than €41,300 annually), whereas 38 per cent earns a low salary (less than €19,200). In Stokhasselt-Noord, this boiled down to 6 per cent and 55 per cent, respectively. Two per cent of those living in Hilvarenbeek have a non-Western background; in Stokhasselt-Noord this rises to 51 per cent. I present these statistics because the traffic control in Stokhasselt-Noord was not marked by the lenience exhibited during the control in Hilvarenbeek. This was a bicycle control (mainly checking for lights) and everyone who was cycling without lights received a ticket. Most people were from ethnic minorities. *This* was the police officers' target group.

Much has been written about ethnic or racial profiling, 'the practice of using ethnicity, race, national origin, or religion as the basis for making law enforcement decisions about persons believed to be involved in criminal activity' (Open Society Justice Initiative 2012, 13; see Fassin 2013a; Goody 2006; Harris 2006; Miller 2010; Van der Leun and Van der Woude 2011; Rodrigues and Van der Woude 2016). For instance, the literature on 'driving while black' (e.g. Larrabee 1997; Tomaskovic-Devey et al. 2004) has convincingly shown that traffic violations or controls are often used as a pretext for stopping and searching motor vehicles driven by minorities. In the main, however, police scholarship reduces such problematic (and, arguably, unconstitutional) police practices to the cognitive biases of individual officers. Thus, when Lipsky (2010, xiii) stated in his preface to the thirtieth anniversary of publication of his *Street-Level Bureaucrats* that 'racial profiling ... arises not from official policy or direct racial orientations but out of the ways police officers draw on social stereotypes in exercising the discretion sanctioned by their departments', he expressed the mainstream view about ethnic profiling.

The problem with this line of thinking is that it fails to specify how cognitive states relate not only to general social stereotypes but also to broader power relations and government logics (Amar 2010). More generally, it can be stated that the 'cognitive turn' in discrimination scholarship comes with serious shortcomings. As Bielby writes:

> First, it reinforces the perception that discrimination occurs simply because of individuals' personal shortcomings, i.e., their inability to overcome the automatic tendency to make categorical judgements bases on race or gender, regardless of social context. Second, as a result, it invites reform proposals that focus exclusively on individual and interpersonal processes ... Third, by highlighting automatic or unconscious processes at the level of individual cognition, it avoids addressing the ways organizations act to structure decision-making context so that cognitive biases are allowed to affect ... decisions. Fourth, it avoids addressing the responsibility organizations have for taking steps to ensure that the impact of cognitive bias is minimized and analysing the effectiveness of any efforts an organization takes along these lines. (Bielby 2008, 57–8)

Recent police scholarship has in fact paid attention to the broader power relations, government logics, and institutional contexts that prompt ethnic or racial profiling and police discrimination more broadly. In their book *Pulled Over*, Epp and colleagues write about 'institutionalized racial framing' that takes place when officers are directed to look not for violations of the law but for suspicious individuals and neighbourhoods (Epp et al. 2014). This kind of (often race-based) spatial policing was also reported in the work of Çankaya in The Netherlands (Çankaya 2008, 2011, 2012; Gowricharn and Çankaya 2015). Converging with my observations, (those, for instance, which arose when I joined Harry and his fellow officers), Çankaya reports about the ubiquity of target-group policing that centres on suspicious and risky individuals (profiled on the basis of group characteristics) instead of actual law breakers. Similarly, in the earlier cited book *On the Run*, an engrossing account of the struggles between police and minority residents for control over the streets and homes of Philadelphia, Goffman does not point to the defects of character of police officers to explain police racism and violence but instead to the tasks that they are assigned (Goffman 2014; Jencks 2014). Finally, Fassin builds a strong case arguing that police racism must be considered beyond merely looking at an individual officer's behaviour (Fassin 2013a, 2018). He describes in meticulous detail how a 'culture of results' that was enforced on the French police and imposed quantified goals in terms of numbers of arrest, led to an over-policing of 'easy prey' such as marijuana users, minority youth, and undocumented immigrants.

That being said, in April 2013 when Harry and I were invited by the District Commander to reflect on the persistent problem of ethnic profiling (in The Netherlands, the term 'ethnic' rather than 'racial' profiling is most often used), Harry's exhilaration made perfectly good. He could finally tell his superiors that his unit had regularly been instructed to focus on ethnically defined target groups. By that time, the public debate on ethnic profiling in The Netherlands had exploded, and I noticed that many uniformed police officers were fed up with being accused of discrimination. Whenever a new report appeared on this topic (e.g. Amnesty International 2013, or the earlier mentioned work of Çankaya), the chief of police automatically responded by stating that ethnic profiling was a breach of professional norms for which individual officers needed to be held responsible. For instance, in his blog the chief of police gave a personal reaction to the Amnesty report, which rendered ethnic profiling as a structural problem. He wrote:

> Selecting someone simply on the basis of descent goes against our sense of justice. It is not integer and not professional ... Does that mean that we cannot be accused of ethnic profiling? Of course not. It is statistically unlikely that all of the 63,000 police officers work without making judgement mistakes ... Just like everyone else, police officers have intuitions and assumptions about minorities ... By means of training we constantly invest in knowledge and insight: what is required to work in a multicultural society? (Bouman 2013)

Such interventions effectively thwarted all efforts to go beyond individual change programmes. The authoritative words of their boss made middle managers heavily reliant upon stereotype and awareness training programmes that focused only on individual shortcomings. In March 2013, I observed a two-day programme called 'Multicultural Craftsmanship and Honour-Related Violence', attended by Harry's unit. During a preparatory talk with the three course instructors (a Dutch policewoman and two Turkish-Dutch policemen, all working in the same team they were about to train), it became clear to me that all three had an inexorable drive to bring ethnic profiling to an end. Yet, despite my attempts to warn them that their use of particular cultural theories were dated and would in fact run counter to their objectives, they went ahead and ran the programme. They wanted to counter ethnic profiling, a process of ethnic boundary construction (Barth 1969), but focused on the 'cultural stuff' instead. Using cultural theories that have been abandoned by anthropologists as the kind of 'culturespeak' (Hannerz 1999) or 'cultural essentialism' (Grillo 2003) that prompts 'groupist thinking' (Brubaker 2002), the instructors started talking in a stereotypes about the unique features of 'Arabic culture' and 'Middle Eastern culture', seeking to dispel some of the officers' stereotypes about minorities.

Unsurprisingly, their theories immediately backfired as officers felt at liberty to defend their tightly held stereotypes and to exaggerate cultural differences. One officer (white, in his fifties) told the course instructors: 'The problem [with minorities] is unsolvable and we should leave it like that'. 'An unsolvable problem that we should leave like that? Why is it unsolvable?' asked one of the course instructors. 'Because you are dealing with two cultures that cannot be reconciled ... Those people have a completely different background. You can live with it, but you can't solve it.' This triggered other officers to murmur in consent.

The instructor made several attempts to show that the officer was fundamentally wrong, but without success, due to inbuilt limits of the course. The officer's comments were pre-packaged for him by the instructor, who had lumped together an immense variety of individuals under the tags 'Middle Eastern' and 'Arabic'. His intentions were good but the result failed them.

After the first session, dedicated to cultural theory, the instructors embarked on an even more sensitive topic: ethnic profiling. One of the male instructors asked his audience to list a number of traits typifying their 'usual suspect':

> 'Drives a dark Volkswagen Polo.'
> 'Between 15 and 25 years old.'
> 'Wearing a hoodie.'
> 'Coloured skin.'
> 'Moroccan.'
> 'African.'
> 'Runs away when we come!' (general laughter).
> 'Scooter.'
> 'An air of indifference.'

Obviously, the instructor had opted to use this method to prompt people to be aware of their tendencies to frame individuals, and to make sure that they understood that this ought to be done differently. To reinforce his message, he shared some of his own experiences as a Turkish-Dutch police officer. One day when he was working for a special unit dealing with repeat offenders, he had lunch with a colleague (John, who appeared at the beginning of the previous chapter), both being dressed in plain clothes. Another colleague, unfamiliar to both men, was telling a story about a bicycle theft. When our instructor pressed for details, he was told that it was none of his business. He was not recognized as a colleague. His interlocutor thought he had come to repair the elevator.

Further entangling himself emotionally, our instructor told another personal story. He and John arrived at the precinct station to pick up a suspect, both in plain clothes. The desk officer frowned at John when the latter inquired about a suspect's whereabouts. The desk officer pointed to our instructor, saying that he was standing right behind him. The instructor then turned to the audience: 'And that's all right. We are all people. We all have *assumptions*. That's all fine. This is just about raising awareness.' He concluded with another story.

A little while ago, there was a symposium about ethnic profiling. An Antillean colleague who works and lives in Rotterdam, and drives a Volkswagen Polo, had been checked 1200 times by Rotterdam police officers when he was off-duty, in six years! Gradually it came to the point that he considered this to be very irritating [alluding to the notion of VIP; Very Irritating Policing]. He went to his chief of police, who advised him to buy another car and to move to another neighbourhood. Which he did. What are your thoughts on this?

'Recognizable', said a male police officer. 'We do it all the time at our road blocks, by saying to some people "you can go through, because you don't belong to our target group".'

Most of the officers in the audience nodded in agreement: they regarded this as standard operating procedure. The course instructor grinned, this time through gritted teeth and clearly pained, saying: 'that's OK. As a policeman you have to start somewhere. I'm not saying that this is good or bad.' 'Yeah, OK, but sometimes, Moroccan youngsters are treated like animals', said a young officer who had only recently joined the team. He told the group about how perplexed he was when he saw some of his colleagues extracting a suspect's submissiveness, which, he said, they felt to be their due. Another young officer came to his assistance: 'I worked with the wrong people and we often indulged in stopping and searching people just for the sake of it.'

It was clear to me that these contributions gave the instructor a ray of hope, enough at least to propose that something needed to be done. To attain 'fair-play policing', he suggested that the team was in need of a new code of conduct. Despite the fact that such codes are rarely coercive and can thus be seen as a soft option, the suggestion alone caused a lot of disturbance: 'We already have such a list and it's called *Code Blue*. The thing is, however, that we keep these codes in mind for two weeks, after which we forget about them. It simply doesn't work because it has no priority.'

Another officer, who had previously said to me that he had had enough of 'all this multicultural bullshit', added audaciously: 'I'm not gonna do it again. I simply refuse it.' The female instructor replied: 'No, of course, if you don't want to do it, that's your right. It is not compulsory; that is not what this is about.'

Downcast, the instructor retreated from her initial path of change, in which she had invested so much hope. As the day came to an end, it was clear that all three instructors knew that a disastrous precedent had been set regarding the immunity of self-will from social control. The majority of their colleagues had no intention whatsoever of altering the ways and means they conducted their policing. And why would they? In the words of one male officer: 'None of this is strange. If you look at our curriculum, it's full of modules about personal development and the like.'

Indeed, as we recall from the previous chapter, officers are trained and *biocratically* governed to mould their personal style of policing to the ideals of personal authenticity and craftsmanship.

Ironically, the three instructors had called their training 'Multicultural *Craftsmanship*'. The title was borrowed from a similarly titled chair held by a professor at the Police Academy, who had argued in one of her publications for an 'inclusive identity' that leaves 'room within the organizational culture for social and personal identities and concomitant expressions, involvements and interests' (De Vries 2010, 78). The station chief of the team that I was working with was a typical biocrat and, logically, fond of personal involvement and expression. In fact, as I will discuss in Chapter 4, he allowed one of the course instructors to talk about honour-related violence from an autobiographical perspective by letting him share with the other team members a personal story about how he once almost committed murder to avenge the family's honour.

Not only can we raise serious questions about this kind of personification (private interests, personal aptitudes, life stories, etc.), it is also only half the truth. Personal liberties and individual forms of expression abound in the biocratic workplace, but we should not forget that biocracy is the workplace correlation of Foucault's biopower and thus a form of control (Foucault 2008). *Bios*, or 'life itself' becomes enmeshed with power relations when the 'whole person' of the employee is encouraged expression by management ideology (Fleming 2014b). That the officers were not simply free to act in accordance with their private caprice (e.g. liking or disliking minorities) became clear from their repeated emphasis on the fact that they were often *instructed* to indulge in ethnic profiling ('target-group policing'). They were actively encouraged to ignore the disinterested and aloof requirements of the bureau and to police *with* regard to person. This turned the problem of ethnic profiling into an altogether different one, perhaps best described by Hall: 'The question is not whether men-in-general make perceptual distinctions between groups with different racial or ethnic characteristics, but rather, what are the specific conditions which makes this form of distinction socially pertinent, historically active' (Hall 2002, 58).

About a fortnight after the training, when Harry and I sat in the office of the district commander to talk about the vexing issue of ethnic profiling, it was interesting to see how management responded when Harry commented that officers were incentivized to indulge in ethnic profiling. For years, a persistent psychologism had relegated ethnic profiling to the domain of 'private troubles' instead of a 'public issues' (Mills 1959), conveniently diverting attention away from leadership and management. Harry's direct confrontation of his colleagues and their attitudes caught people off guard. I felt stimulated by Harry's courage and decided to support him. I told our audience that I also considered it strange that ethnic distinctions were highly salient in policing at a time that diversity and anti-profiling campaigns had become central to defining norms of police professionalism (see also Amar 2010). I admitted that I considered ethnic profiling an institutional problem and told them about several e-mail messages I had recently received from a (native Dutch) female police officer, Karin, in which she lamented being forced to demand that individuals from particular minority groups leave the city centre:

Part of e-mail (9 March 2013)

Hi Paul,

A while ago we talked at [the police station]. I have finished my training some time ago and now work as a senior constable. For a while now I have been experiencing some things at work that bother me. Serkan [one of the instructors] advised me to contact you, because of your expertise.

In a nutshell, I notice that colleagues discriminate a lot. In the 'war on burglaries and muggings', people are singled out without any mercy for scrutiny on the basis of their skin colour and descent. I try to stay away from this sort of thing and continue to control people on the basis of behaviour [not their looks].

Lately, I've been shocked by some of the assignments I was given by my superior. For instance, during a road block I had to check 'a

> group of Moroccans who are always loitering'. I asked why. 'Because they are our target group.' I asked in return why they are a target group: because they are known to commit burglaries or because they are Moroccans? On his turn he asked me [sarcastically] if I didn't know what a target group looked like.
>
> At another occasion, a control which took place due to some recent muggings and shoplifting, all people with a 'Romanian look' had to be stopped and frisked. At the briefing, I inquired into the purpose of this control. Were we supposed to look for suspicious persons or to simply control everyone with Romanian looks? And what do we do next? The answer was: 'All Romanians need to be expelled from the city centre. Check them and send them away. Well, you don't have the authority to do so, but you can fake it. If they don't leave, follow them until they do.' I couldn't possibly explain this to the Romanian guy on the street.
>
> As time wears on, I increasingly get the idea that I can't do a proper job in the eyes of my colleagues if I don't discriminate. It makes me feel very sad. The *WOS*-culture [WOS = Burglary, Robbery, and Mugging] forces me to discriminate and indulge in racist behaviour, and I am not comfortable with that. That is not my job. I feel horrible as a human being.

Asserting their authority, the officers mentioned by Karin were involved in what I will describe in the next chapter as 'micro-deportations' (cf. Mutsaers 2014a). Very much in line with the work of Çankaya on race-based spatial policing, such forms of banishment are only possible due to a very broad conception of police discretion that borders on illegality (Çankaya 2008, 2011, 2012).[2] In his work on Parisian anti-crime squads and urban policing, Fassin provides similar examples, which he describes as 'petty states of exception', defined as 'temporally, geographically and juridically limited forms of non-respect of the law within democratic regimes' (Fassin 2014, 2015). Based on a long-term ethnographic project, he calls the French police decidedly unconstitutional in their battle against urban crime. He describes the arbitrary character of police punishment (cf. Harkin 2015), that is, the needless use of physical force and provocation which produces a sense of (and actual) insecurity amongst those who

[2] Again, I do not define police discretion as the idiosyncratic behaviour of individual officers, but more generally as police behaviour that is not 'fully brought under the rule of law' (Bittner 1990, 119). Such a definition asks for a sociological rather than psychological understanding of the issue.

are disproportionally policed. Fassin shows that it is the security actor who is causing these feelings of insecurity (see also Mutsaers 2016a). The resemblances with the Dutch case are evident.

Again, the discretionary authority described cannot be relegated to the level of individual decision-making. The micro-deportations that Karin cited were prompted by a particular framing of minorities, in this case rendering Romanians as burglars, robbers, and muggers. Karin explains that it is very difficult to engage in out-of-frame activities ('I can't do a proper job in the eyes of my colleagues if I don't discriminate'). As Goffman stated, frames organize more than meaning; they also organize involvement: 'During any spate of activity, participants will ordinarily not only obtain a sense of what is going on but will also (in some degree) become spontaneously engrossed, caught up, enthralled' (Goffman 1974, 345). Involvement, he stressed is an 'interlocking obligation':

> Should one participant fail to maintain prescribed attention, other participants are likely to become alive to this fact and perforce involved in considering what the delict means and what should be done about this—and *this* involvement necessarily removes them from what they themselves should be involved in. So one person's impropriety can create improprieties on the part of others. (Goffman 1974, 346)

This interlocking obligation may explain why Karin's colleagues had nothing but scorn for her. Her 'frame-breaking', as Goffman would call it, might have had a knock-on effect on the rest of the police department. This way, one maverick can challenge the accepted way of doing things.[3]

I encountered another maverick when I was carrying out ethnographic work in Amsterdam-West. The Moroccan-Dutch

[3] In this sense, frames are very similar to institutions. The relationship between individuals and institutions is an old enigma in social theory and it will most likely continue to be so in perpetuity. Do institutions straitjacket individual minds and bodies or can individuals also wreck institutions? What is the interplay between the two? My police ethnography has brought me closest to Douglas' take on this matter. She argues that:

> [i]nstitutions systematically direct individual memory and channel our perceptions into forms compatible with the relations they authorize. They fix processes that are essentially dynamic, they hide their influence, and they rouse our emotions to a standardized pitch on standardized issues. Add to all this that they endow themselves with rightness and send their mutual corroboration cascading through all the levels of our information system. (Douglas 1987, 92)

policeman in question, Abder, turned out to be very aware of his position as an outsider. Adopting a social Darwinistic frame, he said:

Colleagues within the Dutch police discriminate, it's as simple as that. They question your loyalty because you have a different ethnic background. To some of them, you're just like the criminal ethnic minority on the street. Due to that image—which is reinforced by contemporary politics—you have to fight an uphill battle as a minority within this organization. What people don't realize is that basic rights are at stake. The right to exist. The right to earn a wage. The right to take care of one's family. This is about whole families. [When I joined the organization] I was at the bottom of the food chain. Carnivores were all around me. I was just a naïve herbivore who had a different idea of the police. I had a great sense of justice, but this changed when I became a member of this organization. It is a jungle in here with racists and all. But it was not my intention to be chased away. So I adapted. Not that I became a carnivore myself; I built protection around myself. A very thick skin.

In his first years on duty, Abder suffered from severe discrimination. None of his colleagues wanted to join a beat with him, he was locked in a wardrobe, and his partner left him outside in the cold when a xenophobic citizen had forbidden Abder to enter his house.[4] Years later, when he was working as a sergeant (at the time I interviewed him, he had already been promoted to inspector), Abder's skin had grown thicker. He was able to avert an outburst of ethnic riots alone. This happened when one of his colleagues confronted a Moroccan-Dutch juvenile who was driving his car in a pedestrian zone. The conflict turned physical and the officer dragged the handcuffed juvenile to the station, holding him by his hair. Relations between the police and ethnic minorities in this neighbourhood had been poor for a long time and incidents like this only made things worse. The officer's behaviour

None of this is to argue that institutions cannot be resisted. Institutions are hardly ever total (unless, of course, they are total institutions, such as those described so famously by Goffman). Douglas agrees on this point. She rejects the 'sociological determinism that credits individuals with neither initiative nor sense' (Douglas 1987, 32). An institution is not a 'superorganic group mind' that leaves the individual in a no-choice situation.

[4] This, by the way, is something that happens regularly to officers from ethnic minorities. As 'social professionals' they are often expected to go along with such demands, in order to attain one of the highest goals of the organization: client satisfaction.

was roundly questioned and within an hour, about twenty-five juveniles marched to the police station, some of them seeking an explanation, others retribution. Unwilling to condone any challenge to their authority, all officers on duty went downstairs in full protective gear. In the words of Abder:

> Our chief always spoke of these 'flash moments', moments that can change the entire situation within the blink of an eye. That's when you get situations like in the Parisian *banlieues*. This was such a moment. If we hadn't managed it correctly, it would have trigger riots, Molotov cocktails, stations under attack, riot policing and what have you more. My task then was to keep the peace and to keep the two parties separated. It is unbelievable that one of these parties was my own ... I was upstairs when one of the students came to get me and said 'Abder, come down! Things are really spinning out of control.'

As the community officer in the neighbourhood, Abder knew most of the juveniles. His first thought was to call the parents of the detainee and settle things with them, but when he went down to the front desk of the station, he saw that they had already arrived and were outraged as well:

> The father had already come to the station, together with the mother, the boy's siblings and the grandparents, who had travelled from Morocco to the Netherlands for a family visit. I asked my station chief 'What are you going to do?' 'We are going to beat all of them out of the station, because they don't want to leave.' 'And then what? Once you've beaten them out of the station, what's going to happen then?' 'Yeah, well, we'll see.' 'They will come back with more people, that is what's going to happen. It will not solve the problem. Beating them out now will mean broken windows and burning cars later.' 'I don't give a shit; at least they'll be out.' 'Let me speak to the parents and talk to them.' 'You have five minutes.'

Seriously disturbed by the fact that he was the only police officer who was handling the situation while the station chief absolved all others from responsibility, Abder turned to the protestors:

> With all due respect, that kid has been arrested for good reasons. I am going to inform his parents now, because they are my prime concern. I am requesting you to step outside, now. I assure you that your friend will be treated decently. Leave now, otherwise things will get out of hand. They [pointing at his colleagues] are ready to kick you out. You will come back in greater numbers, but that will only deteriorate the already negative image of this neighbourhood. What good will that do to you, the neighbourhood, your mothers?

After some time, Abder convinced the detainee's father to talk the juveniles outside the station, and he settled the conflict peacefully. When everyone had left and Abder retreated to the back office to inform his colleagues about the positive outcome of his intervention, he found nothing but clubs and batons lying scattered on the ground, symbolizing his colleagues' desire for physical expression. 'No-one came to me except one colleague who had to look over his shoulders when he whispered, "I can't tell you this in front of the others, but you did well".'

To my knowledge, there are few districts in The Netherlands where police never venture afoot—'no-go zones' in popular terminology—but if I were asked to name one area that comes close to this, it would be Amsterdam-West. Abder's narrative on this 'flash moment' concerned the police station where he previously worked (at the time I interviewed him he was stationed elsewhere), but such moments occurred regularly at other police departments in this part of the city. At Abder's new workplace, I interviewed many of his colleagues who told me about similar events. Shortly before I started my fieldwork, for instance, a group of Moroccan-Dutch juveniles had marched to the police station where I was about to start my study, to protest against police discrimination. In the words of the station chief, who was interviewed in 2012 and talked about some of the events that led to the march:

> Within a month after I started, in March 2007, I had a letter on my desk signed by 70 Moroccan juveniles who complained about police discrimination, intimidation, violence, abuse of power, you name it. It was sent to me, to the mayor, to the chief of police and the National Ombudsman. This was one of the public relations issues [I was confronted with] when I started.

Five years later, police–minority relations had not yet begun to improve: about sixty juveniles marched to the police station to rally against officers who they considered to be racists. When I talked with rank-and-file officers about the march, it struck me that some of them felt personally threatened. This had partly to do with the fact that two of the organizers of the protest march were suspected of terrorist activities at that time, making the event particularly grim. In addition, officers felt intimidated due to the architecture of the police station, which, befitting a post-bureaucratic organization, was an open and windowed space in which it was very hard to hide from the outside world. The fact that many of the juveniles were staring through the windows and locked gaze with those inside while pointing at specific officers brought no relief. Again, as in Abder's case, it was left to one officer who had to 'repair' the social relations. He stepped outside, smoked a cigarette with the youngsters, and successfully encouraged them to leave.

It is noteworthy that state proximity can be interpreted as both the problem *and* solution in these cases. While they can be read as extreme examples of zero-tolerance policing, I will argue that community policing is the actual, underlying problem. In Amsterdam even more so than in the rest of The Netherlands, community policing—that 'benchmark for democratic policing' (Hornberger 2013)—has been rolled out on unprecedented scale. This has generally been hailed as a positive development and some analysts have argued that it is due to the fact that Dutch officers are deeply embedded in society that the police here have so far managed to stay clear from large-scale riots such as those which have occurred in France, the United Kingdom, or the United States (e.g. Adang et al. 2010). During ride-alongs, bicycle, and foot patrols, I saw the fruits of community policing. Officers often took ownership of their beat and were generally accepted by the community as a legitimate authority.

However, I also recognized the limits of 'community' in community policing (Herbert 2006). It is useful to quote Herbert's critical work on community policing at some length:

> State actors employ certain grids of legibility upon the input they receive from the citizenry; they recognize some and not other forms of input as legitimate, they sort that input into categories, they react to it via certain prescribed routines. James Scott provocatively refers to this broad phenomenon as 'seeing like a state'. Community is thus not some independently existing entity, but is rendered sensible through a particular state epistemology. The police are not different in this regard. As we will see, they construct community in particular ways that fundamentally impact the manner in which they respond to citizen concerns and demands. (Herbert 2006, 72–3)

I was given various banal and everyday examples of how 'community' is constructed by police when I accompanied a female community officer, Patricia, in Amsterdam-West. As mentioned earlier, Dutch police officers are very good at maintaining joking relationships with members of the public. Patricia was a master joker. As we strolled through the neighbourhoods, she made one joke after another. Because these neighbourhoods are very heterogeneous, many jokes had to do with people's ethnic backgrounds. For instance, with native Dutch residents who complained about street pollution caused—in their perception—by ethnic minorities, she joked that this is simply how they 'do it' in the Rif Mountains of Morocco. Another example: one day we encountered a Moroccan Dutchman who was parking his car illegally. Patricia started her usual business of joking and the man reciprocated the joke. This joking relationship, however, turned out to be asymmetrical and he was given a ticket. Then something peculiar happened. Patricia joked that 'Allah would never permit illegal parking.' The man laughed, submissively, and in response, Patricia teared the ticket up. The man could keep his money but lost face.

The result of such informality is an unmediated proximity between police and the people, which works out quite well for some people but has deleterious effects on others in the community. As my fieldwork advanced, I noticed that ethnicity often (but not always) played a role. These observations converge with Herbert's work and I agree with him that a state agency like the police force needs to be aloof from the vicissitudes of community pressure in order to keep unjust dominance by the majority out of the game. In line with the thesis that I developed in the Introduction, Herbert argues that separation is a means of protection—of both members of the public *and* police officers, as we will see in more detail later in this chapter. State proximity, caused by intimate forms of community policing, takes away the protective shield that ought to protect minority juveniles from invasive policing and—in the reverse—officers from overly personal relationships with juveniles (who, as we saw, targeted individual officers when taking their grief to the police station).

However, in both cases proximity also appeared to be the solution to the tense situations that had developed in and around the police station. Both times escalation was prevented by the intervention of a community officer who personally knew the (small nucleus of) 'troublesome' youth and immediately engaged in 'social repair work'. While reading my notes on these events, my thoughts drifted to Göpfert's work on the Nigerien gendarmes and their *gyara,* or repair work (Göpfert 2016). As he carried out his ethnographic project in the West African Sahel, Göpfert observed how gendarmes often tried to find alternative solutions to disputes and conflicts than force, and as such did not have to bring down the full weight of the law on people's heads. The aim was always to forge a consensus between the conflicting parties and to reinstate harmonious relations. Drawing on Gluckman's idea of the 'norm of the reasonable man', Göpfert provides us with detailed case descriptions to illustrate this repair work, used to balance between a foreign power (the Nigerian *Code Pénal* and *Code de Procédure Pénale* still contain elements from the colonial era) and the expectations of a post-colonial citizenry. The difference between Göpfert's and my own materials is, of course, that his centred on conflicts between citizens whereas my data concern 'mediated' conflicts between police and youth (in the words of Abder: 'my task then was to keep the peace and to keep the two parties separated. It is unbelievable that one of these parties was my own'). The resemblance, apart from both forces using the same kind of 'repair work', lies in the fact that in both contexts police officers mediated between different conceptions and ideas of justice.

To what extent does state proximity—in this case expressed in the close relationships between particular community officers and minority youth and their kin—really offer a sustainable solution? Obviously, it can lead to intolerable conditions for ethnic minority officers. Abder's is a case in point. He was already considered an outsider by his colleagues and cases such as those described in the previous pages only led to more alienation and mutual hostility. The same thing happened to many other officers, including Sergeant Mo, a Moroccan-Dutch community officer in Gouda. I interviewed Mo and some of his colleagues in the spring of 2008, when he had resigned as a community officer to focus on the assessment and selection of new police recruits, processes which he considered to be coloured by 'whiteness' and which he wanted to make more neutral and fair. At first, it was not entirely clear to me whether Mo had abandoned his post because he was marginalized in the community policing team or because he simply considered the other job more important. When I returned to the department about a year later for another round of interviewing, it slowly dawned on me that both reasons were very much entangled. Mo felt like he was 'crying in the wilderness'. He assured me that if diversity is banished to the organizational backwaters, the situation in his former watch area (the notorious

Oosterwei neighbourhood) would deteriorate. An all-white police team could never bring peace to this neighbourhood, so increasing the number of ethnic minority officers was vital.

Oosterwei was built in the 1960s and initially inhabited by lower middle-class residents (Adang et al. 2010). In the mid-1970s, the first immigrants—mainly 'guest workers' from Morocco—arrived, which initiated a flight of the Caucasian population to the suburbs. From the 1990s onwards, predominantly negative news was broadcast about Moroccan-Dutch juveniles who allegedly spent their days loitering in the streets and committing petty crimes. The situation deteriorated around the turn of the century, when the police lost all their authority and considered Oosterwei a no-go area.

Here is an extract of Frank's narrative (Frank, then in his mid-fifties, was a colleague of Mo): 'Yeah, with these people it was just a zero-tolerance approach. "Cleaning the streets", that sort of thing. It was war when I came here as a community officer in '95. Flipped cars, broken windows, a lot of confrontations".'

Richard, whom I met in a dual interview with Frank, confirmed this: 'Our relations with "the Moroccan world" (my emphasis) were of a highly problematic nature. A lot of violence. It became ever more hostile. All we did was hunting. A car with a Moroccan in it was by definition stopped and searched. It was turned inside out.'

In 2005, a new station chief of Moroccan descent was installed. One of his first priorities was to improve the security situation in Oosterwei, which was why he recruited a Moroccan-Dutch community officer, who was instantly promoted from senior constable to sergeant: Mo. My interviewees in the district, as well as other researchers (Adang et al. 2010), confirmed that things swiftly improved. Police–minority relations got better, which resulted in de-escalation of tension and greater police legitimacy in the community. In his appraisal of Mo, Frank said 'It's such a pity that management let him go, though. He lived in that area, he went to the Mosque, he knew everybody. You only had to show him a photo and he recognized who it was. He really proved his merit.'

Frank, however, was equivocating, because this was not the whole truth. The fact that Mo was hired by a station chief with the same ethnic background *and* who promoted him to sergeant aroused envy:

At a certain point, he was promoted, just like that. There was no procedure, no job interview, nothing. And I was like 'Hey, maybe I wanted that job as well. This is not how these things are supposed to go.' They'd created a special job profile for him, some mixture of community policing and ethnic minority relations.

Richard backed Mo up: 'We had that before, that Moroccan colleagues were actively recruited, while other candidates were simply not hired or promoted. We were simply not allowed to apply. But many [Moroccan-Dutch officers] have failed and have left the force. Some couldn't adapt because of their background.'

Talking about his first days in the department, Mo told me that he knew from the start that it was not going to be easy for him: 'There was no warm welcome. Jokes about Moroccans were a daily thing around here and then someone like me [i.e. a Moroccan-Dutch officer] joins the team. It was one group and they did things their way.'

Not ready yet to embrace the way of acting as expected by their new station chief, Richard and Frank complained as they supported each other:

Before [Mo came], people would come in after a fight cursing like hell: 'Fucking Moroccans.' Hard talk about certain groups, still shaking with a cup of coffee in their hands. But now, that is no longer possible. And if Mo happens to overhear such cursing, he tells you what's on his mind. But I think that people should have a chance to express themselves, to vent their feelings. Perhaps a separate, isolated room where you can curse for five minutes. 'Those fucking Moroccans.'

This 'new way' of performing the police function (closer to the people) was actually not that new. In their review article of the different 'generations' of community policing in The Netherlands, Punch and colleagues distinguish beat officers (dominant in the 1960s and 1970s) from neighbourhood teams (mainly seen in the 1980s and 1990s) and community officers (emerging in the 1990s) (Punch et al. 2002). Theirs is clearly a description of policy, not street reality, and by and large we can indeed state that over the years, community policing *policies* have shifted from external (the relation between community officers and the public) to internal (integration between community policing teams and other divisions of the police force) integration. Following this categorization, beat officers have often been labelled as 'social workers', mainly occupied with solving social problems (cf. Herbert 2006).

They have often been adopted by the public who view a particular officer as 'our' police officer (Punch et al. 2002). In contrast, community officers are said to strike a better balance between proximity and distance, adopting problem-solving and crime control rhetoric equally, and they are better protected from the temptations to be in unmediated proximity with members of the public, and all the risks involved, by the line that separates them from the public.

During my ethnographic work across the country, I encountered different combinations of external and internal integration. Some community officers clung to the idea of state externality as an important protection mechanism, while others, like Mo, conformed to the old-style beat constable. Operating closely to the people he policed was particularly easy for Mo because he had grown up in the same neighbourhood (where he still lived at the time of our interviews) and shared his Moroccan identity with most of the residents. As a consequence, his contacts with the public were very informal. Often, he would skip the early morning briefing at the station and go into the neighbourhood straight from home, in plain clothes. His external integration was encouraged by the station chief, who considered it a necessity in order to counter the public's alienation from the police. Most residents contacted Mo on his personal e-mail account or phone number, and Mo was available almost all the time. He drank tea with people in the tea house, joined them during the *salat al-djuma*, the Friday prayer, and helped them with their tax administration and other paperwork.

Despite the positive results it yielded, Mo's external integration gradually led to his alienation from other community officers. He was accused of 'mingling with the enemy' and was increasingly avoided by his colleagues. Whenever he was accused of 'talking with the enemy', he would give a simple rejoinder: 'Of course, that's what I'm getting paid for.'

Despite his resilience, Mo ended up embittered about the whole situation and quit his job. He stood alone, 'crying in the wilderness', as he put it. Soon after he resigned as a community officer, the situation in Oosterwei escalated again. In September 2008, a bus driver was assaulted and mugged by a juvenile from Oosterwei's ethnic minority group. Some bus drivers decided to avoid the neighbourhood for days, despite the fact that the assault had occurred in an adjacent neighbourhood. Resembling the mugging incident in London in 1972, analysed by Hall and his associates, a 'moral panic' occurred which further escalated the situation (Hall et al. 1978). A member of the Dutch Law and Order party (the VVD neoliberals) spoke on national television about a 'nation on fire', and the party boss of the Freedom Party (known for his hostility towards migrants and his highly political exaggerations) publicly suggested withdrawing the Dutch army from Uruzgan and deploying it in Gouda. Oosterwei was plunged back into the same wretched situation it found itself in before Mo's beat-style conduct had brought a ray of hope to residents in the area. The ties that he had established were instantly broken after he left, because personalized trust had never been scaled up to trust in the organization as a whole.

Additional Comparisons

In this chapter, I have described several scenes that offer insight into the troubled history of relations between the police and ethnic minorities in the various places that I have studied for some years. By focusing on the different kinds of state proximity (literal, relational, symbolic), I have tried to demonstrate the paucity of alternative explanations of police discrimination that centre on individual shortcomings. I have argued that blame should not be assigned to individual officers at the bottom of the pyramid but instead assigned to the institution and its post-bureaucratic spirit. The post-bureaucratic organization of the Dutch police force merits our chief attention, because it endangers some hard-won rights and liberties. We have seen how sentimental texts such as tweets can turn supposedly neutral civil servants into agents of popular justice; how the instructions that are given to police officers on the basis of 'target groups' accentuates the presumed correlation between group traits and criminality, and encourages generalized ethnic suspicion; how the embrace of authenticity and craftsmanship as key competences for police officers allows migrant hostility entry into the organization; and how intimate forms of community policing can have adverse effects on those communities, despite its intent to reduce antagonism.

Throughout this chapter, I have made some ad hoc comparisons with studies carried out by police anthropologists in other national contexts (e.g. Fassin 2013a; Göpfert 2016; Owen and Cooper-Knock 2014). In conclusion, I will describe some of the resemblances I have detected between the work of fellow police anthropologists and my own. Again, I am fully cognizant of the contextual differences that exist and it is not my intention to claim that all cases described are somehow identical. Rather, I simply wish to point at some similarities that, if given more attention, help us advance the *anthropological* study of police.

I continue with the last two cases of the previous section, more specifically with the 'provisional authority' of Abder and Mo. I borrow this notion from Jauregui's book on police in India (Jauregui 2016). The modifier 'provisional' for police authority has to be understood in relation to both definitions of the word. First, Mo's and Abder's authority 'may be considered chronotopic, expressing variance across different time-spaces' (Jauregui 2016, 14; Mutsaers forthcoming). In contrast to the ideal of officers in which stable authority is vested by their office and its surrounding legal bureaucracy, Mo and Abder saw their authority fluctuating across time and space. Peculiarly, their authority was often questioned *within* the police station and *by* their colleagues. As time passed by, their 'intra-station' authority faded due to a chain of events that eventually led to their transfers. Outside the station, their authority was continuously negotiated. In a service context, they sometimes literally had to stay outside in the cold when a native Dutch citizen refused to let them in (for reasons that obviously had to do with their ethnicity). As stated earlier, they had to accept such ordeals due to a radicalization of police discourses on 'social professionalism'. By contrast, their authority was widely accepted in minority communities, where they were indeed perceived as 'one of us'.

Second, provisional authority refers to 'conditions of supply and demand, and exchanges of resources, material or otherwise, as in provisions that may be expected, offered, distributed, traded, or taken among multiple interested parties' (Jauregui 2016, 14). As will be discussed shortly, such provisional authority takes more extreme forms in India but it also played an important role in Mo's 'life' at work. I mean this very literally, as he took his non-professional life to work and vice versa. For Mo, no boundaries existed in his highly personalized style of what we can call 'cultural policing'[5]:

[5] Others before me have used this notion of cultural policing. For instance, Comaroff and Comaroff (2004), in their work on law and (social) order in

I am not the kind of person who works from nine to five. You can't get away with that, not when you're working in a Moroccan community. If someone takes the effort to come to you, you can't say 'come back tomorrow'. You can't do that, it's an unwritten rule. People come to you with certain expectations ... Often I didn't even start at half past eight, because it simply isn't effective [implying that everyone is still asleep at that time]. So, often I didn't even come to the station; I directly immersed myself in the community, sometimes in plain clothes.

Mo talked at length about the importance of trust relationships—of building 'rapport', as anthropologists call it—and argued that this requires investment:

Building up trust takes time and investment, if necessary by idle chatter, by filling in people's forms, or by helping them out with phone calls [in Dutch] ... Sometimes it only takes five minutes, but the return on investment is enormous. The person will start to talk in a positive way about me, as will his son, his wife, his neighbour, his cousin, you name it. Then, when something happens, they will tell me who did it.

Such 'provision' also enabled Mo to exert particular forms of 'social control' (his words) that would otherwise not have been possible. Referring to his discussions with parents on the criminal activities of their children, he said:

I often invite parents to the station, not individually, but collectively in sessions. And I say 'this is your son.' That makes them vulnerable, because I am very hard on them; I include religion and all the rest of it. I tell them that they've failed in the eyes of their God. That's really painful, isn't it? That they have failed as parents, failed in the eyes of the Creator. Then there is no way out for them ... I ask them 'haven't you listened to the Imam last Friday? I am not saying these things as a policeman but as a fellow Muslim.'

As a member of the Moroccan-Dutch community in Oosterwei, Mo knew exactly which strings to pull. Talking about communal violence, he stated:

To get them talking, you need to dig deep. Sometimes the root cause can be found in the family; it may even go back to the villages [in Morocco], where they come from. That's where the misery started ... [To understand

post-colonial South Africa, discussed cultural policing in the context of occult-related violence—violence against alleged perpetrators of magical evil such as witchcraft. These practices can be best understood as the policing *of* culture. What I am referring to, though, is policing *through* culture.

> this] you need to start with the first generation; that's the outer circle. That's where you can win trust ... You shouldn't go straight to the core. No, no, no. Take your time and pay attention to the contextual factors that may not seem important at first, but which may turn out to be crucial later on. And then slowly, slowly, slowly, you go to the core.

In her ethnographic study of police practices in Uttar Pradesh in India, Jauregui came across the notion of *jugaad*, which refers to goal-oriented improvisation, especially the use of informal social networks (Jauregui 2014, 2016). This is a useful concept because it falls in line with the community work of Mo and others like him. Although in India, *jugaad* is often used by police officers to advance their own interests (and, as stated earlier, I did not encounter any of this during my own fieldwork), Jauregui argues that it can also be conceived of as a necessary practice to 'get by', or even as a virtuous practice: '[t]his analysis is centred on how *jugaad* mobilizes relationships to conduct everyday exchanges that work to allocate or provide a social good, thereby constituting a (potentially) virtuous practice' (Jauregui 2016, 36). The important point, however, is that with *jugaad,* this mobilization of relationships always involves a transgression of public–private boundaries—of the lines dividing state and society.

Notably, such transgression was also definitive in Mo's excommunication. Mo's *jugaad*—that is, the second definition of provisional authority—made his authority provisional in the first sense of the word, as explained above. His informal exchange networks across the public–private divide eventually corroded his authority at the police station. His colleagues were increasingly unwilling to treat him as a fellow officer; instead, they considered him 'one of them', the enemy. This corresponds to Jauregui's remarks on *jugaad's* provisionality in the sense of its temporality, 'marked by impermanence, instability, and iniquity' (Jauregui 2014, 88).

Jauregui calls for a comparative anthropology of *jugaad* and related practices, and while reading her discussion of comparable concepts in other places (such as *blat* in Russian, *wasta* in Arabic, *ubuntu* in Zulu, *o jeitiñho brasilerio* in Brazilian, or *guanxi-wang* in Chinese), I wondered about the place of *jugaad* in the digital world of policing. How does goal-oriented improvisation, specifically the use of informal social networks, look like in the age of the Internet? Is the police tweet discussed earlier an act of *jugaad* as well, and if so, what new avenues are opened up for us to study police authority, agency, oversight, and accountability? As I asserted earlier, a police tweet ought to be seen as a text that transgresses public–private boundaries in the sense that it is 'composed in the language of the law [but] intersect[s] with the fabric of particularistic "*sentimental feelings*" that define the political textures of local community life' (Martin 2007, 684, emphasis original). As such, like *jugaad*, it blurs the line between formality and informality. This time, however, the social networks that are mobilized are digital networks that exist by virtue of officers' social media activities. In these digital networks too, services are exchanged. In the example discussed, we saw that police served the public by warning them about particular forms of criminality. In exchange, they expect people to be vigilant and to act as the ears and eyes of police.

Notably, as in the case of Mo, such social/digital network-based policing may easily lead to 'your police, my police' situations (Hornberger 2004, 2011, 2013). Hornberger discusses such situations in the context of the South African Police:

> If a person successfully 'captures' a police officer through some relationship of familiarity, friendship or indebtedness or the concurrence of particularistic interest, then that officer can become 'my police': a private police officer, providing protection for that particular individual through a personalized relationship. As such, it contradicts the image that the government aspires to create, both of an effective, modern, democratic state, and of a police service as a modern, public institution with a disinterested and unbiased relationship with the public. When practice deviates from this ideal model—as it does frequently in contemporary South Africa—isolated corruption or incompetence are usually identified as the cause. However, the imaginary of 'your police, my police' suggests that these contraventions are in reality fairly routine. (Hornberger 2004, 216)

They are also fairly routine in The Netherlands. In the case of Mo and other Moroccan-Dutch community officers I spoke to, there was a direct relationship between the officer in question and community members.[6] The Twitter relationship is more mediated, but

[6] Hornberger too writes about such direct relationships:

'[P]eople would know particular police officers by name, would have their mobile phone numbers, and could call on them when necessary. They would have long histories of exchanging personal favors with them, ranging from sharing food with them to giving them special prices on goods that they were selling on the streets or in small shops. While a human rights ethos and an

when taken *in toto*, police tweets may amount to a form of 'police vigilantism' (Owen and Cooper-Knock 2014) that privileges particular segments of the population, which may try to harness it for their own ends. What these specific segments of the population look like is more difficult to establish due to the complex, interlinked, and often pseudonymous nature of online or 'plugged-in' publics (Mutsaers and Van Nuenen 2018)—but it is likely that the tweets of the kind I have discussed further reinforce social divisions in society. As a result, they may increase the legitimacy of the police in particular circles, but leave it wanting in others.

All in all, it may be concluded that the culture of the Dutch police is changing, and, arguably, not changing for the better. Culture is a promiscuous concept that can be used to talk about a wide range of different things (Martin 2018). Here, I am not referring to it as a collection of dominant traits such as masculinity or group loyalty, conventionally used to grasp police culture (Loftus 2009). Rather, I refer to culture as historically persistent but not necessarily stable 'patterns of meaningful organization' (Martin 2016, 463). In earlier times, Dutch police culture could without doubt be classified as the ideal rule-of-law type, characterized by procedural regularity, bureaucratic order, and what Whyte called the 'organizational man' (Whyte 1956). Under the pressure of various calls to 'humanize' the police, a different model emerged and it is the corollary of this post-bureaucratic model that has been described in this chapter. With reference to the earlier discussion on the humanization of police, I agree with Cabot that police are often becoming dangerous, discriminatory, or corrupt, precisely when certain 'human' aspects begin to shape their actions (Cabot 2018). This is what we have seen in the various cases described in this chapter: the chokehold death, the paternalism, the mugshot, the road blocks, the prescribed target-group policing, the micro-deportations, the jokes about Allah, etc. We will see more of it in the next chapter.

ideal of community policing provided proximity between the migrant and the police, what was actually created through these interactions was not a public but rather a private police.' (Hornberger 2013, 609)

3

Thickening Borderlands

'Who can forward this to the alien police?' (municipal official 1)

'That's just a matter of calling them. You can do it, I can do it ... Police. Check. When did it [his residence permit] expire? June 16? I can ask it during the break, then we have it uh ... (police officer 1)

'[Sarcastically] Oh, we have a party today, it's his birthday! (youth worker)

'Today is his birthday?' (police officer 1)

'Yes, he is turning 18!' (youth worker)

'So, he can just scram. He wanted to go to Bosnia anyway, he said. We can speed things up for him.' (police officer 2)

'It is no longer in a state of war.' (municipal official 2)

'Nope, nothing wrong there.' (police officer 2)

'Our approach is working.' (municipal official 3)

'We have a new item on the agenda: making a birthday calendar. We can visit them at home. HAPPY BIRTHDAY!' (police officer 1)

'Congratulations with your eighteenth.' (municipal official 2)

From Police to Policing

So far, I have dealt with one aspect of the lost art of separation almost exclusively, also described as the non-modular constitution of present-day policing, and its relation to police discrimination. This aspect—biocratic governance and the blurring boundary between the private and the public—has been described as a crucial instigator of the corrosion of the public character of policing in The Netherlands. Reading our times more broadly, I have also argued that non-modular policing appears across the globe in various guises and as such, colours the global security landscape.

Police Unlimited: Policing, Migrants, and the Values of Bureaucracy. First Edition. Paul Mutsaers. © Paul Mutsaers 2019. Published 2019 by Oxford University Press.

In some contexts, it surfaces as officers extracting private 'taxes' from individual citizens and other forms of police corruption (Jauregui 2013; Roitman 2006); in others it manifests in amicable arrangements between the police and citizens and out-of-court-settlement of cases (Göpfert 2016), moulded by personal ties dominant in 'your police, my police' situations (Hornberger 2011). In other contexts, such as in The Netherlands, biocratic governance opens the door to a form of policing affected less by the law than by privately held thoughts and beliefs about the world and how it ought to operate. As we saw in the preceding chapter, when such policing *with* regard to person is combined with a migrant hostility that pervades the institution, police discrimination is an obvious consequence.

Biocratic governance is an important manifestation of the lost art of separation and it remains a central focus in this chapter (and the next). However, here I extend the analysis to a different sort of separation: not the separation of (public) institutions from (private) individuals but the separation of different institutions. With the celebrated demise of bureaucracy as well as the 'phoenix-like emergence of the "post-bureaucratic or network organization" out of its ashes' (Coupland and Reed 2004, 5), this separation has increasingly been under attack. With respect to law enforcement, since the 1970s the kinds of political forces have arisen that critique the (putative) closed nature of police bureaucracies (see the Introduction for the Dutch situation). To meet the demands of an increasingly articulate public, as well as those that emerge with new and complex security problems, police organizations worldwide have been eager to develop strategic partnerships and networks (see Diphoorn and Grassiani 2016 for a recently published overview of 'pluralized policing', 'security assemblages', etc.). That police power is often 'divided across a multiplicity of organizations and institutions' is now a social fact (Karpiak 2016b, 109).

In a way, this *generalization* of the police function—as we may call it, as long as we acknowledge this term as an exaggeration—means a regression to earlier times. Like my interpretation of biocratic governance as a (partial) return to a pre-modern organization of labour (undifferentiated, no distinction between role and person, etc.), I interpret the contemporary notion of law enforcement as a network-based public service as a (partial) return to a time before the police function was rigidly demarcated by its bureaucratic organization. Clarifying his distinction between police-as-governance and governance-as-police, Garriott states that

> [t]here is a deep and abiding relationship between police and governance. Indeed, as the etymology of 'police' reveals, the two terms were once virtually synonymous. The term 'police' emerged in Western political discourse as early as the thirteenth century. It is generally traced to the French term '*police*', which was used to capture the meaning in the Latin term '*politea*' (Greek '*politeia*')—the source for both 'police' and 'policy' in English. Indeed, in its early European usage, 'police' is the term used to refer to the power to govern and/or the act of governing itself, suggesting a closer affinity to the contemporary notion of 'policy' than police. (Garriott 2013, 4)

The renewed expansive notion of police (which Garriott calls 'police-as-governance') urges us to look beyond the police organization proper. It means that in order to understand discriminatory *policing* (the practice) we must look carefully at *the police* (the institution) as well as behind it (Hallsworth 2006). This holds true especially for a case study of The Netherlands, because the Dutch police have long been cutting edge in this respect. Not only have the Dutch been among the first to de-bureaucratize the organization, they have also been early adopters of plural policing and other strategies that led to vibrant security networks (Jones et al. 2009; Van der Sluis et al. 2011). Converging with the Dutch paradigm of community policing, police strategists in The Netherlands have developed a 'diffuse kind of policing that marries welfare to discipline, care to coercion and prevention to repression' (De Koning 2017, 4). In this chapter, we will see that this has led to a broad institutional security landscape inhabited by penal and welfare actors and public, semi-public, and private institutions. These are collectively responsible for what De Koning calls 'diffuse policing', an exercise that encompasses law enforcement, order maintenance, and social control, as well as public health.

Although the epigraph of this chapter shows that members of a local security network (in Tilburg) talk in jest about the policing of migrants and migration, it is especially in this field that diffuse or networked policing has advanced so quickly. The Netherlands is at the frontier of the so-called policing of migration that is characterized by a blurring of boundaries between criminal and administrative measures 'in the sense of direct police involvement in the enforcement of immigration laws and the control of "immigrant" communities', and, conversely, in the sense that 'police-like activities of immigration authorities and other agencies are acquiring new coercive powers' (Weber and Bowling 2004, 195). Whether it comes to the introduction and implementation of specific migration control measures—such as the pledge to meet specific deportation targets (already extant), the drive to criminalize illegal stay (a recurrent political topic), or the introduction of mobile biometric devices for police officers to conduct on-the-spot checks of the residence status of migrants (tested in Rotterdam)—or the growing number of government agencies, semi-public bodies, and private companies operating together to counteract the presence of migrants, the Dutch approach is innovative.

The rest of this chapter unfolds as follows. First, inspired by the 'sites of enforcement' framework of Weber and Bowling (2004), I will offer a critical take on several policy developments in The Netherlands with regard to *external* and *internal* border control. The emphasis will be on the latter, but both forms of migration policing are discussed in order to demonstrate the zeal in Dutch migration policing and the increasing risk of inequitable treatment of migrants who already live in—or are planning to come to—this country. Second, I present a detailed discussion of empirical materials obtained during my ethnographic work in Tilburg and Amsterdam. Although I was mainly interested in the police, I have also assembled materials from a variety of other sources—including a number of public, semi-public, and private organizations engaged in migrant-related activities and who work in coalition with the police. Because empirical research on the internal policing of migrants is scarce (Leerkes et al. 2012a; Loftus 2013), this part of the chapter is quite detailed. I hope to respond to Loftus' (2013) call for sustained empirical examination of the inner world of border policing by discussing in some depth how Somali immigrants in Tilburg are confronted with internal border policing and how the police in Amsterdam partnered with the military to police migrant groups. Finally, I will deploy the concept of 'thickening borderlands', introduced by anthropologists, to argue that the social geography of borders has changed radically as a result of the ever-expanding powers of agencies involved in the policing of migration.

Migration Policing: Internal and External Border Control

While the powers to stop, frisk, interrogate, and physically remove people places criminal justice agencies at the coercive end of social control, this control function no longer lies exclusively in the hands of the three 'C's—cops, courts, and corrections. Being frequently subjected to controls may antagonize the relationship between controller and controlled, and due to the 'pluralization of governance' and the rise of 'networked policing', such relationships may now be experienced in citizen contact with a whole range of state and non-state actors.

This holds increasingly true for migrants who have come to (live in) liberal democracies, for fluid and nodal strategies of policing now permeate the world of migration control (Loftus 2013). As a result, the policing of migrants now reaches beyond physical borderlines. Although the various refugee flows, which have plunged Europe into a deep crisis, have made the development of new borderlands visible to all who seek them, they are experienced in highly unequal ways. As Rumford wrote: 'borders exist at multiple sites within and between policies [and] mean different things to different people, and work differently on different groups' (Rumford 2012, 894). For instance, the fact that many rights do not accrue to undocumented inhabitants in countries such as The Netherlands, Belgium, or Germany means that a marginalized and vulnerable population is actively created that is 'beyond the pale of protection' (Zedner 2010, 394).

From the 'sites of enforcement' framework (Weber and Bowling 2004, 202; see also Bowling and Sheptycki 2012, 103), it becomes clear that borderlands are expanding both inwards ('in-country enforcement') and outwards ('pre-entry controls'). I will briefly discuss various modes of external and internal control over Dutch territory and mobility in(to) The Netherlands to shed light on the current state of Dutch migration policing. As stated earlier, The Netherlands is an interesting country to study because of its pioneering and aggressive role in the policing of migration. In countries such as the United States, new forms of migration policing—such as police officers checking the status of anyone resembling the profile of an illegal immigrant, the targeting of criminal aliens, prolongation of the period of 'probationary citizenship' for legal migrants, rising detention rates, proposals to make illegal stay a felony, or President Trump's recent executive order on immigration that bars citizens of seven Muslim-majority countries from entering the United States—have been answered by massive support for immigrants' rights (Coutin 2011). No protests of this nature have occurred in The Netherlands in response to new migration bills, laws, and policies. Unsurprisingly, therefore, immigration law enforcement is now diffuse and includes a wide range of parties, such as asylum officials, immigration officers, the Border Police, the Aliens Police, and regular police departments, as well as transport companies, private security companies, the Labour Inspectorate, employers, local officials, school administrators, landlord, social service workers, and housing companies. These are now co-responsible for checking the residence status of migrants.

A good example of external border control is the delegation of responsibilities to private transporters, such as airlines, which have taken over core tasks from immigration and customs officers. By means of carrier sanction legislation, governments have enabled a sort of 'remote control' that has shifted responsibility away from their own physical borders (Bosworth and Guild 2008; Scholten and Minderhoud 2008). By imposing financial penalties on private transport companies who permit people with 'inadequate documentation' on board, governments have taken an important step in the privatization and 'de-territorialization' of migration control. In The Netherlands, carriers' obligations have been firmly laid down in various forms of legislation, such as the Aliens Act 2000, the Aliens Decree, and the Alien Regulation (Scholten and Minderhoud 2008).

A completely different example of external border control is the 'pre-departure integration strategy' (Bonjour 2010; Groenendijk 2011). In the early 2000s, the European Union (EU) Council adopted a range of EU directives that allowed member states to 'select' immigrants for family reunification. These directives made it possible to demand that immigrants pass an integration test as a condition of their entry visa. The Dutch government was among the first in the world to impose such requirements on family migrants from certain countries outside the EU (Australia, Canada, New Zealand, the United States, Japan, and South Korea were exempted). The Dutch Law on Civic Integration Abroad stipulates that passing an integration test abroad is a prerequisite for family migrants to being admitted to The Netherlands. Groenendijk pointed out that the lawfulness of this act is doubtful as it may violate the constitutional protection of family life and is arguably incompatible with the EU Family Reunification Directive and Article 8 of the European Convention of Human Rights, dealing with the right to family life (Groenendijk 2011). Discussions about the right to family reunification have recently been given new vigour, as a result of the lengthy waiting time that Syrian refugees in Europe have to endure, in total desperation, we may add, considering the ongoing war in their homeland.

With respect to asylum seekers and refugees, tactics of externalization are also deployed and have helped governments to distance themselves, both legally and geographically, from immigration control (e.g. Andersson 2014; Scholten and Minderhoud 2008). The Dutch Advisory Committee on Aliens Affairs advised the Dutch government in 2003 to adopt a border management strategy that is modelled on the idea of 'concentric circles' rather than the classical borderline (Scholten and Minderhoud 2008). In this model, inner circles (e.g. The Netherlands or the EU) are to be protected by outer circles or 'buffer zones' (e.g. Turkey and North African countries) to which asylum procedures can be outsourced (in so-called Transit Processing Centres), to which, in turn, asylum seekers can be readmitted when a so-called safe Third Country Nation was part of their migration journey and where refugees can be located so that they stay in their regions of origin rather than seek refuge in an EU country (Fekete 2005; Weber and Bowling 2008; Andrijasevic 2010).

One obvious example of this border management strategy is the EU–Turkey joint action plan, the result of an agreement between the EU and Turkey to increase cooperation on migration management. It essentially boils down to the bargain that all 'irregular migrants' crossing from Turkey to the Greek islands will be returned to Turkey, and that for every Syrian being returned to Turkey from the Greek islands, another Syrian will be resettled to the EU. In exchange, the EU promised a visa liberalization roadmap for Turkey.[1]

[1] As an aside: when I was interviewing Syrian refugees in The Netherlands for a project on their experiences with border police, one of them complained about the cold logic of EU politics. When asked about the EU–Turkey joint action plan, Nadiyah, a former pharmacy student, said 'It's human smuggling on a higher level. They send people back to Turkey and then they take a few people and send them to Europe.'

With respect to *internal* border control, Leerkes and colleagues distinguish between two types of control (Leerkes et al. 2012a). One pertains to all practices intended to trace, apprehend, and deport migrants from state territories; the other aims to exclude migrants from societal institutions and public provision.

While detention and deportation were for a long time considered secondary techniques to police immigrant populations, they are now ubiquitous in liberal democratic countries such as the United States, The Netherlands, and the United Kingdom (Gibney 2008). Throughout Europe, detention facilities have sprouted in which people are kept in light of 'pre-admission detention, pre-deportation detention, detention for the purpose of transfer to a safe third country, detention for the purpose of transfer to the responsible state under the Dublin Convention and criminal detention linked to illegal entry/exit or fraudulent documentation' (Broeders 2010, 175). Europe, in the words of Walters, is a wide archipelago of detention centres (Walters 2002).

On this point too, we can establish that The Netherlands is particularly hostile to migrants. The political discourse on migrants is influenced by politicians who want special stop-and-searches for Antillean juveniles and deportation of convicted criminals with Moroccan nationality (see Van der Leun and Van der Woude 2011). Compared to other EU countries, the length of migration detention is very long in The Netherlands. In fact, it has no fixed duration and immigrant detention of up to eighteen months is not exceptional (Broeders 2010). The capacity for immigrant detention rose from 45 places in 1980 to 3,320 places in 2006, and its share of total prison facilities has similarly risen from 9.1 per cent in 1999 to 18.1 per cent in 2006 (Broeders 2010). Moreover, in 2010, for example, 6,100 migrants were detained for an average of 76 days without charge or process (Ombudsman 2012; Mutsaers et al. 2014). International institutions like Human Rights Watch, the Parliamentary Assembly of the Council of Europe, the European Court of Human Rights, and the European Court of Justice have recurrently denounced the Dutch government for systematically violating the human rights of asylum seekers (De Leeuw and Van Wichelen 2012; see Mutsaers et al. 2014, 181–2). This may not come as unexpected, considering the fact that the Dutch government reached, for instance, a readmission agreement with Iraq (Fekete 2011) and now seems to make the same mistake, this time in a European context, with another illiberal regime (Turkey) where human rights violations abound. Also, in December 2005, news emerged that the Dutch Immigration and Naturalization Service (INS) had made it a standard procedure to deliver information gathered during interrogations of asylum seekers from Congo to the Congolese authorities when these asylum seekers were sent back to Kinshasa. Something similar has taken place in the case of asylum seekers from Syria (before the war). Whether or not these people survived deportation is unknown (Mutsaers and Siebers 2013, 21). Weber (2002) argued that such mistreatments of asylum seekers ought to be described as a state crime.

The enforcement of migration laws may not be considered an obvious topic for criminologists; it remains an administrative rather than criminal justice matter in The Netherlands (although political pressure to criminalize irregular migration is mounting), for example. However, migration policing is increasingly attaining a 'criminal-justice-like' status (Weber 2002) and the measures that are taken have become more and more punitive. For example, the conditions in immigration detention centres are often worse than in regular prisons (Broeders 2010). Aside from that, regular Dutch police departments are an integral part of migration policing (see following) and have ample juridical mandates to apprehend migrants who are reasonably suspected of illegal residence (Leerkes et al. 2012b). This makes the line between administrative and criminal justice policing of migrants very thin in this country.[2]

With regard to the second type of internal border control referred to by Leerkes and colleagues, we can establish that the Dutch government is equally zealous (Leerkes et al. 2012a). Entitlement

[2] An example of another EU member state that is known for its criminalization of immigration, or 'crimmigration' (Aas 2011) is Denmark, where in 2016 a former children's ombudsman (Lisbeth Zornig) was prosecuted under trafficking laws and fined £2,328 for driving a Syrian family to Copenhagen (Crouch 2016). Aliverti (2012, 2017) has argued that such a deterrence with criminal sanctions of immigration offences that are typically tackled by administrative law (e.g. illegal entry, possession of fraudulent documents, overstaying an expired visa, or non-profit assistance in unauthorized mobility) is unfair. After all, many immigration offences (profit-based trafficking and smuggling excluded) fall short in fulfilling the harm principle and are often based on weak or no *mens rea* or *actus rea* requirements, yet license excessive imposition of pain when followed by detention and expulsion (Aliverti 2017). The 'normative justification of criminal law in immigration matters is weak' (Aliverti 2012, 417).

to public services (social security, housing, health care, etc.) and access to social institutions (e.g. the labour market or public education) are severely restricted for undocumented migrants, who only have access to legal assistance, emergency healthcare, and education in the case of children under eighteen years of age. The Netherlands was one of the first countries in the world to make undocumented migrants ineligible for social services and to exclude them from the labour market (Leerkes et al. 2012a). A crucial piece of legislation is the *Koppelingswet*—literally translated as the Linking Act—which was implemented in 1998 and has amended the Aliens Act and twenty-five other acts (Scholten and Minderhoud 2008). It obliges public and semi-public agencies (welfare departments, housing associations, etc.) to check the residence status of their clients, which is registered in the Aliens Administration System of the Aliens Police. These kind of 'asylum austerity laws' (Eakin 2016) make life so precarious for undocumented migrants that many of them are automatically exposed to 'everyday criminogenic situations' (Zedner 2004) and forced into criminality (involving, for instance, black labour, illegal housing, subsistence crime, or counterfeit documentation). Research in The Netherlands has demonstrated that increased vigour in exerting this kind of internal control has pushed undocumented migrants towards petty crime and drug-related offences (Leerkes et al. 2012a).

As the opening extract of this chapter reveals, the two types of internal control that have been distinguished here can conflate in practice. I observed during my police ethnography that the very same agencies involved with the police in migrant-related activities to regulate the access of migrations to particular services and provisions can also, in very unobtrusive ways, be involved in dispelling activities. This has to do with the partnerships that exist with the Dutch police, which have a remarkable position if it comes to migration control. Just like, for instance, the Australian state police (see Weber 2011), the Dutch police hold wide-ranging powers with regard to the policing of internal borders. In contrast to many other countries, all police officers may apprehend undocumented migrants, regardless of whether they are suspected of committing a particular crime or not. Since the early 1990s, all police departments have access to the Aliens Administration System. Consequently, between 1997 and 2003, for example, a majority of the apprehensions of unauthorized migrants (in total

107,322) was conducted by the regular police (57 per cent versus 24 per cent by the Aliens Police and 19 per cent by the Military Police; see Leerkes et al. 2012b).

The objective of the next part of this chapter is to show how different agencies work together to police internal borders on the basis of sustained and thoroughgoing collaborations. An increasingly diverse spectrum of agencies (e.g. housing companies, social service, police, municipalities, youth workers, and other welfare organizations) work together and form a microscopic system of control that uses pervasive surveillance techniques (O'Neill and Loftus 2013). In these 'multi-agency networks' (Weber 2011) or 'constellations of social control professionals' (O'Neill and Loftus 2013), hordes of personal information are shared about people, which extends and intensifies the policing of internal borders. The ethnographic materials discussed below correspond, by and large, with De Koning's study of the police in Amsterdam, in which she reports that:

> In order to understand such racialized policing, we have to go beyond a narrow focus on the police itself, and instead examine the broader institutional landscape tasked with security. This institutional landscape is made up of penal and welfare actors who together enact what I call diffuse policing. Such diffuse policing envelops targeted persons and spaces in a dense web of surveillance, and disciplinary and reform interventions that are hard to escape or challenge. (De Koning 2017, 1)

Dutch Somalis at the Internal Border

At 11 a.m. on 28 November 2012, John and I were patrolling the shopping mall that is close to the police station in Tilburg. As is typical for the Dutch police, we did so on our bikes. Slightly embarrassed by my rusty city bike that creaks with every stroke of the pedals, I was aware of the contrast between us. John, the sportsman, six-and-a-half feet tall, his appearance betraying his Vietnamese/Indonesian ancestry, on a police bike, versus me, the not-so-sporty police ethnographer, pale winter skin, and six inches shorter. In addition to his physical strength John is the embodiment of proper police ethics, the sort of officer who gives confidence in law enforcement as a neutral force.

While talking to a florist who complained about parking issues around the shopping mall, we noticed that something is amiss about 300 feet down the road and we headed in that direction.

A group of children, whispering and giggling, was circling around a man in his fifties who has crashed down on the pavement. Too sunk into apathy to pose any threat, he did not resist when the kids delivered soft punches and kicks. We sent them away and turned to the man, his eyes vacant and his talk gibberish. I now recognized him as Abdi, who was not only known to the police for his long record of petty crime but also to me due to the various swift and inconsequential encounters we had had in the neighbourhood where I grew up. Abdi was a homeless man who had been dwelling in Tilburg for almost two decades. I later learned from a police report that he was born in Ethiopia in 1957 and had lived for many years in Somalia. He arrived in The Netherlands in 1992 and applied for asylum. In July 1997, he appeared on a list of the INS as a candidate for deportation to Somalia and was given the status *verwijderbaar*—removable. He was on the list until October 1997, but the deportation never occurred. Another deportation to Somalia—this time escorted—was planned for October 2004, but in September 2004, the court decided that Abdi should be immediately released and had a right to a financial compensation of €1,600. Following this, he made several attempts to get hold of a residence permit, but to no avail. On 27 July 2006, he was declared an 'undesirable foreigner' and was again detained. Almost a year later, in June 2007, he was released *again* because there was no prospect of deportation due to the unstable situation in Somalia and the psychoses from which Abdi suffers. His run-ins with the police started in 1993, mainly because of subsistence crimes and misdemeanours. Because of his status as an illegal migrant, he had no rights to any kind of public assistance and was barely able to subsist.

A light drizzle had begun to fall and it had grown chilly, so we helped Abdi to his feet and crossed the street to seek shelter from the rain. The laboured shallowness of his breathing had us worried and we called an ambulance, following the advice of a general practitioner who happened to walk by and who checked his vital signs. While waiting for the ambulance to come, John asked me not to mention anything in the presence of the ambulance personnel about Abdi's previous contacts with the police, which John framed as a problem of his homelessness rather than his lawlessness.

'If case they find out, they'll leave him on the streets; it has happened before', he said, implying that with this knowledge in mind, the ambulance personnel would deem the man unworthy of hospital treatment.

The ambulance came and I sealed my lips, partly because I wished Abdi well and did not want to aggravate his condition, but also because I was stunned by what my companion had just told me. I had no inkling then that the police shared that attitude with ambulance personnel. What followed when John and I returned to the station reveals something of the punitive mentality shared by the police in that area. Around noon, we came back for lunch and shared our story. I stood transfixed and had to clench my teeth to stop myself from responding when a police trainee said: 'Yeah, I know that guy. We sometimes force him in the back of our vehicle and throw him out at the outskirts of the district.'

'Last time we did this', a senior constable recounted to me in a separate conversation, 'he managed to get back to the neighbourhood sooner than we did, and we had a car!' Then a sergeant chimed in: 'They are just waiting for him to die, so that he can no longer cause any trouble or cost any money.' He shrugged his shoulders and walked away.

According to the grapevine, these sort of 'micro-deportations' are habitual not only in this district but also elsewhere.[3] Because of their clandestine, almost invisible nature, it is easy to dismiss them as a 'rotten apple' instead of a 'rotten orchard' problem

[3] Coincidently, on that very day in November 2012 when I was in John's company, a judge in Rotterdam deemed the evidence presented in court sufficient to pass sentence on two police officers employed by the Rotterdam police (case file ECLI:NL:RBROT:2012:BY5995). The case: two officers of the Rotterdam police received a message from the operator that a homeless Polish migrant was causing nuisance. When they arrived, the man was sleeping on the grass. The officers decided to wake the man with their clubs, to put him in their vehicle, and drive to a dead-end street at the border of the police district where the forest begins. One officer stayed behind to watch over the car and lit a cigarette, while the other escorted the Polish man into the woods with a shovel in his hands. Expelling 'undesirable migrants' to the outskirts of the district has become a routine practice within the police unit both officers worked for—it is even known to their superiors. However, this time things seemed to take longer than usual. The officer who stayed behind started to look for his colleague and walked deep into the woods where he witnessed what the papers now call a 'fake execution'. His colleague stood behind the Polish man, who knelt on the ground with the shovel in front of him. Apparently, all this was done to ensure the man would never return to 'their district'.

(Punch 2003). However, such acts of police deviance ought to be understood in reference to a broader context.

First, as we saw in the previous part of this chapter, 'deportation', in the sense of forced transnational mobility, has become a dominant feature of the Dutch politics of migration control. That a 'deportation turn' (Gibney 2008) has taken place in The Netherlands becomes clear from the statistical fact that the number of foreigners (*vreemdelingen* in Dutch) removed by the Dutch Repatriation and Departure Service (DT&V)—with or without consent of the deportee—nearly doubled between 2013 (9,730 people) and 2016 (17,080 people) (DT&V 2017). As we saw earlier, this deportation turn inevitably implicates regular police officers, who apprehend a large part of unauthorized migrants and must meet specific deportation targets. Granted, transnational authorized deportations differ in many ways from the illegal micro-deportations described earlier, but parallels between the two can easily be drawn. One parallel concerns the idea of zones, which operates at both scales. The similarity between, on the one hand, EU policies of concentric circles that distinguish inner zones, buffer zones, and outer zones for immigrants, and, on the other hand, spatial policing on the basis of zones, tolerating migrants in one part of the city but not in others, cannot be denied. Even without officers' awareness, zoning mechanisms can become entrenched in their minds and become part of police ideology. Another parallel that can be drawn concerns (micro-)deportation as a form of punishment. The Dutch law already enables the state to deport an immigrant when he or she is convicted of particular criminal offences, depending on the sentence (Alien Decree 2000, Sec. 3.86), and political pressure is mounting to carry out policy and legislative reforms that lower the threshold (*Kamerstuk* 2015/2016, 19 637, no. 2188, p. 2).[4] Such political decisions transform

[4] For more information, see Van der Woude et al. (2014, 11), who state that:

> In 2001, the government introduced the so-called sliding scale that provides the Immigration and Naturalization Service (INS) with powers to deport legally residing migrants who are seen to be endangering public order, in most cases because of (prior) convictions (Alien Decree 2000, Sec. 3.86). The decision to deport a migrant with a criminal record is determined by the length of residence and the seriousness of the offense. In cases of short residence, a relatively small offense can result in deportation. In the case of a longer residential stay, the infringement of the public order requires the penalty to be more severe. The decision whether a criminal alien is threatening public order

deportation into the enforcement of migration *and* criminal law, de facto rendering it a form of punishment. In the same vein, micro-deportations can be thought of as a form of punishment that takes place outside the regular criminal justice procedures and thus present us with a violation of due process norms.

During my fieldwork I also discovered that in addition to the national contexts, local politics also bore some remarkable resemblances to the practice of micro-deportation. For clarification we must return to the case of Abdi in Tilburg.

Somali immigrants in Tilburg are known to occupy their time chewing Qat in public places.[5] Qat is a mild drug that has a sedative effect but can also cause insomnia, apathy, aggression, and stress (De Jong and Van der Veen 2011). At the time of my research, Qat was an illegal product almost everywhere in Europe, but not in The Netherlands. It was only in 2013 that Qat was added to the opium list by the Dutch Minister of Security and Justice and had become an illegal product (*Staatsblad van het Koninkrijk der Nederlanden, jaargang* 2013, nr.1). However, in the Tilburg neighbourhood where I conducted my field research, it was already forbidden by means of a municipal by-law (a local zoning ordinance). This ordinance had imposed severe restrictions on the trade and consumption of Qat in this area, forcing traders and users to conduct their business at the industrial compounds surrounding the neighbourhood. Notably, these are the same compounds Abdi was expelled to by police officers.

depends on the maximum length of imprisonment for the criminal offense(s) committed. Since 2000, the requirements for deportation via the sliding scale have been eased twice, once in 2002 and once in July 2012. Before that, aliens with residence periods of less than one year could be deported for an offence punishable by more than nine months' imprisonment (Alien Decree 2000, Sec. 3.86); in 2002, this threshold was reduced to one month (July 17, 2002, *Official Gazette of the Kingdom of the Netherlands*, no. 371, 17 July 2002, 371); and in 2012, the minimum imprisonment length became only a single day (July 1, 2012, *Official Gazette of the Kingdom of the Netherlands*, no. 286, 1 July 2012, 286). The 2012 amendment is the product of a zero-tolerance policy for migrants. Migrants are deportable from Dutch territory on the basis of any imprisonable offense during the first fifteen years of their residence (Parliamentary Papers 2011–2012, 19637 no. 1494, February 17, 2012).

[5] The official name of Qat is *Catha edulis*, a chewing tobacco from the Horn of Africa and the Arabian Peninsula.

Such a zoning ordinance is yet another example of internal border control, a form of control that draws boundaries by dispelling 'unwanted others' to areas that are largely invisible to law-abiding citizens. Here is why the ordinance was implemented several years earlier. A group of Somali men had assembled in a park in the neighbourhood to chew Qat and to socialize. Abdi was present too and, being homeless, defecated in public. This event was photographed by a group of (native Dutch) residents, who forwarded the photos to a district manager working for the municipality. Via this district manager, the photos reached the mayor, who was known to be severely opposed to Qat (he called it a 'noxious product' according to a municipal official who I interviewed) and not particularly circumspect about his views on migrants.[6] Soon thereafter, the local zoning ordinance was enacted. According to one police officer, the mayor regularly called the police department to make sure that officers would vigorously crack down on Qat-related activities in their neighbourhood. Such a strict policy is remarkable for a country that is known for its liberal drugs policies (and it is a good example of the earlier mentioned concept of 'police vigilantism').

A case like this shows the profound impact of by-laws on how—in this case—Somali immigrants experience (their right to) the city and communal life within it. Regretting its past housing policies that brought together large families (which Somali immigrants in Tilburg generally have) in particular neighbourhoods, the municipality later actively started dispersing migrant groups (interview with municipal officials in 2013). The local ordinance banning Qat may have fulfilled this purpose precisely. De facto, it countered group formation of Somalis in the neighbourhood and simultaneously gave police officers an additional reason to stop and frisk them. If the stop reveals that the person lacks legal status, this may even result in what Dutch police officers call a 'by-catch'—a coincidental apprehension of an undocumented migrant (Leerkes et al. 2012b).

We begin to get an idea of the involvement of multiple organizations in the policing of internal borders (e.g. the police, the municipality, citizen watch groups). As I became more interested in the

[6] In 2010, he resigned as mayor to become Minister of Security and Justice, a position that enabled him to implement many of the migrant-hostile policies discussed in the previous section.

life and times of Abdi, I discovered that various criminal justice and welfare organizations were involved as well—often collaborating in security networks. Indicative of the pervasiveness of the surveillance methods used by these networks is the fact that all the information that I retrieved about Abdi's whereabouts (his imprisonment, his hospitalization, his detainment, and his planned deportation) came from a report titled *Problem Approach in Security Networks: Project [Abdi]*. This report, which is specifically about Abdi, was written by a police officer who distributed it among several network partners with whom she intended to collaborate in order to tackle 'the problem'. Among her partners were the municipality, a regional mental healthcare institution, and the so-called Care and Security House of Tilburg (*Zorg- en Veiligheidshuis*), a collaboration of around twenty partner organizations across the public and private sectors. Such security networks have appeared across the country and are best described as 'constellations of social control professionals' (O'Neill and Loftus 2013). Through these partnerships, hordes of private information and personal data about specific individuals and families are collected and shared in order to intensify surveillance and, sometimes, policing (see also De Koning 2017, for The Netherlands). For example, a senior employee working for *Bemoeizorg* (best translated as 'Meddle Care', a collaboration of four welfare- and healthcare organizations that intervene in people's private lives if they disturb the public order but refuse to accept help) said in an interview:

> We are often visiting [people at home] in pairs with external partners [like police officers] and use the 'good guy/bad guy' principle. The other one is exerting pressure in the sense of, if you don't do this then you are evicted from your house, you lose your entitlement to social benefits, you get locked up and so on. And then we come in: 'Perhaps I can help you to do this or that.'

Similar tactics were used with Abdi. In the earlier mentioned report, we can read that the initial attempt to put pressure on him was by overwhelming him with financial penalties. It reports on an interaction between a patrol unit and Abdi on the streets, which was registered in the Police Information System:

> [The unit encountered Abdi who was surrounded by beer cans] We asked him if these were his, to which he answered 'no'. When we attempted to dispose of the cans he shouted 'fuck you police'. We handcuffed him ... At

> the same time some people at the shopping mall headed in our direction. To our surprise, they supported us and were glad that something was done against the nuisance [Abdi] is always causing ... Unfortunately, [Abdi] had nothing on his name. He was sent away with a bunch of other *mini's* [police language for petty criminals].

When it turned out that this strategy was not working because Abdi often simply could not pay his fines, we read in the report, the network, together with the public prosecutor, decided that fines were to be swiftly converted into an irrevocable restraint on freedom. One of the arguments given in support of this was that by isolating his location it would be easier to administer his medication. Prison was the only intramural facility where this was possible, it was argued, because none of the mental healthcare organizations was willing to admit Abdi (remember the reluctance of the ambulance personnel to transport 'clients of the police'). Medication was seen as key to the solution of 'problem Abdi' because—in the words of the author of the report: 'Even though he will still have to scrape out a living, he will no longer fall into a psychosis and start screaming at and spitting on people and grabbing them and chasing them.'

In an outstanding article about the sociolegal aspects of law and order, Bauman argued that 'spatial confinement, incarceration of varying degrees of stringency and harshness, was at all times the prime method of dealing with the unassimilable, difficult to control, and otherwise trouble-prone sector of the population' (Bauman 2000a, 208). However, in what he calls the 'post-correctional age', prisons increasingly become factories of exclusion rather than places for correction and rehabilitation. In the poignant example of Abdi, this becomes instantly clear. Not a lot of people seem to care about his destitution, only about his troublesome behaviour and what it does to 'innocent' others. Isolating him from the innocent is deemed more important than working on the legal and economic conditions that obviously make rehabilitation a sheer impossibility. Bauman states that maintenance of order is increasingly occurring by resort to a paradigm of exclusion, a paradigm in which mobility (immobility) has become a key indicator of inclusion (exclusion). It is evident that Abdi ranks lowest in what Bauman (1998) calls the 'hierarchy of mobility'. Not only does he have no place to go and finds himself in a legal limbo (he cannot be deported to Somalia, nor can he legally reside on Dutch territory, nor can he be sent away to other European countries due to the constraints of the Dublin Agreement); he has also spent many years of his life in prisons and immigration detention facilities, waiting for others to decide the course of his life.

Life decisions were not in the hands of his family either. One night his brother was 'beaten up in a bestial manner' by three white men (case file ECLI:NL:RBBRE: 2002:AE0485). He barely survived, but the men came to his house a few hours later, blocked the entrance, and set the house on fire. Abdi's mother, who was also present, survived, but his brother suffocated from carbon monoxide poisoning. The front of the house was plastered with racist slogans ('White Power') and with Sig Runes (a Nazi symbol). These concrete and symbolic forms of violence had a deep impact on the Somali community in and around Tilburg—not because the culprits were not convicted for the arson attack (they were), but because none of the criminal justice agencies would acknowledge that this was an act of racial violence.

Like some of the relatives of the Somali women I spoke with in the community (see the Introduction), Abdi's mother fled from the country and started a new life in the United Kingdom. Their experiences may relate closely to what Weber called a 'second exile', which asylum seekers may experience when they go through the things described earlier (Weber 2002). Abdi's mother belongs to an estimated group of 10,000 to 20,000 Dutch Somalis who left The Netherlands for the United Kingdom since the turn of the century (Van Liempt 2011). Based on narrative interviews with Dutch Somalis in Leicester and London, Van Liempt shows that this might very well have to do with feelings of insecurity and lack of protection experienced by Dutch Somalis (and other migrant groups). One of her interviewees told her about the vulnerability that Dutch Somalis experience due to the current political climate of The Netherlands:

> I really felt at home in the Netherlands, but it is the political climate, the whole country has changed, they keep bothering you about your identity, it is always you, you Muslim, you Somali, they always point at you ... It started with September 11, then there was the famous column of Paul Scheffer, what was it called? The Multicultural Drama, and then it went from one thing to the other, Ayaan Hirsi Ali, Pim Fortuyn, I thought my life is short and I don't want to be involved anymore, enough is enough.

The Netherlands was not the country I knew anymore. (quoted in Van Liempt 2011, 259)[7]

All this confirms the experience of (legal) alienation about which the Somali women, who were given a voice at the very beginning of this book, narrated. Feeling overpoliced and underprotected and distrusting both legislators and law enforcers, these women had a very weak idea of the police, which we defined as a measure of faith that the state police will reliably resolve exigent crises. It was felt that the police were a security risk, instead of security providers.

PSYCOPS and the Outer Bounds of Police Power

In the previous chapter, I chronicled the ways in which 'security' played out on the ground in Amsterdam-West and I elaborated on several incidents in which the police station was transformed into a stage on which Moroccan-Dutch juveniles expressed their opposition to police. I now want to continue using this locale in order to discuss another security partnership in addition to the ones already covered.

After the situation at the Amsterdam-West police station, described in Chapter 2, ceased to be acute, time arrived for reflection. Restoration of good relations between the police and the community were clearly needed and it was plain to the senior officers at the station that stop-gap solutions would not suffice. The dossier covering this issue was entrusted to a project leader, Superintendent Carl, who wrote a proposal to the Ministry of

[7] Some of these names may require explication for those who are not familiar with the changing political climate in The Netherlands. Paul Scheffer is a Dutch publicist and member of the Labour Party (PvdA) who is famous for his newspaper column *Het Multiculturele Drama* ('The Multicultural Drama', 2000) which signalled a more generalized enthusiasm for the dissemination of national awareness, meant to reinforce Dutch culture and nationalism as a prerequisite for dealing successfully with migrants in The Netherlands (see Mutsaers and Siebers 2013, 14). Former MP Ayaan Hirsi Ali (VVD) became a controversial subject of debate in the Dutch press after she released a short film, Submission, with Theo van Gogh (a controversial filmmaker and columnist who was murdered in 2004 by a radicalized Muslim) about the submission of Islamic women. Pim Fortuyn was a well-known politician who acquired fame and popularity due to his anti-immigration politics. He was murdered in May 2002.

Security and Justice to apply for a budget for his plans. In an interview, Carl told me how thrilled he was, as he had just received the news that his proposal had been approved and that the ministry was willing to pay his department a large sum of money to implement the plan. In our discussion, he emphasized what he thought was the main problem: police–minority relations. These were below par, he argued, which made it very difficult to establish meaningful contact with minority groups and to talk with them about criminality, social problems, disorderly behaviour, and the like—all signs of a phenomenon we discussed in the Introduction: legal alienation.

Carl and his associates were thus right when they urged their colleagues that something needed to be done about police–minority relations. But what did they do?

At first, Carl told me that he deemed police–minority *communication* to be the main problem. This problem was not relational but had to do, he argued, with the illiteracy of many people in the neighbourhood. Carl told me that many could not read the brochures, flyers, or digital newsletters that the police distribute every now and then to inform people about security issues, crime prevention, and so on ('many people in our district are completely illiterate, anno 2012'). During the interview, however, his focus shifted from language to a much broader spectrum, including culture, politics, religion, kinship, etc. Gradually, miscommunication was no longer framed as a problem of people's language skills but of their different place in and view of the world:

> I want to know everything about them. Knowledge is power, also in this case. So, for instance, I have a Moroccan '*target group*'. I want to know: where do their parents come from, exactly? Which specific areas? What kind of religion do they adhere to? Who has contact with whom? (my emphasis)

In a confidential document that I accessed through my research, it was stated that intelligence needed to be gathered about kinship ties, political affiliations, cultural values, religion, race, gender, age, and so forth. Such information was deemed necessary to determine what 'lines of persuasion' were to be followed to 'psychologically influence target groups'. In the interview, Carl told me about how he discovered what was, in his opinion, the most expedient method to achieve such persuasion and psychological influence:

> So I was thinking, in my own network (I have a substantial network), who do I know, who can I get around the table to brainstorm with me about how to take up this challenge? At a conference, I bumped into someone who worked for a communication agency and I said to him 'Who are you working for, normally?' And he said 'The military. They have a lot of communication targets.' ... And I said 'Who are your contacts there?' 'Major [name]', he said. So I became acquainted with this major and he told me about PSYOPS, which made me very enthusiastic. 'The Dutch military has a target group [*doelgroep*] in Tora Bora, Afghanistan', he continued. And Carl here has a target group in [name of the neighbourhood] in Amsterdam-West. Simply replace Tora Bora with, you know, I thought 'that is perfect'. I was eager and said [to the major] 'Can you tell me more about it?' So, what PSYOPS does, it is a micro-analysis [*haarvatanalyse*, literally translated as 'capillary analysis'] of a particular area. They go from macro to micro ... And they make a network analysis.

PSYOPS—psychological operations—is far from uncontroversial. It is used in war-torn countries such as Iraq and Afghanistan to win the hearts and minds of the local populace. Critical scholars have described it as a military strategy that weaponizes information and aims at 'cultural symbols that elicit intense emotional reactions in audiences that are important within the target society (achievement, power, affiliation, intimacy, unity) to express the desired message' (Anderson 2011, 217). It has been called a 'militarization of inner space' as it targets people's psychic and emotional life (Orr 2004). Obviously, the deployment of PSYOPS by a state actor for internal affairs cannot be thought of lightly, something of which Carl was very much aware: 'Imagine the headlines: police work together with the military in warzone ... [meaning: Amsterdam-West].'

When PSYOPS—which was playfully changed into PSY*COPS*—was introduced to the police team by another project leader, the audience was advised not to search on the original term on the Internet as it would immediately direct them to Nazi Germany within ten hits, it was said (which was not true; the US army, however, came out as top in the search). To make PSYCOPS operational, the mayor of Amsterdam had to submit a Defence Support of Civil Authorities request to the Ministry of Defence (in Dutch: *Bijstandsaanvraag militaire steunverlening in het kader van het openbaar belang*). Two requests were submitted (for two different neighbourhoods) and approved, which allowed the 1st Civil Military Interaction Command of the Dutch army to assist police officers in Amsterdam in PSYOPS methods. The defence support group consisted of a tactical PSYOPS team, a target audience analyst, a culture analyst, a tactical coordinator, and a specialist in behavioural influence (Dijkstra 2014, 213). They trained a selection of police officers in what is called the 'Target Audience Analysis Process', a defence method that is used to select, study, and exert influence upon specified target groups (*doelgroepen*, ethnically defined). In the report that was published—but never made publicly available—the words PSYOPS and PSYCOPS were carefully avoided (Dijkstra 2014).[8]

PSYCOPS became a topic of interest to the media. On 12 June 2015, the Dutch high-quality newspaper, *Trouw*, for instance, published a critical article (discussing the discriminatory character of PSYCOPS) in which a PSYCOPS project leader was cited stating:

> PSYCOPS improves our contacts with diverse groups in society ... I don't see why that is discrimination. The police are not only there to catch crooks; they are also here for prevention. For this, we need the public. The beauty of soldiers is that they are used to look with an open mind. They drive their tanks in foreign land and need to figure out the cultural codes.

Her intentions may have been genuinely good, but that is not the issue. The issue is, after Cicourel (1968) and Becker (1967), that police definitions of a situation cannot be seen as neutral descriptions of existing problems. In fact, sometimes the solutions that are proposed turn out to be part of the problem. Bringing in the military to deal with migrant groups on Dutch soil may not improve contacts; it may make them worse, especially when militarized psychological techniques are used that can be easily interpreted as a form of manipulation or even indoctrination. That not everyone shared the 'police definition of the situation' became clear from the public debates. Social media exploded with expressions of outrage and indignation. In addition, the newspapers quoted experts such as a Dutch professor in military ethics, who stated that PSYCOPS 'is not something you would want from the police, which is supposed to be keeping order' (Professor Désirée Verweij in the same

[8] It was given to me by a journalist who had retrieved it on the basis of the Dutch Freedom of Information Act (*Wet Openbaarheid Bestuur*).

Trouw article). Despite these critical voices, the National Police (NP) simply repeated its good intentions in a press release: 'The basic assumption of the project is that every group has its own codes, rules, key persons, needs and sensitivities. The police takes these into account in order to improve cooperation.'

Although motivations only have fringe relevance to the much more important question—what are the effects of PSYCOPS and similar police projects?—it is nonetheless important to find an explanation for the confusion about PSYCOPS and its underlying intentions. I believe that the confusion is concerned with the earlier mentioned expansive notion of policing (the practice) that has become dominant in The Netherlands. Converging with the Dutch paradigm of community policing, police strategists in The Netherlands have developed a diffuse kind of policing that marries welfare to discipline, care to coercion, and prevention to repression (De Koning 2017). This has blurred the boundaries between service and adversarial policing, allowing the police to engage in a sort of Orwellian doublespeak that obscures and distorts meaning. This blur enables make-believe; it makes it possible to account for the most intrusive and pervasive forms of policing as well-intended interventions, meant to help people with their security problems and boost their well-being. Such intentions may or may not be real—after all, the heart is unknown country (Rebhun 1999)—but the fact remains that part of the problem, the migrant-hostile policing described in this chapter and Chapter 2, is kept completely out of the limelight. In the process, a problem between two groups (of police–community *relations*) is transformed into a problem of one group, minority communities: *their* culture, *their* religion, *their* politics, *their* kinship structures.

Following my analysis thus far, it is precisely the expansive notion of policing that is an important part of the relational problem. This notion squares well with security strategies centred on 'pluralized policing' and 'security assemblages' that divide police power across a multiplicity of organizations. Such developments should not be underestimated as they epitomize a shift away from the social organization of police forces as legal bureaucracies characterized by clear institutional delineation. PSYCOPS epitomizes the post-bureaucratic police in at least two ways. First, it suspends that specific aspect of Walzer's art of separation that isolates the police from its organizational environment. The post-bureaucratic organization is a network organization that values strategic partnerships. In this case, the Dutch military possessed skills and tools that proved useful to the police. However, when *internal* security agents such as the police make use of the knowledge and resources of an *external* security agent such as the military, a merger or fusion of internal and external security takes place whose legitimacy must be questioned rather than taken for granted (Bigo 2006). It frames the selected 'target groups' as external threats. In addition to other scholarly work (e.g. Epp et al. 2014; Fassin 2013a; Zoettl 2017), this is yet another example of how police define race/ethnicity and citizenship.

Second, PSYCOPS also suspends the art of separation in the sense that it leads to an unmediated proximity between police and policed. This is a problem that is closely related to the permanently relevant question: wherein lie the outer bounds of police power? The proximity I mean is both literal and symbolic in kind. The police entered the most intimate and private spheres of targeted people, quite literally. The reason I declared PSYCOPS controversial in my media appearances (see Chapter 5) was the fact that sometimes very private information was gathered about groups of people rather than about individual suspects or offenders. Moreover, with respect to symbolic proximity, it must be noted once again that the police uniform ought to be a symbol of neutrality. State externality demands of the police that they operate without regard to the person, that is, without regard to class, ethnicity, race, religion, etc. The fact that a Target Audience Analysis was performed on the 'codes, rules, key persons, needs and sensitivities' of targeted ethnic groups (to quote from the NP's own press release) means that the art of separation had become dysfunctional, to put it mildly.

Critics may downplay the meaning of PSYCOPS by calling either the project itself or my interpretation of it 'exceptional' or 'extreme' (as the NP did in the media and in personal communication; see Chapter 5). However, the fact remains that it is congenial with other partnership-based and invasive police practices discussed in this chapter and Chapter 2. 'Behind the front door programmes' (De Koning 2017) such as PSYCOPS always merit critical attention.

Additional Comparisons

Throughout this chapter I have dealt with additional cases that reveal the problematic consequences of state proximity as described in the previous chapters. These cases bear close resemblance to those described by other police anthropologists.

First, the micro-deportations that were mentioned are reminiscent of Zoettl's work on 'extrajudicial punishment' by police officers in Portugal. Such extrajudicial punishment is often 'imposed for the sake of anticipating or substituting uncertain judicial punishment' (Zoettl 2017, 10)—a rationale I also encountered among Dutch police officers who talked about the 'punitive gap' between police and the judiciary (see also Fassin (2013a) on this punitive gap in France). Such illegal police violence was recorded by Westley in 1953 in his article 'Violence and the Police', in which he concluded that the means of violence, which are originally a property of the state, are often 'in a psychological sense confiscated by the police, to be conceived of as a personal property' (Westley 1953, 41). Numerous other studies on illegal or extrajudicial police violence can be mentioned, covering both the Global North and South (e.g. Beek and Göpfert 2012; Cabot 2018; Caldeira 2002; Nuhrat 2018; Pausschinger 2017; Verdery 2018).

Second, we can compare the local zoning ordinance that led to the criminalization of Qat in Tilburg with Martin's study of police in Taiwan, specifically with his analysis of how forces of public opinion call the police to act (Martin 2007, 2013b). Martin describes how patrolmen are mainly busy trying to strike a balance between law and sentiment: 'the working environment of policing is a complex social topography in which a variety of often deeply conflicted relationships between legal instrumentality and intimate solidarity must be carefully managed' (Martin 2007, 667). He offers us detailed descriptions of the dense fabric of 'particularistic' relationships in the communities for which individual patrolmen are held personally responsible. They take this responsibility 'not by driving around in cars looking for predefined problems, but by hanging out in the back rooms of local businesses and participating in the social processes where problems are defined' (Martin 2013b, 161). Importantly, he adds, 'the bureaucracy is not the primary mechanism through which police power is concentrated to define and solve problems' (Martin 2013b, 162).

Rather, these problems are defined and solved by social forces that operate largely outside the scope of the legal bureaucracy. In a similar way, we saw how particular social forces, embodied by a vigilant group of concerned citizens who coalesced around Qat as the symbol of migrant pollution, as matter 'out of place'. Public sentiment quickly led to by-laws that mobilized police to banish Qat—as well as its traders and users—to its proper place.

Third, PSYCOPS and comparable invasive programmes are reminiscent of the work of other anthropologists on policing as a double-edged sword, as a mode of operation that marries community service with surveillance, care with coercion, and intimacy with discipline. In the Global North, there is the work of Johansen on the *mise-en-scène* of urban policing in Denmark, particularly the policing of radicalization (Johansen 2017). She describes how the city is reconfigured through the war on terror, which has shifted the focus of police and other state agents from 'troublesome' ethnic minority youth in poor neighbourhoods to relatively well-educated and well-off Syrian youngsters. However, this 'war on terror' has a very particular manifestation in Denmark, where Johansen studied the Crime Preventive Section in Aarhus, Denmark's second city. The local counterterrorism programme, the Aarhus Model (which has been exported to other parts of the world due to its success) 'is a brilliant empirical example of how the Scandinavian welfare states have turned the western wave of counterterrorism into an extensive welfare project, in which risk and security become a subject of biopolitics, family intervention and a matter of assimilation' (Johansen 2017, 5). Like the security networks in The Netherlands, the Aarhus Model is a multi-agency effort involving a whole range of institutions (youth services, civil services, social services, law enforcement agencies, civil associations, and security representatives from urban neighbourhoods). One can imagine that this approach is preferable to other, much more violent counterterrorism approaches that can be found across the world, but like PSYCOPS, it has its downsides: 'police officers are also pointing out that they are dealing with something new and they are explicitly concerned about the questions, dilemmas, and paradoxes involved in walking the thin line between mind policing and the prevention of a terror attack' (Johansen 2017, 6). As in The Netherlands—which is another example of a traditional welfare state—police become very close to the youth and the families and faith communities they serve.

In the Global South there is the work of Hornberger on the rather quaint combination of militarized and community policing in South Africa (e.g. Hornberger 2013). Chronicling the various transformations of the South African Police, which have been taking place under the aegis of the increasingly populist-oriented ANC administration, she points to the curious fact that a forceful state has forged increasingly intimate relationships with the public.

In conclusion, I would like to discuss a concept that I believe best covers the empirics of this chapter: 'thickening borderlands'. The term was coined by Rosas who, on the basis of ethnographic research in the Mexico–US borderlands, insisted, very much in line with the literature on policing of migration/internal borders, that the border can no longer be seen as geographically fixed (Rosas 2006; see also Rosas 2012). As described in this chapter, borders can expand both outwardly—so that, for example, a Syrian refugee can experience the Dutch border in Turkey—and inwardly, giving people an experience of 'deportability' (De Genova 2002), that is, the sense that deportation is always a real possibility.

Thickening borderlands does not only adequately capture the changing geography of borders; it also gives us an idea of the new *social* geography of borders, that is, of how they are experienced by social actors. The adjective captures precisely the embodied experience of migrants who are immobilized and stuck in their locality, whose lives slow down and become inert and sclerotic under the pressure of an increasingly thickening control apparatus that keeps them in check and in place. This holds true for people who experience in-country controls, like the Dutch Somalis in Tilburg or the migrant groups targeted by PSYCOPS in Amsterdam. To them, the border of the nation-state is reproduced in everyday life and in innumerable places throughout the 'interiors of the migrant-receiving state' (De Genova 2002, 439). For some migrants, boundaries are virtually everywhere because mundane activities such as working, learning, driving, residing, or travelling are turned into illicit acts due to a person's illegal status. As a result, physical and social mobility are severely restricted because deportation becomes a possible risk in every sphere of life (De Genova 2002). This signifies a form of captivity in which prison walls become unnecessary. There is excellent anthropological work around, such as Gonzales and Chavez (2012) and Willen (2007), that focuses on the experiences of undocumented migrants in, respectively, the United States and Israel. Gonzales and Chavez have scrutinized what they call the 'biopolitics of citizenship and governmentality' that works through 'surveillance, immigration documents, employment forms, birth certificates, tax forms, drivers' licenses, credit card applications, bank accounts, medical insurance, car insurance, random detentions, and deportations' (Gonzales and Chavez 2012, 255). This kind of biopolitical control frustrates the lives of Latinos in Orange County, California, through a combination of physical and social immobilization. Consequently, they live 'liminal lives' that unfold *in* the nation but are deemed unworthy to *be part of* the nation. Just as Abdi's, their lives are literally 'on hold'. Similar conclusions have been drawn by Willen, who conducted more than two years of field research in Israel on undocumented West-African and Filipino migrants in Tel Aviv (Willen 2007). She tells the stories of the undocumented who live underground lives and try to hide their bodies from what they perceive to be an omnipresent gaze.

It is important to stress that the concept of thickening borderlands must be understood in terms of embodied pain and physical harm. A thickening of borderlands is accompanied by what anthropologists have called 'infrastructural violence' (Ferguson 2012; Rodgers and O'Neill 2012). These researchers emphasize that destitution and deprivation often come about through exclusion from important infrastructures (at a subsistence level, including essentials like water, electricity, and the wires, pipes, and buildings that are part of a citizen's protective infrastructure, but also at a more advanced level, such as exclusion from the city's public places). For homeless and 'illegal' people like Abdi, it is exactly through the working of such infrastructural violence that thickening borderlands become operational and palpable. The concept reminds us that 'social suffering is often experienced in material terms' (Rodgers and O'Neill 2012, 405). Placing emphasis on the social and material suffering of migrants such as Abdi may help to build a counter-narrative that opposes dominant national narratives about states suffering hardship at the hands of migrants who are accused of causing harm by taking public benefits, by acting in criminal ways, and by 'polluting' the nation's culture (cf. Coutin and Vogel 2016). Considering the fenced world in which we are currently living, such counter-narratives seem to be more important now than ever before.

4

Psycho-Technicians and Greedy Institutions

On the 16th of July 2009, Cambridge, Massachusetts police Sergeant James Crowley arrested Harvard Professor Henry Louis Gates Jr, a prominent African-American scholar of race, literature and history who serves as Director of the W.E.B. Du Bois Institute for African and African-American Research. Sergeant Crowley, although white and named after an Irish militant nationalist, identified strongly with new post-racial professional norms and was described as a leader in implementing anti-racist reforms within a racially integrated police department. In fact, Sergeant Crowley had been promoted by a black mayor of Cambridge; and a black police chief of Lowell chose the sergeant to lead a training course on ending practices of racial profiling within the police, which he had done since 2004. But at Professor Gates' front door, the achievements of decades of police reforms around race seemed to evaporate. In an emergency call to the police, a neighbour had reported seeing two men possibly attempting to open the door to Gates' house. In fact, the men in question were Gates and his driver, who were simply prying loose a screen door that was stuck. The cautious neighbour had not reported the men as black and had underlined that they might, in fact, be residents of the home. But when the police operator relayed the message to the officers on duty, the operator raised the urgency level by misstating that the neighbour had reported two black men breaking in. When Sergeant Crowley arrived, Gates was already inside and settled in his own home. The officer demanded to enter and ordered Gates to produce his identification. Gates complied, but also angrily demanded to see Crowley's identification and badge number. Crowley refused to comply and decided to punish Gates for his pride. Crowley did not, it would seem, draw upon his own sensitivity training and the

Police Unlimited: Policing, Migrants, and the Values of Bureaucracy. First Edition. Paul Mutsaers. © Paul Mutsaers 2019. Published 2019 by Oxford University Press.

> new values of anti-racist professionalism that he had taught others for so long. Crowley arrested the professor in Gates' own home, charging him with a baseless disorderly conduct charge that was dropped after Gates spent a few hours in jail. (Amar 2010, 575–6)

I took this short narrative from Amar's introduction to a special issue of *Ethnic and Racial Studies* titled 'New Racial Missions of Policing', which I re-read after the fatal shooting of the seventeen-year-old Rishi Chandrikasing by a police officer at a railway station in The Hague (24 November 2013). The officer who pulled the trigger while Chandrikasing was running away from him after being ordered to nail his feet to the ground, was acquitted after he was charged by the Chandrikasing family for murder. A police controversy was born. The railway station where the shooting took place borders a neighbourhood (*Schilderswijk*) that is known for its diversity and is notorious for tense relations between the police and the ethnic minority communities. It was in this neighbourhood that protestors voiced their anger towards police and used slogans ('No Justice, No Peace!') which they borrowed from the US Black Lives Matter movement, after police officers killed Mitch Henriquez in a chokehold (see Chapter 2). In contrast to former US President Barack Obama, who had invited Professor Henry Louis Gates Jr and Sergeant James Crowley to the White House for a reconciliatory beer, the former mayor of The Hague reacted much more defensively. He ridiculed the protests which occurred in response to the killing of Henriquez, implying that people had gone mad due to a combination of hunger and heat (it was exceptionally warm in June that year and Ramadan was underway). Two years earlier, only one week before the shooting of Chandrikasing, a local news agency had broadcasted a documentary in which former police officers voiced their critique on police violence and discrimination in the notorious district. The mayor responded by saying that he saw no need to further investigate this matter and assured the local police commissioner that he could count on his full support.

Yet, in addition to contrasting these forms of political leadership, we can also draw an interesting parallel. As in Sergeant Crowley's case, the officer who shot the young Chandrikasing must have had excellent training in post-racial professional norms and values (see Chapter 2). In fact, among public sector institutions in

The Netherlands, the police stand out in terms of investment in diversity management (see Boogaard and Roggeband 2010, for a brief overview). The point of introducing Professor Gates' ordeal in combination with the shooting of Chandrikasing is to draw Amar's argument into the Dutch context. Amar argues that racial and ethnic distinctions have become increasingly salient in policing at a time that 'diversity and anti-racial profiling campaigns [have] become central to defining norms of police professionalism' (Amar 2010, 578). According to Amar, this is the case for a significant part due to the nature of these campaigns and the training that accompanies them, which almost exclusively focus on the cognitive or psychological aspects of police discrimination against ethnic minorities.

In Chapter 2, I concentrated on the effects of biocratic governance on migrant-hostile policing 'out there', on the streets. I will now turn from external affairs to internal affairs, and place inter-ethnic labour relations and work floor interactions under the microscope. My aim in this chapter is twofold. First, I will try to explain why the cognitive turn in diversity management that is lamented by Amar and many others is highly problematic. The general critique on psychological diversity management as decontextual and ignorant of power relations is easily proffered, but rarely do we encounter studies that scrutinize the effects of diversity management (DM) on human relations and interactions. In the first part of this chapter, I seek to enhance our understanding of the role of 'psycho-technicians' in this matter and look at the 'domaining effects' of their productions. What happens when DM techniques leave the context of production and become operational in different contexts of usage? I will build on various concepts from the field of linguistic anthropology (e.g. entextualization, interdiscursivity, intertextual asymmetry, pretextuality, and strategically deployable shifters) to answer this question. Second, returning to the starting point of this book, I aim to show that the convergence of psy-frames and diversity management is an important aspect of biocratic governance as it enlists the whole police officer, including his or her private considerations, social identity, and personal ties. Such an enlistment, or better, submission, turns the Dutch police into a prototype of what Coser called *greedy institutions* (Coser 1974). Whereas earlier I aimed to shed light on the risks of such greediness for those who are policed, I now also turn to the risks for police officers themselves. A quotation taken from Coser helps to highlight this point:

> When the desire for wholeness leads to an enlistment in greedy organizations, it may end in an obliteration of the characteristics that mark the private person as an autonomous actor ... Commitment to greedy institutions requires that the autonomy gained by men who stand at the intersection of many circles is relinquished, and is replaced by heteronomous submission to the all-encompassing demands of organizations that greedily devour the whole man in order to fully fashion him into an image that serves their needs. (Coser 1974, 16–17)

The Psychological Turn in Labour Management

Before I continue with the case analyses, I must emphasize that the dominance of psychology in diversity management and labour management more generally is, of course, not new and not limited to the Dutch police. As far back as 1989, Rose wrote, in *Governing the Soul*, that organizational life in its broadest spectrum has taken on a psychological hue, as life at work is increasingly rendered intelligible through psychological language, rationalities, strategies, and technologies. Psychological expertise has become an increasingly important factor in matters such as selection, promotion, job evaluation, performance appraisal, work design, job enrichment, etc. It indeed seems true that different applications of psychology in the workplace are now more highly regarded and more insistently mobilized than ever before, and academic interest has developed accordingly (e.g. Costea et al. 2008; DiFruscia 2012; Miller and Rose 1988, 1994; Shields and Grant 2010; Tucker 1999). Many employees around the world will, for instance, be familiar with the 'Big Five' test (featuring five personality traits, namely extraversion, openness to experience, conscientiousness, agreeableness, and emotional stability) or other techniques of psychological profiling through which employers claim to find a match between an employee and the organization. What's more, it is not only the match that is considered important; labour management theory and practice increasingly solidify around the idea that the employee's soft characteristics (e.g. attitudes, character traits, predispositions, emotions) are key to organizational success, hence, 'the expansion and intensification of demands on the self to become ever more involved in work with its whole subjectivity' (Costea et al. 2008, 672; see also Blommaert et al. 2012).

Back in the 1960s and 1970s, critical work had already appeared on the psychological turn in labour management, such as Baritz's *The Servants of Power* (1960) and Anthony's *Ideology of Work* (1977; see Grey and Willmott 2005 for an insightful reader). They were among the first seriously to open the discussion about the politics of psychological techniques and expertise in the workplace. This discussion on the politics of psychology was essentially a discussion on the politics of freedom. Was psychology used to increase the freedom of workers, the freedom of managers, and what kind of freedom was this exactly? Baritz and Anthony were clear on this matter. Baritz had suggested that industrial psychologists had put themselves on auction to the power elites by giving managers increasingly nuanced and effective means to control employees. Similarly, Anthony never concealed his ideas about the laws of psychology being put at service of management to inculcate workers with certain beliefs and expectations. Theirs was a critique on ideology, on the belief that the worker's self-actualization and self-fulfilment (the psychologist's boost of the 'humanization of work', to use a hackneyed phrase, which harks back to our discussion in Chapter 2) and increasing efficiency in work processes are not mutually exclusive but mutually stimulating. This was dismissed as false knowledge at best, manipulation at worst.

Such an ideology critique could itself be criticized from at least two angles. First, in certain ways it could be seen as an individualization or even personalization of the problem ('servants of power'), despite its fierce Marxist critique on the obsession with the individual that was said to characterize the psychological profession. Second, such a critique merely focused on psychological expertise in the negative, as something that adjusted workers to exploitative conditions or further caught them in hierarchical relations of domination and subordination. Miller and Rose (1988, 1994) and Rose (1989) argued against this and discussed how the various 'psy' disciplines, as they called them, have acquired the capacity to render themselves *technical*, able to produce an effect that is not only negative, but that stimulates subjectivity, shapes desires, and creates new knowledge.[1]

[1] This debate soon spilled over to other (sub)fields and human resource management (HRM) was one of them, as it was clear from the outset that 'psychological

In the first part of this chapter, I offer my own views on this debate by centralizing the role of the technician; this is a complicated matter. Baritz and Anthony and Rose and Miller worked with different definitions of the technician. Baritz's view was that technicians are not concerned with problems outside the delimited sphere that is assigned to them and are concerned with means only, not with ends, which prevents them from taking up a critical role in society. Baritz quoted Coxe who suggested that the technician should begin with an 'analysis of [his] own place in [his] present-day social organization' and should start worrying about his 'responsibility for the use to which the results of his work are employed' (Coxe 1940, 96–7). From this viewpoint, it is exactly their withdrawal from politics that turns technicians into political servants. Rose and associates (e.g. Barry et al. 1996) on the other hand, argued against the relation between the technical and the political as an explicit opposition. Technology itself is political, they said, because it carries with it a certain directive capacity.

I will take up this notion of directive capacities and build two arguments around it. First, the technicians discussed here—who work in the tradition of the 'psy-disciplines', making it sensible to dub them 'psycho-technicians'—often do not oversee or cannot imagine the consequences of the directive capacities of the management instruments they provide, because their expertise is often used in governance at arm's length. Such modes of ruling disconnect the substantive authority of expertise from their actual uses in real-life settings and can thereby be distinguished from more embedded forms of governance, which take local contexts more seriously (Rose 1996).

expertise is vital for the maximization of the use of HRs in institutional life' (Rose 1989, xxviii). In her landmark book on the rhetoric and realities of HRM, Legge positioned HRM in a broader political-economic context (Legge 1995, xvii; as did others, e.g. Thompson 2011) and deconstructed it 'as a phenomenon whose importance lies largely in its existence as a rhetoric and discourse that serves the interest of a range of influential stakeholders who have an interest in hype-ing the extent and depth of its facticity.' She concurred with Braverman (1974) that human relations and industrial psychology experts were the 'maintenance crew for the human machinery' (Braverman 1974, 60 and Legge 1995, 18). On this terrain, we also find critique on the ideology-critique, and it is spearheaded by Watson who has consistently dismissed Legge's critique on HRM as an ideological apparatus that simply masks the antagonisms in capitalist society for being too much about appearances (Watson 2004, 2010).

Second, this lack of imagination is a lack of 'sociological imagination' (Mills 1959), which makes it hard to understand peoples' personal troubles at work as public issues or 'going concerns' (Hughes 1984); that is, as situated in a broader social fabric with particular structural problems that cannot be addressed from a distance and cannot be solved by a singular focus on the individual. Forcing through such a distanced focus on the individual while obscuring the larger social landscape must, according to Mills, lead to what he called 'psychologism'. The contribution of psycho-technicians to freedom at work is therefore a contribution to a particular form of freedom, which is best captured by Rose who wrote that the psy

> has come to celebrate values of autonomy and self-realization that are essentially psychological in form and structure ... human subjects ... are 'obliged to be free' in this psychological sense. That is to say, however apparently external and implacable may be the constraints, obstacles and limitations that are encountered, each individual must render his or her life meaningful as if it were the outcome of individual choices made in furtherance of a biographical project of self-realization. (Rose 1989, viii–ix)

Psychologism at the Dutch Police

We have seen before that psychology is not something that is foreign to the Dutch police organization. However, not all psychology equals psychologism. For instance, all police recruits are psychologically tested in The Netherlands before their training at the Police Academy can start, and for good reasons: these recruits are about to wield the monopolistic powers of legitimate violence. Having started work and begun enforcing the law, some officers may again find themselves in front of a psychologist. For instance, a considerable number of them may have to see a psy-expert to treat post-traumatic stress disorder (PTSD). However, this sort of psy-expertise is not likely to be defined as psychologism the way Mills meant it. Yes, such treatments and tests centre on the individual. However, larger social landscapes are not ignored; often they simply cannot be managed. For example, it is largely out of the hands of a police organization when , for example, a poverty-induced burglary leads to a gun fight that involves an officer who is subsequently diagnosed with PTSD. The individual officer can be treated, but the deeper causes of the gun fight cannot—at least not by a police organization in itself.[2]

The sort of psychology that I would like to place at the centre here is the sort that is involved in diversity management and labour control more generally, as it is this sort of psychology that is more likely to fuel psychologism.[3] Psychologism may, for instance, develop when a career trajectory, which is institutionally determined, is rephrased as a personal development plan, as if an individual's career is shaped only by personal growth and thus independently of organizational constraints, asymmetric power relations, and favouritism. I have encountered numerous instances of such psychologism throughout my ethnographic project. Here is an example. A Turkish-Dutch officer had himself transferred from one police force to another because he had heard chances were better for him there to get promoted to sergeant. In this new environment he applied for job openings repeatedly but was rejected because each time his personal development plan was considered to be below par. He tried to build a discrimination case but his superiors claimed that their assessments were legitimate and fair rather than discriminatory. It was argued that the officer simply lacked the right personality traits, and they mentioned various identity profiles (such as 'entrepreneurial', 'sociable', and 'open-minded'). These are the sort of fuzzy and

[2] I would like to thank an anonymous reviewer for clarifying that this is in fact a moot point. There is an incongruity between my assertion and the fact that much police policy is actually designed to address 'deeper' social problems. While it may be true that the police cannot adequately solve such issues, this does not mean that attempts aren't made. Looking at the central topic of my ethnographic research—that is, the role and function of the Dutch police in a multiethnic society—multiple attempts have been made (and are continuously made) by the police and their partner organizations to address issues at the intersection of ethnicity and crime. In the closing years of multiculturalism this was done progressively and with a general idea of some goodness of fit between immigrants and Dutch society. Now, however, monoculturalism dominates and the Dutch police seek partnerships with a plethora of public and private organizations to address crime-related issues among immigrants in a repressive and prohibitive manner. See Chapter 3.

[3] Again, see the work of Siebers, who has demonstrated that the introduction of post-bureaucratic and psychological control and a very personalized language fuel the emergence and continuation of ethnic conflicts and exclusion in Dutch organizations (Siebers 2009a, 2009b, 2010b; Siebers and Van Gastel 2015), including the police (e.g. Siebers 2009c, 2017).

ambiguous criteria that have been widely documented to fuel ethnic inequality in work settings (e.g. Campbell and Roberts 2007; Moss and Tilly 1996; Siebers 2009a) and can be interpreted as the kind of organizational constraint that is largely beyond any individual officer's control. In our case, they may impede a particular segment of the workforce (ethnic minority officers) because they expand the room of selectors/superiors to prejudge. We will see later in this chapter that the use of such criteria in human resource (HR) decisions allows superiors to shift their ground constantly.

Here is another example. A group of minority policemen who experienced similar problems were invited by a deputy district commander (DDC) to an informal grievance talk to discuss their experiences with discrimination. These men told me that this talk was misleading. One officer said: 'There was no sympathy for our feelings of exclusion; it was just a one-way street.'

The DDC had enticed the men into confessing their deepest feelings and emotions but had given nothing in return. In the end, she had used the same kind of identity profiles to justify the stagnant careers of these men. They too were deemed insufficiently open-minded, flexible, sociable, and entrepreneurial. Remarkably, these identity profiles can also be found in the *Multicultural Personality Questionnaire* (see Van der Zee and Van Oudenhoven 2001), which had been circulating within the police organization for some time and was used by HR officers and diversity managers to measure whether officers have a personality that allows multiculturalism to flourish within police teams.[4] It is telling that such a questionnaire can be used to harm the career paths of ethnic minority officers. This is reminiscent of the critical work on HRM by Townley in which she stated that personality tests and attitude measurements are 'arrangements for ranking', which 'provide a grid of codability of personal attributes', placing individuals on comparative scalar measures (Townley 1993, 528–9). Such tests and measures may gain notoriety among employees, for they can

[4] The Multicultural Personality Questionnaire has been developed by Karen van der Zee, an organizational psychologist at Groningen University and registered as expert at the Dutch Foundation for Psychotechnics (*Nederlandse Stichting voor Psychotechniek*), an organization that will be discussed in some depth in the next sections.

easily ratchet up competition between employees (i.e. from competition on the basis of output and work performance to levels of the psyche, the hearts and the minds, cultural values, and so on). They are, as Rose states, 'the apotheosis of the celebration of the individual in capitalist ideology'—that is, of some individuals (Rose 1989, 219).

Ethnic minority officers' experiences with what they framed as structural discrimination were always counter-framed as personal troubles they ought to manage themselves in order to become empowered and increase self-assertion (i.e. to set themselves free from the limitations of their current role). At best, they were offered empowerment courses or therapeutic talk sessions to work on their 'mental resilience' (a key word at the Dutch police) so that they could cope better with discrimination in the future. Such coping was considered to be a key quality of a professional police officer, who must know how to roll with the punches. This conforms to official police policy.

In 2008, I conducted an interview with members of a committee that was heavily endorsed and fostered by senior management. This Diversity Steering Committee (DSC) was charged with managing the range and depth of human diversity within the organization. In the interview, I elicited the interviewees' response to the recent reforms of the organization's diversity policies, which no longer framed diversity as a 'social issue' but instead as a 'business case'. This metamorphosis had occurred under the auspices of the National Expertise Centre Diversity (LECD) of the police, whose former director was an advocate of the business case of diversity:

> Formerly, diversity was animated by the unions and by politics. From these viewpoints diversity was about the quality of labour and about political correctness. From this period comes the enforcement of diversity through percentages. The surplus value of diversity for the organization was insufficiently recognized and, furthermore, the notion of diversity as a social issue triggered the idea in certain police forces that target groups were sad ... Diversity as a business issue entails the pursuit of diversity driven by the organization's self-interest: Surviving and maintaining efficiency in a changing environment. (Poelert 2006)

He continued discussing some, in his opinion, formidable examples taken from the private sector such as banking and insurance (this was just before the global financial crisis). The DSC members had appropriated this new policy in full two years later:

> It is interesting to have a conversation with certain allochtonous colleagues: 'The world is unfair and rights are taken away from me.' Well, that is all very interesting, but I don't go along with that. Yes, the world is unfair and that unfair world does not stop at the boundaries of our organization, but what do you need as an individual member of this organization to stay active? That doesn't relieve us of the task to intervene when things happen that we don't like, but we are not there day and night. So people need enough resilience to deal with these things. And what you see is that those colleagues who are prepared to invest a bit more—no matter how unfair that is (that is not even an interesting question to me)—are doing well ... This has something to do with professionalism.' (interview with two DSC members in 2008)

This new diversity policy is demarcated by three important parameters. First, with the abolition of a conception of diversity as social justice, we witness an abdication of the effort to intervene in cases involving injustice or inequality.[5] 'That is not even an interesting question to me', said one of the DSC members. Moreover, the LECD director experienced the interference of unions and politics in the matter of diversity at work as burdensome and bad for business. Second, unionism and other forms of social action for minorities are dismissed because they are considered political, whereas individualization ('you as an individual member') and the business case for diversity ('the organization's self-interest', 'surplus value', 'efficiency') are depoliticized. Third, when all political matters are ostensibly dismissed, we see an *en passant* redefinition of professionalism. A professional is resilient in the face of unfairness, continuously active despite setbacks, autonomous (not leaning on others), and always willing to invest a bit more of his or herself in the job. This definition of professionalism is consonant with the police reforms described in previous chapters, intended to give police officers more 'professional freedom', to have them operate as 'craftsmen' who know how to wield the powers of discretion. Throughout the life of my ethnographic study, I noticed, however, that the fruits of such freedom seldom accrue to ethnic minority officers. In fact, often they had to take the brunt

[5] For such an outmanoeuvring of justice considerations and, basically, 'law enforcement' see also Siebers (2009c, 2017) whose work was very important for my understanding of this abolition.

of laissez-faire management styles and had to fight an uphill battle for recognition and promotion by themselves.

From what follows it will become apparent that these three parameters ostensibly lead to a technical—and thus depoliticized—DM agenda but that they bring politics back into the situation when enacted in real-life situations. It is important to note in this light that both the LECD director and the DSC members are executive managers who come from the police organization, and more specifically have a background in street work rather than desk work, but that their ideas and statements (which are metonymic for the organization's diversity policies at large; e.g. LECD 2006) show a great deal of interdiscursivity with DM texts produced by experts who have no direct relation to the actual work being done by rank and file officers and are able to shape managerial activities from a distance.

Discourse Itineraries

To have a good grasp of the empirical materials in this part of the book, I suggest we use the notion of 'itinerant diversity management' (Mutsaers and Trux 2015). It instantly makes clear that police managers in the organization almost never produce DM techniques themselves. The production site, so to speak, is often the preserve of technicians, who are either in-house diversity experts or external consultants, and who often work remotely. Their services trickle into the organization and with each transfer (e.g. between a subcontracted diversity consultant and an in-house expert), a new step in a process of entextualization occurs.[6] It is exactly because of this itinerant character that DM technicians lose track of their services. It is therefore the anthropological analysis of these travelling devices and their 'domaining effects'[7] that can provide the critical punch.

In my analysis, I deliberately do not speak of a crossing of domains as *intertextuality*—which implies a directionally neutral

[6] I define entextualization following Blommaert: 'lifting text out of context, placing it in another context and adding metapragmatic qualifications to it, thus specifying the conditions for how texts should be understood, what they mean and stand for, and so on' (Blommaert 2001, 18).

[7] Defined following Shore and Wright: the effects that occur when a certain logic (or constellation of various concepts, i.e. a semantic cluster) associated with

comparison of texts (Silverstein 2005)—but as *interdiscursivity*, because this highlights the strategic use of texts and thus connects nicely to the notion of directive capacity discussed earlier. It is because of this strategic use of and directive capacity in textual productions that we need to take into account both the origin/production and uptake/use of the discursive management techniques under study (Blommaert 2013a; Cameron 2000). Especially in institutional communication processes, we see a lot of shifting of texts between contexts of production and contexts of uptake, and it is exactly this shifting that involves crucial questions of power (Blommaert 2001). As we will see, language may appear devoid of power in certain domains (e.g. the domains of HRM, policy, and research) but can become severely styled, codified, regimented—in other words, 'policed'—in other domains (e.g. on the work floor).

One of the most influential partners of the police regarding DM that I came across is the Dutch Foundation for Psychotechnics (*Nederlandse Stichting voor Psychotechniek*, or NSvP). The NSvP presents itself as a capital fund that invests in activities at the intersection of consultancy and science, and mainly concentrates on applied sciences such as HRM and organizational or industrial psychology. It was taken over in 2001 by a leading and international occupational psychology company, SHL Talent Measurement (see Campbell and Roberts 2007) and has multiple connections to the Dutch police.[8] For instance, NSvP associates regularly conduct DM research at the police (e.g. the earlier mentioned Multicultural Personality Questionnaire, developed by an NSvP expert who used it in a research project to test police officers) and an endowed chair at the Police Academy—Multicultural Craftsmanship—was held by an NSvP member for several years.

The NSvP has fully embraced the business case of diversity; on their website, DM texts feature keywords such as resource optimization, innovation, success, entrepreneurship, surplus value, productivity, customer satisfaction, competition, effectiveness, image improvement, flexibility, competence, and excellence.[9]

a particular domain migrates to another domain where it receives new operational power, often with unanticipated consequences (Shore and Wright 2000).

[8] Now CEB Talent Assessment (see <https://www.cebglobal.com/talent-management/talent-assessment.html/>).

[9] See <http://www.innovatiefinwerk.nl>. All Dutch texts are translated into the English by the present author.

Further, a very strong and manifest intertextuality exists in terms of mutually approving links between various NSvP texts (with different authors), both regarding vocabulary and grammar. The grammatical mood in the documents is declarative, lacking hedging expressions or modality: 'Diversity *is* part of a business case' and 'diversity *offers* opportunities to increase the innovative capacities of the organization'. This lexico-grammatical stance implies that we only need to measure to what extent diversity is profitable and competitively advantageous.[10]

A few years ago, I attended a DM conference in Amsterdam that was organized by the NSvP. The day was opened by an NSvP expert who, at that time, held the endowed chair in Multicultural Craftsmanship at the Police Academy. She introduced five new DM methods that were about to be presented separately in workshops. After several minutes, a hand was raised in the audience and the owner of the hand asked: 'Are we all supposed to go into therapy now?'

The setting reminded me of what Costea and colleagues called a 'therapeutic habitus' (Costea et al. 2008). In the book that was distributed at the end of the conference, dialogue was presented as the bedrock of the five DM methods (cf. Siebers 2017): '[Dialogue is a] special form of conversation that is focused on inner search. Not the solution of a problem is central, but a quest to find the essence of a problem. Dialogue is a self-exploration that you go

[10] An interesting side remark is that meta-analytical studies on the business case of diversity find no conclusive evidence that diversity is, in fact, good for business (often measures in terms of creativity, team performance, innovation, and the like). Explanations of these meta-analytical findings are readily sought in the fact that different criteria are used to measure work-related outcomes of diversity (e.g. Groeneveld 2015). If only our measurements are better attuned, our results will become more intelligible. This is a technical approach to the problem and technical malfunctioning can be progressively handled through scientific improvement, it is said. This brings us back to the role of technicians and we must warn again that when the social study of human variety becomes monopolized by technicians, i.e. when social, moral, and political concerns are no longer of interest to those who have been given authority over knowledge through their profession, life for some individuals may become fraught with risks. In our case, we must ask a usually unposed question (apart from some brave exceptions like Carter 2000 or Noon 2007): What will happen when meta-analytical studies irrefutably demonstrate diversity's impediments to business? Does that give sufficient reason to homogenize the workplace? These sorts of ethical questions are generally not asked in the DM literature.

through together' (De Vries 2010, 8). These DM methods were thus translated into management techniques of which inner search and self-exploration constitute the quintessence. The way we understand and govern ourselves is central, not the actual solution to a social problem: these techniques present themselves as 'liberation therapies' that offer a sort of 'social vaccine' to keep the self-governing individual healthy and productive (Cruikshank 1996).

The prominence of such introspective approaches—which had already been in vogue at the Dutch police for a number of years—prompted me to explore how they were enacted in real-life situations at work.[11] Here is one case at the Rotterdam police, where I interviewed a Turkish-Dutch female community officer, Ayşe, who, at the time of the interview in 2008 had recently switched from the alien police division to a community policing team. She was transferred because she had clashed with two of her colleagues. During an early-morning briefing at which about thirty officers and the station chief were present, these colleagues had taken newspaper coverage of a clash between Islamic and Catholic leaders as a pretext to approach Ayşe aggressively: 'You Muslims have to knock it off. You think you can allow yourselves everything. We Christians will attack the Turkish consulate and teach you what violence is.' A second colleague had the audacity to add that it was 'about time to take our white cone hats out of the lockers.'[12]

Before we consider how cases like this are dealt with by police managers, it is important to stress that this sort of politicization was a recurring theme throughout my police ethnography. For instance, Karin, who sent me the emails about the micro-deportations in Tilburg, lamented the tendency of her colleagues to parrot the most extreme statements of Geert Wilders, the right-wing leader of the Freedom Party (PVV), known for its anti-immigrant sentiment. In March 2014, Wilders had caused a stir while campaigning in The Hague when he asked if his audience

[11] For an analysis of how this personalized discourse in organizations works out negatively for minority officers at the Dutch police, also see Siebers (2009a).

[12] The impact of migrant-hostile discourses in the media and politics on inter-ethnic labour relations was demonstrated by Siebers (2009c, 2010a, 2010b, 2017; Siebers and Dennissen 2015) who showed that discourses in Dutch politics and media have turned into outright hostility towards migrants, triggering ethnic conflicts between migrant and non-migrant employees in Dutch work settings, including the police force.

wanted more or fewer Moroccans in The Netherlands. When they chanted 'FEWER, FEWER, FEWER!' Wilders promised that he would take care of matters. He went on trial for his comments—a trial which he exploited politically by complaining about the (in his eyes) deplorable state of the Dutch *rechtsstaat*, the constitutional state. If it was up to Karin's colleagues, Wilders would have been acquitted for his comments (in 2016, he was convicted of inciting discrimination). Karin told me that her colleagues strongly agreed with Wilders.

Similarly, a superintendent in Breda (Surinam-born Dinesh, who will play a more substantial role later in this chapter), told me that he felt ill at ease with the website that the PVV launched in 2012 to allow people to complain about Central and Eastern European migrants if they caused a nuisance or steal jobs (at this time, the PVV was supporting the Dutch minority government):

> The government creates problems, because people, including police officers, begin to think like 'there you have that Polish guy again, or that Romanian.' People at the station talk about these things. For example, this morning it was broadcasted that the PVV has this website where you can file a complaint about Polish people. Colleagues discuss this and say 'hey, shall we do that as well?' I think I have to do something with that, as a police manager. So this morning I said 'I don't think you can say these things. Of what will it be the beginning?'

As in the French case (Fassin 2013a), political messages abounded in Dutch police canteens. Often they reflected anti-immigrant sentiments. Majority rule kept newspaper articles of this kind firmly in place, and when an officer wanted them removed, (s)he had to make sure nobody saw her attempting to remove such an article. Aziza, a Moroccan-Dutch female superintendent working in the same police team as Karin, wrote in the diary that she kept for me:

> I was cleaning my desk today when I noticed this newspaper article. An argument was made in it for the mass deportation of Moroccans in the Netherlands. A very blunt piece. I saw it in 2003 in the canteen of the station, where I was working at that time for about six months. I copied it and put it back. I didn't do anything with it.

A couple of weeks after she handed her diary to me, she told me in an interview how taxing it was for her to work in an environment populated with colleagues so hostile to immigrants:

> That something like that is in the papers, fine. That Geert Wilders exists, also fine. But that this can be displayed in the canteen of a

police station. I was like … Where in heaven's name have I ended up? What kind of organization is this? I know of course that it was only one person who did it, but it says something about the entire organization. I secretly copied the article but didn't do anything with it. This had to do with the fact that I was new in the organization. I didn't know it that well.

Aziza felt that it was only by keeping her opinions to herself that she managed to climb the career ladder and make it to superintendent.

Back to Ayşe. According to her, the station chief, who was present when her colleagues referred to the white supremacist Ku Klux Klan, did not intervene and continued with the briefing as if nothing had happened. Ayşe, who thought of herself as an articulate person, clammed up completely. She filed an official discrimination complaint but to no avail; it was not processed. She went on sick leave for three months, as she could not go to work:

Then you fall back upon your old life, you see? I want to integrate in society, I want to do things, but then you withdraw, you go back to your own culture. Well, you have the need to talk about it, but in your own language. You only wish to talk to people who understand you. For me it was very hard to explain to a Dutch social worker what I experienced inside. Many Turkish people live for their honour, you see … Maybe this is unthinkable for a Dutch person, but at that moment, your sense of honour and pride is extremely affected. They rather could have kicked me to death … So then you find yourself sick at home … [I wasn't] able to go to work while the other colleague was unaffected and could simply go on with his life and his work. But it is supposed to be the other way around. How can the victim be stuck at home for three months, while the aggressor can continue with his work?

After these three months, Ayşe was invited by the station chief for conflict mediation, a dialogue session involving herself and her two colleagues. With a quaver in her voice she said: 'Now, I am willing to go into mediation about how we use our keycards, for instance, but this is something completely different … These people have made up their minds. They are no kids of 16, 17 years old.'

She declined the invitation, which she saw as sheer rejection and betrayal of hew views. The station chief had not intervened in the heat of the moment and now she felt she was about to be thrown to the wolves again. She was convinced that she did not have a fighting chance in the mediation because it would just enable her colleagues to air their grievances and aggravate her condition. Declining the invitation was unacceptable to the station chief, and Ayşe was forced to leave the team. She was told that she lacked the mental resilience deemed essential to teamwork and to handle situations like these. It was argued that she had a deficit in terms of openness, flexibility, and assertiveness, competences considered necessary to stand one's ground as a professional police officer.

This course of events invites several comments. To begin with, there is no doubt that this case can be assessed in light of NSvP discourses on dialogue as a technique for inner search and self-exploration, rather than an interactional device that can be used to solve a problem that is much broader than personal troubles between individuals. It is a clear instance of psychologism, to refer back to Mills, in which the most central 'going concern' (Hughes 1984) of the police institution is simply forgotten or ignored: security. Ayşe's *idea of police* had deteriorated so much due to her colleagues' verbal assaults that she no longer felt safe in their presence. Put differently, the insecurity that Ayşe felt because of the demeaning treatment was magnified by the particular context in which it developed. It is always easy to impute a wide range of imperfections on individuals whose personalities or biographical backgrounds may be seen as the cause of the emotional release in the dispute. It is more challenging, however, to realize that it can be problematic to leave a dispute like this to private recourse when it stems from a significant ongoing concern that guides the course of collective action in a particular institution such as this, and that works as an important backdrop to recorded troubles.

As my ethnography advanced, I realized that ethnic minority officers often have to endure structures of racism or cultural exclusion that permeate the organization as migrant-hostile discourses in Dutch politics and media (Siebers 2010a), which are then copied and reproduced by officers at work. Ayşe's case is certainly not a singular case; it is part of a pattern that is characterized by migrant hostility. This hostility is often left unchallenged by police managers who cannot or dare not intervene. The reasons of individual police chiefs need not all be malignant; in fact, I prefer not to contribute to such a depiction of the problem as one which stems from particular individuals (the 'servants of power' argument). The outcome of many interviews on this topic suggests that some police managers too felt constrained by these new leadership discourses, such as those that developed under NSvP aegis. Others believed in the ameliorative and emancipatory potential of mediation and dialogue as inner search.

In any case, such dialogue techniques need radical rethinking after they are put to a test in practice. The question that needs to be begged, because it will otherwise go unasked is: what do we make of the business case of diversity when a victim of blunt racism is being doubly victimized when she is harassed out of her job based on psychological qualifications such as open-mindedness, flexibility, and assertiveness? Ayşe was indeed 'obliged to be free', to echo Rose (1989): free to engage in the verbal competition with her colleagues. And this freedom was essentially perceived as psychological in form and structure.[13]

There was a deficit of sociological imagination—not psychological strength—in the case at hand; the sort of imagination needed to understand that this was a clear matter of intertextual asymmetry (Blommaert 2007), a case in which some people are burdened with particular forms of intertextuality while others are not. Blommaert gives the example of the term *slavery*: when uttered in a classroom it triggers different intertextual worlds for Afro-Caribbean children than for Caucasian children. Such terms operate on different scales and at different levels for different people. Phrases such as 'you Muslim', 'attacking the Turkish consulate', or 'white cone hats' were automatic phrases for Ayşe's colleagues, but they had a lasting impact on Ayşe as they immediately invoked categorical, collective, and transcontextual images for Ayşe. It is no wonder, therefore, that she fell back on her old life, the Turkish life she led before she became integrated into Dutch society, and on group thinking ('your own culture', 'Turkish people live for their honour', 'this is unthinkable for a Dutch person'). In this light, it is easy to understand how difficult it was for Ayşe to participate in the individual change efforts proposed by the station chief. She was well aware of the fact that she did not lack the *capacity* to communicate (a psychological

[13] Siebers (2009a, 2017) discusses in detail how the application of post-bureaucratic management approaches encourages police team leaders to outmanoeuvre concerns for justice and law enforcement.

understanding) but that she was *incapacitated* to engage (a contextual and sociological understanding). During the interview, she struck me as a fluent and powerful communicator; it was her colleagues' aggression that had rendered her mute.

This brings me to a final issue that I want to mention briefly, that of pretextuality and pretextual gaps. Pretextuality is defined as the 'preconditions for communication that influence communicative behaviour', and pretextual gaps refer to the 'differences in such preconditions between participants in communication' (Maryns and Blommaert 2002, 12). Obviously, Ayşe did communicate. She filed an official discrimination complaint but that was not the kind of communication that was expected from her. This would make the whole thing political and obstruct a professional solution (remember the viewpoints of the DSC members and the LECD director). However, the intertextual asymmetry already discussed had already politicized the situation in the sense that the preconditions for people to participate in communication (the mediation) were uneven. It is exactly this kind of unevenness in real-life situations that is missed by technicians who contribute to arms' length management and do not become involved in the intricacies of everyday life at work.

The case of Ayşe shows, as I argued earlier, a high level of regimentation of communication, which is at odds with the liberation technique that dialogue—as defined earlier—is taken to be. Dialogue is de facto turned into what Du Gay called a 'discourse register': 'a particular, institutionally sanctioned way of talking' (in Cameron 2000, 14) in which talking is not seen as an activity that involves at least two interlocutors but is seen instead as an individual or even psychological capacity or skill. The station chief valued his employees in proportion to their communication *skills*, from which it follows that Ayşe's problems would automatically begin to recede if she would be willing to improve these skills. This brings us to the notion of 'soft skills' (e.g. Urciuoli 2008), particularly to a soft skill that is highly esteemed within the Dutch police: authenticity. Let us turn to two text fragments, the first from a dissertation that was supervised by an NSvP board member (and published on its website), and the second coming from an official employer's statement published by the national HR division of the Dutch police:

> Accommodating authenticity allows for individual differences and 'being different' and creates possibilities to experience these differences and

let them co-exist, rather than disappear ... More specifically, in diverse working contexts, research shows that when group members give recognition to the unique qualities of other group members, this recognition moderates the relation between diversity and performance ... Creating a working climate that stimulates authentic behaviour is contingent upon authentic leadership. Authentic leadership means that managers are a reflection of themselves and are in contact with all dimensions of their self. (Raaijmakers 2008, 92)

The police organization pursues diversity and this requires a variety and authenticity of leadership in the police organization ... Leaders coach and impassion employees in order to let them excel in the things they are good at; this gives employees a chance to act in accordance with their own views ... Leaders must be capable of touching upon the authenticity of employees. (Werkgeversvisie Politie 2008, 77–8)

The mainstay of the argument in favour of authenticity as a relevant factor at work is that, if managed (accommodated) in a proper way, it allows for diversity and 'being different' in a team, which in turn improves performance and stimulates employees to excel (the business case for diversity again). This works at different levels in the organization in the sense that authentic leaders are needed to 'connect with the authenticity of employees'. Again, we will observe what happens when certain ideas originating from the fields of HRM, policy, and research trickle down to the work floor, where they are confronted with the everyday complexities of social interaction. This time the notion of soft skills—a category to which authenticity certainly belongs—as strategically deployable shifters (SDSs) is central to the analysis (Urciuoli 2008). Urciuoli characterizes soft skills on the basis of two semiotic properties: denotational indeterminacy and strategic indexicality.[14] They are vague, hard to describe, and cover a wide range of disparate practices, but at the same time invoke images of corporate success, mission, vision, strategy, etc. (see also the NSvP keywords listed earlier). The combination of these two semiotic properties turns them into SDSs. Urciuoli explains: terms that are related to soft skills are semantically variable and therefore become strategically useful linguistic elements that have 'no context-independent lexical meaning' because they 'can only be fully interpreted in terms

[14] After Blommaert: '*indexical* meaning: social meaning, interpretive leads between what is said and the social occasion in which it is being produced' (Blommaert 2005, 11).

of the speaker's position in a specific place, time, social context, or some combination thereof' (Urciuoli 2008, 214). SDSs' 'semantic value seems obvious yet hard to pin down'.

In the autumn of 2011, I followed a district commander (DC) for a couple of weeks. At a certain point, I joined him in a personnel review, a meeting that is periodically held by the DC and his HR advisor to discuss the career development of police officers, as well as other HR-related issues. That day they discussed a job interview they—and a team leader—had had earlier with an operational commander (OC) who had applied for a job as deputy team leader. During the personnel review, they were finalizing their decision to reject the candidate, Surinam-born Dinesh, because both were of the opinion that he was not 'authentic' and therefore unfit as a team leader. When I asked at the end of the meeting what they meant by authenticity, how it fit the job profile, and how it could be assessed, they clearly felt uncomfortable. The HR advisor was visibly ashamed to confess that it was mostly a gut feeling and that authenticity is applied as a criterion in various ways in the force. However, in separate interviews that I conducted afterwards with the DC, the HR officer, the team leader, and the applicant, a different story arose. Several weeks after the meeting, the HR officer had regained confidence when I posed the same question. She said:

> Leaders must be themselves, that is, authentic ... In a job interview you are primarily looking for the true self of a person. And you know what ... an answer is not right or wrong—I mean, substantively right or wrong. No, it's about how you come to it. This means that you look for who someone really is.

When I raised the same question in a separate interview with the DC, he superimposed another category on authenticity, 'assertiveness', defined as the courage to stand up against your superiors. He did not refer to himself but to the Turkish-Dutch team leader Dinesh would work for as a deputy. I had a lengthy conversation with this team leader, Meryem, and it turned out that her employment record contained a number of ethnic conflicts that caused her to be expelled from another police district. Before I spoke to her for the first time, I had heard many positive stories and was looking forward to meeting her. From hearsay, I understood that Meryem had a promising career and was widely regarded as having 'high potential', on her way to the top level in the organization. However, when I spoke with her, she told me this:

> I did very well [in the organization]. I have been working here for 20 years and I managed pretty well to climb the ladder. I was on my way to the highest level. But all of a sudden, everything changed. I wondered whether it had something to do with the political climate. Is it because of the new government [the migrant-hostile Freedom Party—PVV—had recently started to support the minority government]? Are people within this organization so easily manipulated by political pressure? Promotion plans were aborted and my superiors distanced themselves from me. Had I become a threat? Did people become afraid of me? One of the things I'll never forget is that my superior told me: 'You and I, we have been enemies for centuries.' Soon I realized that this was about Christianity and Islam. I am not a Muslim; I had never even read the Koran. But then I bought one and I read it, twice! I started reading about the prophet Mohammed. I wanted to. For nights I had been awake, crying, considering to 'go back' to Turkey, where I was not even born. I am born in the Netherlands.

It turned out that Meryem was given the assignment to reorganize an all-white team of which she was the OC. This had caused so much resistance among the seasoned and entrenched officers that Meryem ended up being transferred. This had happened after she had called in sick, angered and incredulous with how she had been treated. After a period on leave, she was only allowed to return to the organization if she 'voluntarily' submitted herself to intensive psychological testing. According to the DC, she has a 'strong personality' and 'need[ed] to be brought back into balance'. He was looking for an authentic person who was strong enough to 'give serious counterweight to Meryem'. In his eyes, Dinesh was too much institutionalized in the sense that his communication style during the job interview gave away his subordinate position relative to the team leader.

I had become acquainted with Dinesh a few years earlier, in 2008. At that time, he was already keenly aware that the organization was increasingly looking at 'who you are', as he put it. At the time, he seemed fairly neutral about this. By 2011, he was more critical. He did not protest against authenticity as a criterion for the job per se, which he considered valid, but against the slippery and shifting use of it. As a result, he experienced the whole thing, the application process and attendant expectations, as alienating: 'I am not willing to change my whole personality... And

I said that to the committee. If you're looking for someone who bangs his fist on the table, that's fine. But that's not who I am.' 'You don't want to change that?' I asked. 'No, because I want to be myself.'

The shifting that had occurred was a one of expectations about personal and institutional registers, something that has been extensively studied by Campbell and Roberts (2007) in relation to job interviews as gate-keeping encounters that exclude candidates with an ethnic minority background from certain positions. Once again, we see the conversion of a psychological technique from a putatively liberating device (which gives people the freedom to 'be different', to have 'unique qualities', and to 'act in accordance with their own views') to a prescription, in this case of a synthesis of personal and institutional registers that is not even clearly delineated by the DC and the HR officer and remains a matter of guesswork for the applicant in question. Dinesh apparently tilted the balance too much to the institutional side, whereas Meryem was judged to make things way too personal. Notions such as authenticity, as used in this particular encounter, therefore amount to 'synthetic personalizations' (Fairclough 1992). 'Strategically simulated constructions of identity, which are called up in appropriate moments of [in this case] the interview, and which present a ... version of the self that is entirely consistent with organizational values and the institutional regime of the job interview' (in Campbell and Roberts 2007, 250).

I consider the cases described here problematic and their aftermath regrettable, particularly so for an organization that has an active policy in place for a long time that is designed to increase (the value of) diversity (Boogaard and Roggeband 2010). The police force, as stated earlier, really was among the first Dutch public sector organizations that started to recruit ethnic minorities actively (as early as the 1980s). I found no indications of bad intentions when it comes to policy developments concerning the management of ethnic diversity *within* the Dutch police. This holds true for the period when the 'social approach' to DM had the upper hand (e.g. Ministerie van Binnenlandse Zaken en Koninkrijksrelaties 1996; Vriesema and Kruyt 1987), as well as the period after the turn of the millennium, when 'business approaches' became dominant (e.g. Flentrop and de Vries 2011; Winthagen and De Vries 2011). The crux of the matter, however, is that since the advent of business approaches—and the concomitant attraction of psycho-technicians—victims of ethnically biased ostracism are invited to solve their own problems as 'authentic' and 'assertive' individuals. Theoretically, this is part of an empowerment programme that sets the individual free from and makes him or her resistant to 'groupist thinking'. In practice, such programmes are unable to break existing patterns of precisely this kind of thinking and they even add to the myth that 'cultural others' are inevitably 'oriented to the point of the compass laid down in their own culture', as Benedict so eloquently described it more than eighty years ago (Benedict 1934, 277).

Before I continue with other case discussions, I will try to cast the problem in the more general terms as introduced at the beginning of this chapter and this book.

What I consider to be the general problem is what Sennett once called the 'ideology of intimacy', the belief that 'social relationships *of all kinds* are real, believable and authentic the closer they approach the inner psychological concerns of each person' (Sennett 1974, 259, my italics). The emphasis is important. It appears that with the advent of psychological expertise at work, things such as authenticity, inner search, self-actualization, and the like have been turned into absolutes that matter not only outside the workplace but also within it. As such, the psychological turn in labour management is blurring the boundary between life at work—where people adopt social roles that have a certain function—and the private sphere—where they have a personality that ought to be relatively free from the dictates of use value and function.

Such blurring may amount to reparation of the unity between personal life and work life, or at the very least encourages its interpenetration (see Blommaert et al. 2012). This unity, as I argued before, was shattered with the rise of modern institutions—of which bureaucracy can be seen as a prototypical element (Du Gay 1994, 2005)—in order to construct separate, enclosed, and protected spheres of life that were to remain relatively independent from one another (Berger 1973; Walzer 1984). What Walzer called the 'liberal art of separation' he considered to be the prime factor that distinguishes modernity from pre-modernity. Its function is to build a world of walls, each creating a new liberty. Walzer writes that 'under the aegis of the art of separation, liberty and equality go together ... Society enjoys both freedom and equality when success in one institutional setting isn't convertible into success in another, that is, when the separation holds'. (Walzer 1984, 321).

This inconvertibility did not work for Dinesh. Although he was very *sincere* about his social role (adopting a subordinate position in the presence of superiors in a law enforcement agency seems to be in tune with the social role), something else was expected from him. The modern distinction between private and public spheres was discarded when Dinesh was asked to bring his private self to work and to show his *authentic* features (see also Berger's 1973 useful remarks on sincerity and authenticity). But of course, these authentic features had to be congruent with managerially defined objectives, hence the relevance of Fairclough's accent on *synthetic* personalizations (see also Alvesson and Willmott 2002). The adjective stresses the continuing relevance of ideology: The psychological turn in labour management appears to tolerate workers' personalities, but in reality, these personalities become highly regimented once they become salient in the workplace (see also DiFruscia 2012; Mutsaers and Trux 2015). As one might tell from my frequent use of adverbs such as 'apparently', 'seemingly', 'allegedly', 'putatively', or 'ostensibly', my view comes close to the critique of Anthony (1977) and Baritz (1960) on the politics of psychology as essentially a critique of ideology.

It is important to stress that Walzer saw the art of separation as something that is to attain institutional rather than individual separateness. The lines we draw under liberal aegis are not drawn to secure and protect the freedom of the solitary individual but to attain institutional integrity through which individuals can become free without being separated from one another. This institutional integrity was clearly lacking in Ayşe's case. As a remedy, solutions were sought in the individuality of each involved. In her essay 'What is Freedom?', Arendt (1961) argues that such a 'retreat to an inner sense of freedom is not a solution but merely a response to a lack of freedom in intercourse with others' (in Bell 1996, 89). The case of Ayşe makes this painfully clear. Freedom, according to Arendt, is not 'experienced in the dialogue between me and myself', and the very idea around it is distorted when transformed from 'its original field, the realm of politics and human affairs in general, to an inward domain' (Arendt 1961, 144).

NSvP experts and their followers (e.g. the LECD director and DSC members) ostensibly take the political out of labour relations. Psycho-technicians, as discussed earlier, present their work as apolitical, value free, and thus neutral. They claim to stimulate freedom in every sphere of life. Dialogue as inner search and self-exploration supposedly sets everyone free (employees and employers alike) to find out who they are, apparently unconstrained by any form of external control. The same seems to hold true for authenticity as a key competence for leaders and those led. The psycho-technician's conception of freedom takes a very specific direction; it is to be psychological in form and structure or else it is nothing. This oxymoronic 'obligation to be free' in a psychological sense (Rose 1989) implies that freedom cannot be organized by anything external to the self. I believe that Rose was on the mark when he described 'advanced liberal' governance (which is different from 'liberal' governance) as a formula of rule that has managed to strip away the self-evidence of social governance—that is, a form of 'embedded' governance that revolves around the social roles people adopt in particular social or institutional settings in which they work and build a life—and replace it with a form of governance by experts who seek to govern not through the social but through individuals, 'now construed as subjects of choices and aspirations of self-actualization and self-fulfilment' (Rose 1996, 41; see also Rose's chapter in Sharma and Gupta 2006, for a bibliographic list). I believe that the profession of the psycho-technician described in this chapter fits quite well into this category of experts.

The psycho-technician is the kind of expert that Gershon describes as someone who is entrusted with the 'reflexive role of explaining to *other* autonomous entities how to manage themselves more successfully' (Gershon 2011, 542, my emphasis). Again, the emphasis is important. Just as how they see workers, experts look at themselves as autonomous entities—as too are employers, for that matter. Rose speaks of 'advanced liberal' governance, but Gershon prefers to describe this as the 'neoliberal' perspective, a perspective that overlooks differences of scale and flattens all kinds of social entities (in our case, workers, employers, and psychological experts) inasmuch as all are viewed as corporate individuals who are, in addition, misunderstood as equivalents. This leaves us with a particular form of freedom, or agency for that matter—one that encourages agents to negotiate with other agents who are either seen as partners or competitors (Gershon 2011). This is what Gershon aptly calls 'neoliberal agency'.

That the different agents in the cases discussed are not equivalent, do not have the same scalar position, and are not connected through symmetrical relations is clear enough. After all, Dinesh could not change the careers of his superiors and neither could Ayşe transfer hers. Second, the intertextual asymmetries Ayşe felt would be further consolidated during the conflict mediation made the verbal competition between her and her colleagues anything but fair play between equals. Third, being disembedded from the particular contexts (in which they drop their pre-packaged set of diversity management techniques and instruments and move on), NSvP experts can permit themselves to transcend the vicissitudes of daily life at work and are absolved from responsibility in case things go awry. They only deliver the techniques and are neither responsible for how these are implemented nor for the potential malpractices that may result (in that respect, I agree with Baritz and Antony; however, their techniques are not apolitical because inherent in them is a prescriptive capacity). Moreover, it is precisely because they are not embedded that they can only see individuals *down there*, rather than the complex social organization that people struggle with (and that require social governance, for example, a stipulation of anti-discrimination regulations as called for by Ayşe).

This brings me to a final point, that of psychologism and its diametric opposite, sociological imagination. Anthropologists have frequently turned to a sociological imagination, Gershon writes, to parse neoliberalism, to reveal its vulnerabilities, and to help people understand their personal troubles as more widespread issues that are shaped by broader institutional and structural forces, which cannot be understood through neoliberal perspectives on agency or introspections of the psyche. It is imperative to cross these levels of scale and to interrogate how they affect each other (Gershon 2011) in order to understand that a single personal agony may be in fact the agony of an entire organization. While neoliberalism and its bedfellow, psychologism, have the power to flatten the nuances of scale, it is exactly the task of the ethnographer, I believe, to bring these nuances back into the analysis. In the particular field of DM in the work context, the anthropological method helps us to unlearn taking notions such as 'diversity' and 'diversity management' at face value. These notions need a good deal of rethinking and that rethinking can be enabled by crossing domains and scales in the analysis, through a focus on the interdiscursive relations between texts in the sphere of production and those in the sphere of usage. Perhaps, the ethnographer can function as the critical counterpart of the technician in order to improve our sociological imagination and therewith (re)confirm that freedom is something that needs to be organized through social governance rather than taken for granted as an automatic point of departure.

Confessions and Entrepreneurs of the Self

Exhausted from commuting every day between his home and the police station in Utrecht, and passing one of the bottlenecks of the Dutch highway system, Senior Constable Fehim was relieved when a colleague invited him to apply for a vacancy at a community policing team in Tilburg, in the province where Fehim lived. After eleven years of service in Utrecht, Turkey-born Fehim moved to Tilburg in October 2007, at the encouragement of Meryem, who was working as an OC in that period. She brought to Fehim's attention the reorganization that was occurring in the south. The move could offer a chance for him to reinvigorate his career as prospects looked good for Fehim, who had his sight set on becoming a community officer long ago. He was hired as a senior constable.

Having worked in his new surroundings for about six months, Fehim applied for a position as a community officer but his application was denied because of administrative and financial difficulties in the organization. His chief of operations, Frank, considered him right for the job but advised him to wait for less austere times. 'He said it was good that I had applied and that I had proven to be entrepreneurial', Fehim wrote in a journal that he kept for himself (and which he shared with me in 2013). Fehim's job evaluation at that time (which he also forwarded to me) reads:

> [Fehim] shows a certain calmness while doing his job. He adapts quickly to his new working environment ... He does well in spotting new work that needs to be done. He takes on new cases on his own initiative and supports colleagues in their work. He is a good colleague with good social skills. He is customer-oriented and maintains good contacts with citizens ... For the sake of financial management, it is not desirable that Fehim leaves the job and accepts another position. (job evaluation 6 June 2008)

About a year later, Fehim informed Frank about another job opening, but Frank advised him not to apply, 'because this would jeopardize [his] career track'. 'I was not aware of such a track', Fehim wrote in his journal. 'Only much later I found out he meant my PDP [Personal Development Plan].'

Fehim was perplexed by the fact that apparently a PDP had been started—a sort of career portfolio in which an employee writes about career aspirations, steps to follow, personal development of talents, abilities, skills, etc. It had been started without notifying him. This was the first of many incidents that made him feel he was being subjected to a sort of personalized rule (i.e. that his position within the organization was personally decided by one or two superiors), a feeling that would perpetuate and intensify.

The only 'track' Fehim was familiar with at that time was the so-called TeMPo track—an abbreviation of the *Turken en Marokkanen Politie* (Turks and Moroccans Police) project, which was a special recruitment and selection programme to attract Turkish and Moroccan migrants, including Fehim, to the organization. Fehim joined this programme in 1996. It is evident that the abbreviation (T.E.M.P.O.) was a wordplay, referring to the speedy progress of migrants within the organization, who were trained and prepared in the 1980s and 1990s via many special programmes at special locations. A particular training camp, in which migrant police students would have to walk around with name tags with *Politie en Allochtonen* (Police and Allochthones) on, was not uncommon during this period, as I learned during interviews. It was only much later that some, though certainly not all, policy-makers and diversity managers became aware that large segments of the workforce considered these initiatives inappropriate. Affirmative action programmes—giving members of ethnic minority groups an edge over ethnic majority police officers/aspirants—continued well into the new millennium under the aegis of the Labour Party Minister of Internal Affairs Guusje ter Horst (2007–2010).

People's experiences of these affirmative action programmes were not universally negative or positive. What came out of the dozens of conversations I conducted with ethnic minority police officers on this topic was that they felt stigmatized by the policy-induced *ethnic boundaries* (Barth 1969) that developed in the aggregate and portrayed them as incompetent ('they are the ones who need extra attention', ethnic majority police officers would say to me). Yet, there were also more positive evaluations of these programmes. People also experienced support from fellow 'co-ethnics'. Sometimes they managed to organize into collectives and thereby preserved some degree of solidarity in an otherwise highly competitive and individualized organization. It gradually became apparent to me that ethnicity-based networks of solidarity served to mitigate some of the cut-throat professional competition, at least among ethnic minority officers. Looking back in 2013 during an interview, Fehim said 'everybody is on his own of course, but the contact between allochtonous colleagues are a bit thicker and warmer'.

During the interview, Fehim was sitting calmly in an armchair in one of the interrogation rooms of the station. Fehim is a middle-aged man, known for his tranquil and avuncular features. Always respectful to others, never offensive or rude, he is the kind of police officer we are glad to have around when we find ourselves in exigent situations. From his armchair, he carefully measured his words and endorsed both perspectives on affirmative action. He also experienced the collateral damage of such programmes, running the risk of being deprived of professional pride and identity, but also found much support within the collective boundaries they have created. Such policy-induced 'groupist thinking' (Brubaker 2002) has motivated Turkish-Dutch and Moroccan-Dutch officers in particular to create strong support networks within the organization, both formal and informal.

Although Fehim was keenly aware of these advantages, as a good officer he was well accustomed to screening potential risks. For instance, after we discussed this groupist thinking and its concomitant group solidarity, he immediately started wondering aloud whether it also led to his superiors' suspiciousness of his contacts with Meryem, who had brought him south in the first place. Reflecting on his second attempt to apply for a job as community officer in Meryem's team, Fehim ruminated: 'I think, I mean it's just a suggestion, I feel that [his superior] thought "if he goes there, he is likely to be hired by Meryem," implying that this would be something unthinkable and unpalatable to his superior.'

At this point, he already felt he was discriminated against but he had a hard time proving it. To make it clear to me that he did not draw conclusions based on inchoate suspicion, he turned to Meryem's case. He confirmed that she was long considered a candidate with high potential who was about to move centre stage at strategic levels in the organization but that, somewhere along the way, she lost her credits and was given unrewarding jobs. These included being assigned to break up a predominantly Caucasian police team and to carry out redundancies. Fehim knew that Meryem was considered a menace by his own superiors and that the emphasis on her ethnicity ('you and I have been enemies for centuries', it was said to her, echoing some sort of Huntingtonian clash of civilizations between Christianity and Islam) was a strategy to outcompete her. He also knew that in combination with the solidarity among 'co-ethnics' referred to earlier, his ethnic identity was considered to be coterminous with Meryem's, both being enclosed within a common boundary (i.e. their Turkish identities were immediately obvious when seen together). This seriously curtailed Fehim's options to join Meryem's team, he argued.

Fehim and I discussed whether the solidarity between minority officers at work was also the reason for Fehim's superiors to confront him with various individualizing techniques, such as PDPs and several other psychological instruments that I will discuss shortly. Could these be interpreted as splintering techniques, employed by management to break up a fairly strongly organized collective? This question cannot be answered easily. Let me first say that I interpret PDPs as psychological applications because they are devoid of any kind of sociological imagination (see Mills 1959 and Gershon 2011, discussed in the previous section). Personal development is seen as something the individual employee is fully responsible for, without any regard to the broader, institutional, social, or organizational context. Having had the opportunity to screen various police PDPs, I noticed a dominant concern with the intrapsychic domain of the employee. This is not arbitrary but prescribed.

Self-development programmes, with all their paraphernalia (such as PDPs) have been interpreted by DiFruscia as pseudo-therapeutic techniques that are part of 'an HR paradigm [that] has helped [to] make a drastic change in how work relations are perceived' (DiFruscia 2012, 91). Such techniques are not about 'assaying the nature of work', to paraphrase Braverman (1974, 20), but about 'the degree of adjustment of the worker'. They help to avert attention away from labour conditions (issues such as workload, payment, fringe benefits, scheduling, etc., and discrimination with respect to any of these issues) that are the ideal locus of attention for collective entities (such as groups of minority officers) in order to improve life at work. In their stead comes a singular focus on the individual and his 'psychometric profile', which can fragment the workplace into atomistic individual that are in competition with one another (see also Siebers 2010b and Siebers and Van Gastel 2015).

This competitive element clearly emerged when Fehim talked about his own PDP and, rather jealously, compared it with a colleague's PDP, which got the latter promoted to the position of community officer—a post which Fehim had long desired. I saw both PDPs, which were almost similar expect for the fact that Fehim's colleague had added an extra classification layer based on identity profiles that were in vogue at that moment within the organization. They distinguished personality types based on a colour scheme, in line with a 'Spiral Dynamics' course that was popular within the Dutch police at that time. In 2009, Fehim was requested, again, to revise and rewrite his PDP in order to give him access to an internship that would prepare him for the tasks and responsibilities of a community officer.

'As I revised my PDP, others were promoted without a PDP', Fehim wrote in his journal. 'My PDP was said to be underdeveloped, so I had to revise it again. I did this immediately and resubmitted, but I received no feedback. This gave much delay, at least six months. After this, I was said to wait for the annual personnel review, even though my team leader had promised this wasn't necessary.'

Towards the end of 2009, he was finally allowed to start his internship. Despite the fact that he had made great progress in that year—he was applauded by most colleagues I spoke to—and had successfully completed his internship, he was not promoted to community officer. After presenting to the district management team a project that he had started and which had substantially reduced burglaries in the neighbourhood, his supervisor concluded that he did not have a 'sparkling' attitude (*bruisend* in Dutch). This course of events was not a demotion in a strict sense, but Fehim felt that he was brought back to the *status quo ante*; he had to start from scratch all over again. After these events, Fehim confessed in the interview that he seriously considered quitting his job. He had communicated this to his superiors in a despairing e-mail but had received no response. This e-mail, which he had sent to the entire team and his superiors, ended like this:

> I thought that integrity, fair play, honesty and righteousness were highly appreciated within the police, but these things are far gone in my view.

> There is an atmosphere of nepotism. Colleagues are promoted *en masse* to get to certain positions. When I ask for something, nothing is possible. I feel ridiculed, mocked and played. I have no longer any trust in the police organization and I feel like being harassed out of my job.

Shortly after this he found himself transferred to another post doing one of the most unrewarding routine jobs within the organization (simple and routine investigation work; a punishment for someone who prefers 'blue shifts', street work rather than desk work). Fehim was overwhelmed by feelings of isolation and loneliness at work. All these events combined to have a substantial impact on his mental health, which led to a period of absence in 2010.

Herein lies the rub: by sending this e-mail, Fehim did what he thought was expected from him, disclosing his most personal thoughts and feelings. This was in line with the expectations of his PDP, in which he eventually would come to write: 'I shouldn't be too modest; I should step in the limelight. Need to be more extrovert. This takes away the impression that I don't dare to say certain things. I shouldn't be self-effacing; need to stand out.'

For all he knew, personal development was about the acknowledgment of and reflection about one's own actions and thoughts, the ways one deals with disappointments, regrets, etc. (cf. Townley 1993). But, as Fehim's case proves, this is a risky endeavour, regardless of the decisions made. Those who refuse to open up to psychological discourses may forgo opportunities, but those who embrace them put themselves immediately at risk. The autonomy of the act is violated, we could say *qua* Goffman (1961), because individual agency is immediately surrounded by punitive structures once anything out of the ordinary tends to occur, that is, once the individual's actions or thoughts diverge from managerial ideas on proper psychological discourse. The notion of risk-taking (closely related to Gershon's earlier mentioned notion of neoliberal agency) will reappear in an even stronger way in what follows here.

In 2010, I sat together with a DDC, as mentioned at the beginning of this chapter, for an informal conversation about the progress of my research. Enthusiastic as always, the DDC openly shared her knowledge about my research subject and told me about a fireplace session she had recently had with five Turkish-Dutch male colleagues at a fancy restaurant in an idyllic village nearby. These sessions took place in comfortable settings: 'We have our feet on the table and sit by the fire', said the DDC. She explained that the sessions were intended to encourage officers to open up about problems at work.

This time she had invited those five policemen, because time and again they failed to get promoted to sergeant, the rank that gives access to community policing. Their careers were stalled despite the fact that their work performances were perfectly up to standard (this was confirmed in their job evaluations, according to the DDC). Toward the end of the session, the DDC concluded that all five did a great job, but that they lacked the communicative and personal skills to make this known to others. They were advised to work on their entrepreneurship, open-mindedness, and flexibility, as these had become key competences within the organization, the DDC claimed.

She was right on that count. As we saw before, two years earlier a new DM expert group (the NSvP) had made its entrance into the organization and many of its activities centred on the five core competences of the Multicultural Personality Questionnaire: cultural empathy, open-mindedness, social initiative, emotional stability, and flexibility (cf. Van der Zee and Van Oudenhoven 2001). The NSvP had designed a programme that propagated these multicultural personality traits as the *sine qua non* of police leadership. Because the five policemen pursued a position at leadership level, the DDC's advice made sense at first.

In the winter of 2012–2013, when I was carrying out my fieldwork in Tilburg, I joined one of the fireplace session participants, Halil, for several weeks, although I was unaware at first that he had in fact been one of the participants. Things fell into place when Halil, during one of our car patrols, shared his concerns about the career-related hardships of ethnic minorities within the organization. He said that he was disappointed with the fireplace session, as nothing had been done with it afterward. Nobody had received feedback, there was no follow-up, and almost three years later, none of the participants had been promoted to sergeant.

'I had the feeling that I was forced to sell myself, which I am unable to do; perhaps I should work at a market or something for some time', Halil said while we roamed around in the district. He complained about the self-commodification (Gershon 2011; Urciuoli 2008) he felt was imposed upon him.

At the end of the month we spent together, Halil was in fact promoted to sergeant, although it remained unclear to him whether this was a result of the large-scale 'road block' (his term) that he had prepared for several months and brought to a successful end ('the best one we ever had, according to one of his colleagues) or because of the empowerment course, 'You're the Director of your Own Life', which Halil had recently begun to attend. This course was originally intended for ethnic minority officers only, to help them become/feel empowered.

At first, it surprised me that Halil was so enthusiastic about the course, in which he was taught exactly the same things he resented earlier, issues that were also covered during the fireplace session. This course was all about flexibility, entrepreneurship, opening oneself up emotionally to colleagues and superiors, even selling oneself to them. Here are some citations from the course material, a book written by the course instructor : 'Liberate yourself from all constraints, which only exist in your head, and learn how to use your power to become happier and more successful. Take matters into your own hands. Only you are responsible for your own life' (Chrifi 2010, 10). 'Dare to show yourself and to be vulnerable' (Chrifi 2010, 20). 'In order to succeed you only have to be open and willing to change' (Chrifi 2010, 23). 'You can turn your personality into anything you like, but you have to choose' (Chrifi 2010, 58). (All fragments translated from the Dutch by the present author).

Only much later, it dawned on me that Halil's case can be seen as a prototypical example of Gershon's neoliberal agency (Gershon 2011). Within the course of a month, he had turned himself into the archetypical self-reliant career manager (Lane 2011) who 'epitomize[s] the neoliberal enterprising self' (Lane 2009, 683). 'This concept of agency requires a reflexive stance in which people are subjects for themselves', wrote Gershon (2011, 539), and this is exactly what happened to Halil. In the end, it was perhaps neither the road block nor the empowerment course alone that gave Halil this promotion: it is feasible that his participation in the empowerment course indicated his willingness to open up to neoliberal agency and that the organization of the road block was a realization of it.[15] Unfortunately, Halil's positive

[15] I would like to thank one of the anonymous reviewers for suggesting this interpretation.

mood did not last long. Several months later, I received an e-mail from him in which he complained he felt burned out. Halil was used as a human resource for a while but eventually became exhausted (turning him into the fourth ethnic minority officer discussed here who suffered from health issues).

More than two years would go by after the fireplace session before I learned that Fehim had been one of the other participants as well. Just like Halil before him, Fehim felt misled and betrayed and talked about the evening as unidirectional ('there was no sympathy for our feelings of exclusion; it was just a one-way street', he said during the interview). The DDC had absorbed the highly personal information that her subordinates had shared with her but had given nothing in return. To Fehim, the cosy setting was farcical, a front to make him and his colleagues feel at ease and reveal as much as possible of their inner selves. His experience might be interpreted as a submission to some sort of Foucauldian confessional technique (cf. Covaleski et al. 1998; Campbell and Roberts 2007) that tricked him into revealing his deepest feelings and emotions, allegedly to get things off his chest, and to rebuild his persona. But his inner psyche was exposed and he gained nothing in return other than several comments about how to improve his personal qualities. Arguably, these comments go directly against the aims of the Multicultural Personality Questionnaire with which they resonate, provided that this kind of questionnaire is designed to improve diversity at work. Curiously, the various measures of this questionnaire were used against people with an ethnic minority background (these are some of the items that are included in the questionnaire: 'is inclined to speak out', 'takes the lead', 'is often the driving force behind things', 'takes it for granted that things will turn out all right'; see Van der Zee and Van Oudenhoven 2001). It is rather difficult to draw general conclusions about the motivations or intentions of the DDC; for all we know, she genuinely believed these five men would score low on these items and were thus not up to the task of supervising staff. Perhaps she was even right but that is not what must concern us here. The problem is that the DDC omitted, or was incapable of understanding an officer's private troubles as reflecting public issues (Mills 1959), that is, to take the structural impediments they claimed they faced seriously. She lacked sociological imagination and committed the error of what Mills called 'psychologism': the attempt to explain social phenomena in terms of facts and theories about the constitution of individuals.

It may help to remember Bauman's *Liquid Modernity* (2000) and interpret these confession techniques as auxiliaries to what he termed 'life politics'. Central to his analysis of life politics is the observation that people who live in this age (liquid modernity) feel constantly coerced to share intimacies (what Sennett, 1974, called the 'ideology of intimacy'). 'When public politics sheds its function and life-politics takes over', Bauman warned, 'the public sphere is likely to be excavated except for the site where private worries are confessed and put on public display' (Bauman 2000b, 51–2). The division of social experience into a public and a private sphere is lost when the various departments of life are thrown together and are mixed into one amalgam.

Despite his fierce resistance, Fehim also hewed to the psychological discourses that circulated within the organization and encouraged officers to act as private individuals, instead of as organizational actors fulfilling social roles. In the numerous conversations we had, he constantly stressed that he felt the urge to reveal himself and to bring his personal life into the discussion as a way of coming across as 'authentic'. This culminated in a climax in March 2013, when Fehim acted as one of the course instructors in the two-day course 'Multicultural Craftsmanship and Honour-Related Violence' (see Chapter 2). I attended both days of the course and it struck me from the outset that Fehim and the other Turkish-Dutch instructor (Serkan) had chosen a much more engaged and autobiographical approach than the Dutch instructor, who presented herself as an expert. Accepting this division of roles was not an easy decision for Fehim and Serkan as they had already anticipated meeting a lot of resistance from the audience. As discussed in Chapter 2, part of the course was intended to address ethnic profiling, a highly controversial and sensitive topic. Honour-related violence, on the other hand, was widely accepted as a legitimate concern for law enforcement agencies (one that did not require much reflection about police practices). Nonetheless, some officers were visibly fed up with the attention devoted to it. For instance, a few weeks before the course I discussed honour-related violence with an officer who was going to participate in the group I joined, and who said: 'I don't know what all the fuss is about; it's plain murder, nothing more nothing less'. Like him, many other officers were getting tired of all this 'multicultural bullshit', as some called it.

The climax I referred to came when Fehim turned toward his own life history to explain to the participants the ins and outs of honour-related violence. I was completely taken by surprise—as was almost everybody else in the room—when he talked about the pressure he once felt to kill his sister-in-law who remarried three months after Fehim's brother had died in a traffic accident. Fehim had approached her with a knife with the intent to kill and would have done so if it were not for his father's last-minute intervention. In the following hour, Fehim elaborated, using many personal details, on the events that preceded and followed the averted attack. He explained to the group the importance of the *namus* (the honour) of the family. However, no matter how nuanced his story was, the only thing that made a lasting impression was the image of the knife, and all Fehim's colleagues talked about while having a cigarette during the break was their shared disbelief. A few weeks later, I conducted an interview with one of the course participants who confirmed that Fehim was regarded with suspicion in many quarters.

I had an informal course evaluation with Fehim and the other instructors afterwards. As we discussed Fehim's part in the programme, he was complimented by the other course instructors for his courage in revealing one of the most difficult and painful episodes of his life to the group. When I asked him if he had given any thought to the potential risks of his approach, his answer was affirmative but he also stressed that above and beyond his fears, he felt the urge to open up: 'I wanted to show all of me'. His remark clarifies the earlier mentioned relation between neoliberal agency and risk-taking. In the words of Gershon:

> According to the neoliberal perspective, to prosper, one must engage with risk. All neoliberal social strategies centre on this. Neoliberal agents are responsible for their own futures—they supposedly fashion their own futures through their decisions. By the same token, regardless of their disadvantages and the unequal playing field, actors are maximally responsible for their failures. (Gershon 2011, 540)

Fehim's was a risky enterprise because he had created a field so mined by designators of group affiliation (by discussing Turkish people who feel the urge to defend their honour, in the context of a course on ethnic profiling, criminality and ethnicity, group thinking, etc.) that it became well-nigh impossible for him to appropriate psychological discourses that prioritize the individual (e.g. ethnicity as an individual instead of a shared group property). He had to give it a shot, but unfortunately it misfired. He was now one of *them*, indissolubly one with criminal migrant groups. When his colleagues started to mistrust Fehim, his superiors failed to intervene. It was his decision; he missed the mark and was made responsible for his own 'failure'.

Greedy Institutions: Some Comparisons

At the very end of the introduction to his book *Greedy Institutions: Patterns of Undivided Commitment*, Coser explains to his readers why he became interested in greedy institutions, that is, institutions that demand undivided commitment of their members (Coser 1974). Coser was a critic of the criticasters of modernity and its differentiated, segmented, and what they saw as its 'alienated' character. I agree with his view. These 'fashionable' critiques on modernity were expressed around the same time the Dutch police started their de-bureaucratization programmes, which, as we remember, were intended to counter differentiation, segmentation, distantiation, and alienation. Now, forty years later, we can see the effects. What started as reform intended for the sake of liberty and legitimacy—through a 'humanization' of police—has arguably led to a reduction of both. We are advised to keep Coser's early warning in mind:

> When the desire for wholeness leads to an enlistment in greedy institutions, it may end in an obliteration of the characteristics that mark the private person as an autonomous actor ... Commitment to greedy institutions requires that the autonomy gained by men who stand at the intersection of many circles is relinquished, and is replaced by heteronomous submission to the all-encompassing demands of organizations that greedily devour the whole man in order to fully fashion him into an image that serves their needs. (Coser 1974, 16–17)

Coser concluded his introduction with a political statement that celebrates liberalism and its art of separation: a *cri de coeur* to protect the open society.

I will argue in this final part of the chapter that the police departments that I have studied can be understood far better if we apply Coser's notion of greedy institutions, those that demand undivided commitment of the 'whole person' and usurp the private spheres of officers' lives.

Four key words can be extracted from the citation above: (1) wholeness, (2) organizational needs, (3) submission, and (4) autonomy. These will help us to improve our understanding of the cases described in this chapter and to locate the theoretical criticism taken here more precisely.

PDPs, fireplace sessions, empowerment courses, autobiographical imperatives, personality questionnaires, conflict mediations, and the role of psychological profiles in assessments have, in my view, caused the loss of contour of labour control, the breaking down of limits between the public and private, in the sense that more than officers' life at work is now under surveillance and control. The ethnographic cases covered here demonstrate that revealing the finer and more intimate regions of personal and interpersonal life can hardly be said to contribute to personal fulfilment or happiness. Fehim, Halil, Meryem, and Ayşe all suffered from exhaustion and called in sick for an extensive period of time. Some of them considered quitting their jobs. The various psychological applications are in place to 'produce the appropriate individual' who is 'deemed congruent with managerially defined objective' (Alvesson and Willmott 2002, 619). In other words, they are there for organizational needs and these were fulfilled. Halil had organized one of the most successful road blocks in the history of the district and Fehim's course participants had gained deeper insights into honour killings. The ideal individual is the self-managing, self-reliant career manager with his 'decidedly neoliberal leanings' (Lane 2011, 162) who competes with his peers. This notion of competition clearly emerged when Fehim confessed to be jealous of Halil (who was promoted to sergeant) and wanted to outcompete his colleague with his PDP.

I emphatically agree with DiFruscia who states that:

> While HR discourse and psychologizing practices require workers to be '*authentic*', to '*reveal themselves*', and to '*be themselves at work*' in order to '*uncover their full potential*', this authenticity and this freedom must adopt a form the employer dictates ... When '*being transparent and authentic*' means that workers are revealing their disagreement with the organization's higher purpose, or showing stress or malaise, or simply disturbing the scrupulously manufactured work environment, suddenly these '*authentic selves*' are viewed as pathological, and the therapeutic-managerial apparatus steps up its vigil. (DiFruscia 2012, 96, emphases original)

Just like DiFruscia's informants, Fehim was puzzled. He was allowed, even encouraged, to 'reveal himself' during the course—a revelation that had instrumental value to the organization. But when he disclosed his dissatisfaction with the way he was treated as an employee (something he hoped to be instrumental to his own career), the managerial apparatus stepped up its vigil and sideswiped him.

This brings us back to risk taking, which we can connect to Coser's ideas on heteronomous submission. In two instances, Fehim took tremendous risks and was rendered submissive: first (the e-mail) by his superiors and then (the course) by his colleagues. Whatever he did, Fehim bore the brunt of psychological discourses. This kind of distortion also applies to the various identity profiles or 'soft skills' discussed in this chapter ('sparkling', 'entrepreneurial', 'flexible', 'open-minded', etc.), which we nowadays frequently find amassed in job profiles (Urciuoli 2008, 2010). As Urciuoli has demonstrated superlatively, these soft skills are characterized by a denotational vagueness and can therefore be easily manipulated and, in fact, used at will. 'What do they mean by sparkling,' Fehim wondered, and 'how does that relate to my ability to be a good police officer?' It is because of this blurring boundary between personality and competency that the allocation of jobs not only becomes dependent upon the personal taste of superiors (the 'personalized ruling' referred to earlier) but also that criteria, which are not even remotely connected to job requirements, are used. We busted that crook and we did so with a sparkling attitude.

This denotational vagueness in job criteria, euphemized into soft skills, does not have arbitrary (non-discriminatory) effects on the workforce. On the contrary, the use of fuzzy and ambiguous criteria in assessment procedures has been widely documented to fuel ethnic inequality in work settings (e.g. Campbell and Roberts 2007; Moss and Tilly 1996; Siebers 2009a and 2009b). The argument advocated by Siebers is that fuzzy criteria exacerbate ethnic inequality because they calibrate and evaluate employees' qualities based on subjective judgment rather than objective criteria, and thus they allow for unequal treatment. This argument is in the same vein as Moss and Tilly (1996) who show that '"soft skills" requirements, such as personal characteristics, attitudes, character traits, predispositions, emotions, and aesthetics, leave much room for majority selectors' subjectivity in their assessment whether a candidate disposes of such skills, due to the vague and fuzzy nature of soft skills (in Siebers 2009a, 65).

Because non-ethnic markers are used, one can never be sure whether or not discrimination has occurred (which leads to the fact that many charges of discrimination that I have come across within the Dutch police have either been dropped or have failed to bring to light any wrongdoing). This uncertainty is also shown by Fehim's hedging, as demonstrated in the preceding, when he talked about his superior's reluctance to let him join Meryem's team: 'I think, I mean it's just a suggestion, I feel that ...'. Again, he felt discriminated against but he could not prove it.

Finally, a few words on Coser's remarks on autonomy. Most of the psychological applications discussed in this chapter are deployed in a general fashion and involve police officers from all kinds of backgrounds. However, as my ethnography advanced, I started to notice a pattern in the sense that these techniques were more often used negatively in the case of officers with a migration background.[16] Where others were given much more latitude, Turkish-Dutch or Moroccan-Dutch officers were monitored much more strictly and were more often confronted with coercion, at the expense of their autonomy. This brings me to a final issue.

As the analysis of the government of psychological life as an enterprise has become an expanding frontier in neoliberal governmentality studies (see Barry et al. 1996; Binkley 2011; Cruikshank 1996; Miller and Rose 1988, 1994), it has become clear that it is generally assumed that such psychological governance takes place in a positive fashion (see the beginning of this chapter). That is, personal fulfilment and organizational performance are said to coevolve linearly. What is good for the individual is good for the organization and vice versa. As such, we have begun to capture the ways in which 'regulatory practices and techniques have come to operate, not through a crushing of wills or a subjugation of desires but through the promotion of subjectivity, through investment in individual lives' (Miller and Rose 1988, 172). A whole range of organizational forms and technical

[16] See also Siebers (2009a, 2010b, and 2017) for similar conclusions on the Dutch police and other Dutch organizations.

methods are deployed today to extend the field of freedom (Maravelias 2007), practices in the form of enterprise, choice, and autonomy (Rose 1996). These insights stem from what Foucault wrote more than forty years ago:

> In defining the effects of power as repression, one adopts a purely juridical conception of such power, one identifies power with a law which says no, power is taken above all as carrying the force of prohibition. Now I believe that this is a wholly negative, narrow, skeletal conception of power, one which has been curiously widespread ... What makes power hold good, what makes it accepted, is simply the fact that it doesn't only weigh on us as a force that says no, but that it traverses and produces things, it induces pleasure, forms knowledge, produces discourse. (Foucault 1972, 119)

Its fruits, however, did not accrue to Fehim, Halil, Meryem, Ayşe, or Dinesh, nor to many other ethnic minority officers whom I have met over the years. They are captured by a belief system that privileges autonomy and individual agency—or better, neoliberal agency—and obscures the broader institutional, cultural, political, or organizational factors that shape their lives (Lane 2011). This belief system became very real to Fehim when he was left to his own devices when things went awry after the course; he was not backed up by management when his colleagues' mistrust became apparent. Intervention was considered the enemy of individual energy and initiative. I can accept that the power effects of the psychological applications under scrutiny in this chapter derive from their *tendency* toward prescription and production, rather than prohibition and repression, but I believe that we need to make a distinction between their use and their function and be alive to their potentially repressive and prohibitive dimensions in certain cases and certain contexts.

My concluding remarks concern the comparative insights that can be derived from other police studies in another national context. These, however, are bound to be brief as there is only one comparable study to be found on this topic and that is Owen's on the Nigeria Police Force (NPF) (Owen 2016). In his article, Owen rightfully posits that academic studies about states are often oddly silent about the people who populate the state and its institutions, and that it is his intention to start filling that gap by examining the life-worlds of officers in the NPF. By doing so, he uses Goffman's concept of 'total institutions' instead of Coser's 'greedy institutions' to conceptualize the empirics that he came across in his field study. The difference between Coser's and Goffman's concept is that the second refers to institutions that erect barriers to prevent social traffic with the outside world, whereas the first refers to institutions that usurp that world (Coser acknowledges and discusses this distinction in his book;)

> Their encompassing or total character is symbolized by the barrier to social intercourse with the outside and to departure that is often built right into the physical plant, such as locked doors, high walls, barbed wire, cliffs, water, forests, or moors. These establishments I am calling *total institutions*. (Goffman 1961, 15–16)

The NPF, as described by Owen, seems to be more of a total than a greedy institution. Owen acknowledges the fact that Goffman's concept requires some modification in order to fit the NPF, but he also argues that the NPF exhibits many similar characteristics. He examined the NPF's training institution in particular, which is a '*closed residential world* in which character is deliberately unmade and remade in the mould desired by the institution's functional aims' (Owen 2016, 39, my emphasis). This institutional character formation differs from the one taking place at the Dutch police. The NPF lays exclusive claims on officers' identity as it recreates personhood along the lines drawn by the police institution. The creation of a 'police corporate personhood' (Owen's term) goes so far that female recruits must be unmarried at the time of joining, they must apply to get married, and the prospective spouse must be approved by the NPF.[17]

Such totalitarian tendencies are unheard of in The Netherlands, where an officer's background is checked on security grounds only. The fact that the Dutch police is not a total institution does not, however, exonerate it from responsibility for the problematic

[17] In his article, Owen also includes a section titled 'Putting agency back in' and concludes that the NPF is 'totalizing in its claims but not totalitarian in its lived realities' (Owen 2016, 56). Officers do have agency, as they 'navigate the postings web' and attempt to mobilize their social networks to get away from particular positions. Owen therefore talks about a creative 'admixture of the bureaucratic and the particular, of prescriptive structure and innovative agency' (Owen 2016, 57). As the reader may immediately intuit, I disagree with his understanding of the total institution as 'bureaucratic'.

conflation of social spheres. For institutional members as well as those who face the consequences of institutional practices, 'greediness' may have effects on their lives that equal the effects of 'totality'. The imposition of cross-barrier social intercourse (sphere conflation) may have the same effects on people as its strict prohibition.

5

Conclusions: Reclaiming the Public in Policing

Unfortunately, Fehim's ordeal did not end with the controversy that he provoked by offering an autobiographical perspective on 'honour cultures'. About two years later, another unexpected event occurred that placed him at a serious disadvantage. Before I can turn to this specific event, some contextual information is required which at the same time prefaces the main objective of this concluding chapter: reclaiming the public in policing.

About eighteen months after my fieldwork had officially ended, I was still working with local police departments, the Police Academy and the National Police (NP), to translate my research into practical solutions to police discrimination. Activities ranged from invited talks to criminal investigation departments, community policing teams as well as the national leadership, to participation in management programmes (as an ethnographer/adviser), to the coordination of a task force set up to devise concrete plans to counter ethnic profiling. The latter took place in Tilburg, in the spring of 2015, with the cooperation of Fehim and several of his team members who also saw the need to combat ethnic profiling in their district. Under the auspices of a new station chief who had recently been installed, we organized several meetings in which we discussed what specific measures we considered viable and effective. Based on my ethnographic work as well as Fehim's notorious two-day training course on multicultural craftsmanship, we agreed that another cognitive intervention—another attempt to remedy perceptual bias—would not do. In effect, we concluded, such interventions can be part of the problem rather than the solution.

All members of the task force underscored the necessity partially to 're-bureaucratize' police work in order to counter ethnic profiling. The intended reform, we concurred, ought not to depend

Police Unlimited: Policing, Migrants, and the Values of Bureaucracy. First Edition. Paul Mutsaers. © Paul Mutsaers 2019. Published 2019 by Oxford University Press.

on the capacity or willingness of individuals to change their attitudes to minority groups. Rather, with the support of the new station chief, we believed we had the momentum to address ethnic profiling as an *organizational* practice. Convinced by the other members of the task force that ethnic profiling is an issue that exceeds the level of individual decision-making, the station chief proved willing to adopt organizational measures and acceded to our idea to experiment with so-called stop forms or stop reports (see Tomaskovic-Devey et al. 2006; Wilkins and Williams 2008, 2009). Stop forms make it possible to survey the selection of citizens for interdiction by police and shed light on ethnic or racial disparities in stop-and-search practices.

Encouraged by the successful application of stop forms in other countries as a method to counter ethnic profiling and improve police accountability (Amnesty International 2013; Open Society Justice Initiative 2012), we came up with a format that was borrowed from the San Diego Police Department (cf. Wilkins and Williams 2008). This format requires that police officers complete a form each time they stop a person (this was deemed necessary because, in The Netherlands, police controls are not systematically registered unless they result in a citation or arrest). The stop form that we were going to use would record the context of the encounter, the reason for the stop, the citizen's demographics (gender, ethnicity, age), actions taken during the stop (search, search authority, search outcome), and the result of the stop (citation, arrest). Making our plans in the spring of 2015, it was agreed with the station chief that the experiment would start after the summer, that it would last for about six months, and that it would involve the entire executive branch of the police team in question. The stop-and-search data would subsequently be used for basic quantitative analysis in order to (a) be able to detect disproportional police scrutiny of minority groups, (b) study the effects of such disproportionality in terms of 'successful' criminal cases, and (c) to write tailored summaries on each team member, providing the station chief with insights on officers' stop-and-search practices. These could subsequently be used in job evaluation interviews. Anticipating complaints about paperwork, we suggested the use of a digital application instead of paper forms.

In effect, we were about to institute the first system, albeit on a small-scale, to monitor law enforcement practices with the intention to detect possible profiling in The Netherlands. In an atmosphere of congenial excitement, I decided to give some publicity to our plans as these coincided with the final preparations for the public defence of my dissertation (12 June 2015), which I had written based on my police ethnography (Mutsaers 2015a; this unpublished manuscript formed the basis for the present book). The public defence served as an occasion for the communication department of my university to publish a press release to promote my work and to enhance its public profile, which echoed the 'public anthropology of policing' I intended my work to be (I will elaborate on this in the next part of the current chapter; see also Mutsaers et al. 2015). When the press officer asked me in an interview about the practical implications of my research, I decided to mention the stop forms as one of the fruits of the study. The press release (published on 4 June 2015) did its job: within a day I was contacted by almost all major newspapers and various television and radio stations in The Netherlands.

I gave one of my first interviews to the *NRC Handelsblad*, one of the national high-quality newspapers in The Netherlands. The *NRC* reporter was particularly interested in the stop forms, keenly aware as he was of the fact that this method had its adversaries (e.g. the NP and the ruling party in government) and proponents (e.g. Amnesty International and other human rights organizations). To give the article more traction, the editorial team had decided to publish it on the front page, including statements by Gerard Bouman, then commissioner of the NP, and Gerbrig Klos, a senior policy advisor at Amnesty International Netherlands. For verification, the reporter in question had asked me to give him the contact details of another member of the task force. After consultation, I directed him towards Fehim. Both Fehim and I had urged the reporter to treat him as an anonymous source, a request to which he acceded.

Then, as the press release and front-page article were going viral in the mainstream media and blogosphere alike—eliciting mixed responses—something peculiar happened. In an early morning press release (8 a.m.), the NP stated that the organization was willing to explore the 'usefulness' and 'feasibility' of the stop forms. Three hours later, however, the press release was changed and now contained the unhedged assertion that the police team in question was not going to work with stop forms, nor had it ever made concrete plans to do so (see also *NRC Handelsblad*, 11 June 2015). Remarkably, the press release concluded: 'The organization is open to all suggestions that can contribute to [professionalism] and is willing to study their usefulness and feasibility. Bouman: this also holds true for the registration of stops and arrests, in relation to ethnic background.' To me, this press release—titled *Police devoted to diversity*—symbolized the strategy of promises and make-believe with which I had become all too familiar (I will substantiate my claims below).

Of all the members of the task force, Fehim took the hardest blow. Faced with contradicting views on the stop forms project, the *NRC* reporter contacted him for elucidation. Fehim reconfirmed the task force and its objectives, but this time, the reporter used his real name, rank, and station, without consent, in order to assure his readership he had used a reliable source. This unexpected and objectionable turn of events put Fehim at the centre of a political forcefield, a position that opened him up to considerable damage. All the polarized responses and contemptuous remarks that the publicity on our stop forms project had triggered among politicians, police officers, policy-makers, pundits, and citizens alike automatically extended to Fehim. As our call for more bureaucracy stood against the tenor of the times, one can only imagine how taxing this was for Fehim, who had to operate in an organization that had learned to think of bureaucracy as a social evil. We were challenging the prevailing common sense.

Some solace was offered by the fact that the publicity that was given to the stop form project had revitalized an earlier discussion on this topic (mainly carried on by the Dutch division of Amnesty International), and activated and encouraged new actors such as Controle Alt Delete (CAD), a young, vibrant group of activists opposed to disproportionate police violence and discrimination. At first, the NP met political support in its decision to cancel the project. Our project was discussed in an annual report of the Ministry of Security and Justice (34 200 VI, no. 15). There we can read what a Member of Parliament (MP) for Wilders' Freedom Party (PVV) thought about the project and my study in general. Even though she had worked as an attorney before she started her political career, this MP asked the minister, by means of a Parliamentary motion, to block any project of this nature and to stop my accusations of police discrimination. The minister responded by arguing that it was impossible for him to stop third party incriminations: 'In my opinion, the police should not be accused of things they don't do. That does not mean, however, that

I can support this motion, because I would not know how to do so. I cannot stop such third party incriminations', he said. With respect to the stop form project, he simply stated that the experiment had been stopped (which is not entirely true; it had never started in the first place). In a written statement to Parliament, he commented: 'Needlessly increasing administrative burdens needs to be prevented. It will not improve the police capacity or performance' (*Kamerbrief Directoraat-Generaal Politie,* 30 June 2015). Instead, he drew attention to an existing awareness training programme ('Brown Eyes, Blue Eyes'), implying that the NP was already tackling the problem. Such awareness training programmes perfectly match the human failure model, cited earlier, reducing the public issue of police discrimination to the level of private problems of an individual.

However, about two weeks after my police ethnography had been made public, Mitch Henriquez died as a result of the police chokehold, described in Chapter 2. The publicized aspects of my work quickly started to intertwine with the 'political life' of Henriquez's dead body (Verdery 1999). As people were promoting their own causes and claims in reference to the case, the intertextuality of my dissertation was greatly enhanced by people who used it to bolster their own claims. The killing of Henriquez led to an outburst of (hashtag) activism that seriously challenged the legitimacy of the Dutch police, turning it into one of the factors that eventually resulted in the resignation of Commissioner Bouman (several corruption cases, sceptical police unions, and a failed reorganization were among the other factors). The killing of Henriquez was pivotal in the reframing of police misconduct, allowing victims of police brutality as well as those involved in research, advocacy, protest, and activism to reframe this kind of misconduct in terms of police *racism* and to forge a shared 'political temporality' (Bonilla and Rosa 2015). The killing, the protests, and the subsequent prosecution of the officers responsible for Henriquez's death all led to a proliferation of 'assholes' in the sense defined by Van Maanen, as those whom the police tag as such because they refuse to take the 'police definition of the situation' for granted (Van Maanen 1978). Obviously, Van Maanen referred to the occupational frame used by police officers in their street encounters to label those who fail to 'meet police expectations arising from the interaction situation itself' (Van Maanen 1978, 309). Here, however, we can also stretch the definition to include those who publically question, contest, disagree with, or otherwise 'talk back' to police (cf. Mutsaers 2016d). The coincidental developments in the fields of research, advocacy, and activism encouraged people to speak up and resist police brutality and racism.[1]

Whereas in 2015, my call for stop forms had elicited strongly negative reactions among police and politicians alike, two comparable methods had since emerged and one was on the table for discussion in 2016. The police-oriented civil rights group CAD had started a crowd-funding initiative that resulted in the development of a mobile application, supported by the NP, allowing citizens to file an online complaint about ethnic profiling. Similar functionality was integrated in the regular police app of the NP itself. Further, in July 2016 a majority of the Amsterdam city council (Labour, the Greens, Socialists, and Social Liberals) had voted in favour of an experiment with stop forms in the Dutch capital. These more progressive parties had also boosted the debate about stop forms in various other city councils across the country, which even led to a political crisis in the city council of The Hague, where the neoliberal law-and-order mayor refused to enact the motion supported by a majority in the council to start an experiment with the forms.

This new political moment was triggered by a complex configuration of actors, situations, and events, of which the public circulation of my ethnography (and its practical implications) was only a small part. Certainly, the knowledge that academics create spirals in and out of social life, as Giddens (1990) states, but this spiralling is slow paced. Ethnographies rarely lead to revolutions. Neither should they. I believe that the public value of ethnography is not revolutionary but democratic in the sense that, when cast as a public act, it can bring the studied object under scrutiny of 'an assemblage of actors and institutions inhabiting a broad swath of political, ethical and epistemological positions' (Mutsaers et al. 2015, 787). From this perspective, police ethnographies can fulfil a democratic function by prompting informed discussions on the very nature, definition, and boundaries of

[1] Especially when such brutality or racism victimizes Dutch celebrities, such as in May 2016, when the Surinam-Dutch rapper Typhoon was stopped and frisked without probable cause, an event which instantly turned him into the public face of the protest movement.

policing among politicians, policy-makers, legislators, police officials, and advocates, as well as an active and engaged citizenry, re-established in its responsibility to participate in public debates on police (Fassin 2013a). This is one aspect of what I call 'reclaiming the public in policing': democratic societies call for democratic policing, a critical societal function that always warrants public scrutiny. Ethnography can be an important facilitator in this respect. Therefore, I will dedicate a substantial part of this concluding chapter to the 'public afterlife' (Fassin 2015) of my ethnography, which I will address in light of a more general discussion on public anthropology.

In addition to this call on police anthropologists to venture beyond the compounds of the anthropological discipline and establish a public presence, I will also *substantially* reclaim the public in policing by calling for a distinctive anthropology of policing—one that is centred on the modular police officer who masters the art of separation and distinguishes public tasks from private sentiments, criminal justice from popular justice, and social standing from legal entanglement. Doing justice to anthropology as an essentially comparative academic exercise, I will argue, once again, that the recent and rapid advancement of the anthropology of police opens up new avenues for the comparison of policing in the Global North and South. This comparison is confronting us with the alarming conclusion that a worldwide corrosion of the public character of policing is saddling us with law enforcement agencies that find it very hard to exclude politics, particularism, and populism from their operations.

Reclaiming the Public in Policing I: Public Anthropology

That ethnography can have a democratic potential when cast as a public act is one side of the story. The public presence of anthropologists who try to make a difference beyond the academy—by intervening in public debates, collaborating with different publics, designing practical applications—will benefit an open and democratic public sphere. If we accept a broad definition of ethnography as the academic practice of registering and inscribing human experience through (hopefully accessible) discourse, it becomes easy to see how it stimulates acts of responsible citizenship and public debate. Ethnographers build their theories and argumentations on the basis of 'face-to-face' and 'soul-to-soul' field experiences (Van Maanen 1988), which makes them ideally suited to bridge academic and public discourse. However, we also need to be realistic about another motor that drives public anthropology: anthropologists need to go public in order to survive as an academic species.

In the early days, anthropologists used to be praised for their 'extra-mural' (MacClancy 2017) or public activities. The inevitable referent in this history, writes Fassin, 'is Franz Boas' denunciation of the spying activity of unnamed colleagues working for the US government during the First World War' (Fassin 2015, 595) Boas, the founding father of American anthropology, was equally praised for the major role he played in the attack on scientific racism. But there were others, like Margaret Mead, who adopted a flowing prose that seemed to work well in popularizing anthropology.[2] Benedict's *Patterns of Culture* (1934) sold millions of copies and turned out to be very successful in challenging popular preconceptions about culture (see also Eriksen 2006). It has been said that her *The Chrysanthemum and the Sword* (Eriksen 1946) changed the lives of numerous Japanese.

However, in the second half of the twentieth century, a profound rupture occurred in the public engagement with anthropologists, which Eriksen, in *Engaging Anthropology*, describes as a withdrawal of anthropology from general intellectual discourse (Eriksen 2006). This aloof period of disengagement is best characterized by the remarks of Evans-Pritchard on applied anthropology:

> An anthropologist within his own scientific field will use the knowledge he acquires by research to solve anthropological problems and these may have no practical significance whatever. It may be held that it is laudable for an anthropologist to investigate practical problems. Possibly it is, but if he does so he must realize that he is no longer acting within the anthropological field but in the non-scientific field of administration. Of one thing I feel quite certain: that no one can devote himself wholeheartedly to both interests; and I doubt whether anyone can investigate fundamental and practical problems at the same time. Moreover, there is a grave danger that the pressure of political and administrative interests, and the allurements that accompany them, may draw away so many of our small band from the investigation of purely scientific problems that

[2] If one is repelled by the word 'popularizing', Beeman suggests thinking of it as a 'public service' (Beeman 1987).

the advance of the science may be seriously retarded. (Evans-Pritchard 1946, 93)

In the article—the text version of a lecture given to the Oxford University Anthropological Society—Evans-Pritchard expounded on his reasons for strictly separating 'scientific anthropology' from 'applied anthropology' (which he did not consider to be proper anthropology anyway), arguing (a) that scientific and administrative objectives rarely converge, (b) that a purely scientific analysis of primitive social structures was immediately required, as primitive tribes were 'disappearing before our eyes', and (c) that this ought to be done by men of 'some standing, experience and seniority'. This approach provoked a 'clubbishness' of self-acclaimed omniscient and omnicompetent anthropologists, one that lasted for decades (MacClancy 1996). Despite some notable exceptions—such as Verdery's work on political socialism (Verdery 1996), Rabinow's ethnography of Morocco (Rabinow 1977), Shostak's absorbing account of the !Kung (Shostal 1981), or Levi-Strauss' travelogue *Tristes Tropiques* (Levi-Strauss 1955)—the half century that followed Evans-Pritchard's remarks could be typified by the sort of Levi-Straussian structural anthropology that only a happy few could read and understand without getting a serious headache.[3]

No wonder then that Peacock, addressing a group of anthropologists exactly half a century after Evans-Pritchard had done, confronted his audience with a simple choice: either we go public or we perish (Peacock 1997; see also Sabloff 2011).[4] His advice: 'while sustaining our fundamentals, probing the deep mysteries of the human species and the human soul, we must press outward, mobilizing our work and ourselves to make a difference beyond the discipline and the academy' (Peacock 1997, 9). If we prove capable of doing so, Peacock stated, anthropologists will have a prominent position in society. If not, we either face extinction or hang on as the 'living dead' (cf. Lassiter 2005).

I, for one, am glad to see that the discipline has survived and become a vibrant discipline that is open, collaborative, and engaged. Not only can anthropologists be found at the forefront

[3] Some say that Levi-Strauss had only written his more popular *Tristes Tropiques* because he thought he had failed as an academic (see MacClancy 1996).

[4] In his Presidential Address at the 94th Annual Meeting of the American Anthropological Association.

of public debates on important societal issues—I am thinking of Ho's ethnography of Wall Street (Ho 2009), Merry's work on the cultural power of law (Merry 2000), Scheper-Hughes' battle against the human trafficking of bodies and organs (Scheper-Hughes 2004, 2009), Rosas' shocking discourse on neoliberal security in the US–Mexico borderlands (Rosas 2012), as well as the abundance of anthropological work on the police, cited in this book—they now also highlight what it means to carry out a public anthropology. The number of reflections on what a public, open, and engaged anthropology is and what it can do is truly staggering (e.g. Abu-Lughod 2016; Brondo 2010; Campbell 1996; Eriksen 2006; Fassin 2013b, 2015; Gomberg-Muñoz 2013; Hannerz 2010; Haugerud 2016; Lamphere 2003; Lassiter 2005; Low and Merry 2010; MacClancy 2002a, 2002b, 2017; Mutsaers et al. 2015; Osterweil 2013; Sabloff 2011; Scheper-Hughes 2009; Vine 2011). Like their colleagues in the adjacent field of sociology (e.g. Burawoy), anthropologists seem to acknowledge once again that after a long period of 'building professional knowledge, translating common sense into science, [they] are more than ready to embark on a systematic back-translation, taking knowledge back to those from whom it came' (Burawoy 2005, 5).

In work written earlier, I have discussed such systematic back-translation in the light of Hymes' ideas about 'ethnographic monitoring' (e.g. Hymes 1996; Van der Aa 2012). Reflecting on our three police ethnographies (in, respectively, the United States, France, and The Netherlands), Jennie Simpson, Kevin Karpiak, and I stated that:

> Anthropological productions can no longer be presented as just-so-stories written by omniscient scientists who presume the capacity to shed light on objective truth. One of the forerunners in this sense was Dell Hymes (e.g. 1996), who called for ethnographic knowledge to be shared, democratic, and open to all. He saw ethnographic practice as a collaboration and 'learning environment for those who were the target of inquiry, bringing ethnographic and ultimately ethnological knowledge back to the community that had provided it' (Blommaert 2013b, 127). For police anthropologists, this has an important implication, related to what Jef van der Aa (2012) has called 'epistemic solidarity'. Anthropologists have documented the profound effects of policing on minority communities as well as the profound creative resistance of marginalized individuals and communities in the face of such ... Conversely,

Van der Aa's (2012, 98) 'epistemic solidarity' calls for a practical knowledge: '[The ethnographer] is driven by praxis: knowledge as a crucial instrument for social change. In order for this knowledge to really address the problems at hand, it needs to be shared and cooperative.' This includes collaboration with police, despite its many challenges and dangers. (Mutsaers et al. 2015, 786)

Initially, I did not face many challenges or dangers. In 2008, I encountered a former Police Commissioner who had openly spoken about 'institutional discrimination' at the Dutch police.[5] There was a great deal of interest in the topic and with his support, my access to the entire organization was secured. In contrast to other police anthropologists who came up against a ban on the continuation of their work (see Fassin 2013a), I could still write in my dissertation (that is, before I had gone public):

Although law enforcement agencies can be expected not to be very keen of being observed by outsiders, I never experienced any difficulty in gaining access to the field … It deserves note that I never met resistance during my fieldwork and was always facilitated to fulfil my job as a fieldworker. Neither was any attempt made to encapsulate me or to deprive me of my relative autonomy as a researcher. (Mutsaers 2015a, 40)

Despite differences in perspectives on the causes of and solutions to police discrimination, my 'intramural' years of fieldwork took place in an atmosphere of congeniality and collaboration. In many quarters of the organization, I encountered a genuine interest in tackling police discrimination, especially among rank-and-file police but also among some higher ranked officers. Acknowledging collaborative ethnography as an important component of public anthropology (see also Lassiter 2005), I worked together, for instance, with a superintendent who was responsible for a diversity

[5] This contact was established by my colleague (and former PhD supervisor) Hans Siebers, who met this former police commissioner in October 2007. The two men decided to initiate a line of research to understand this 'institutional discrimination' of police officers with a migration background. They approached me with a research assignment to undertake fieldwork along the lines set out by them. My fieldwork started in the spring of 2008. An interesting side note: at that time, the former commissioner was working as the director of the National Expertise Centre Diversity (LECD) at the Dutch Police Academy. He was already discussed in Chapter 4 as the epitome of those who used psychological discourses on diversity management. This confirms, once again, that nothing could be observed in the 'guided doings' of police managers that suggests that the *institutional* in 'institutional discrimination' was taken seriously (Goffman 1974).

training course in the police district in which I was working in 2010 (the course was given to 1,500 uniformed police officers, employed by the 22 teams in the area). After several exploratory talks, he had invited me to his course, which I had attended and subjected to some critical reflections. I shared my ideas with him and he turned out to be very receptive. One thing led to another and before we knew it, we were presenting a co-authored paper at two criminal justice conferences in Australia in which we combined his diversity training and my research, promising ourselves and the audience to end the 'dialogue of the deaf' between police scholars and practitioners (Bradley and Nixon 2009).

In the same year, I submitted a research plan to the Police Academy, which eventually led to the PhD project (2011–2015) that I carried out while being employed by the academy. This plan already contained a critical literature review of psychological approaches to diversity and discrimination and emphasized the need to explore the police-specific contextual and structural dimensions of these phenomena. My proposal was accepted and throughout these years, I collaborated with the police, recognizing the ethical obligation to co-construct knowledge, 'feed back' my findings to the police teams I studied, and to allow the output of my study circulate in productive ways (see the Appendix). The work coming out of this engagement can be seen as an implementation of ethnographic monitoring, a programme developed by Hymes to meet the requirements of epistemic solidarity. In essence, ethnographic monitoring consists of three basic steps: (1) consulting informants to identity issues that concern them most; (2) observing behaviour relevant to that issue; and, finally, (3) feeding back the findings to informants and thus committing to a fair construction of knowledge that balances and checks different perspectives and interpretations thereof (Van der Aa 2012; see also Mutsaers et al. 2015).

The process of re-engaging analyses with actors in the field was not taken lightly. At the heart of this process lay regular reporting back to both rank-and-file officers and the police leadership. Activities ranged from invited talks at local police departments, participation in management and leadership programmes, a keynote presentation at a diversity seminar at the Police Academy, a talk at a strategy meeting of the NP, as well as the organization of various work groups and task forces to translate my research into practice. In addition, I regularly published in professional police and public administration journals and magazines and on websites to make my work more widely available (e.g. Mutsaers 2012, 2013, 2014c, 2014d, 2015b, 2015c; Mutsaers et al. 2012). I consistently made an effort not to cloak my publications in 'the thickest of prose' (MacClancy 2002b, 4), as I was cognizant of the fact that texts adorned with jargon have little extra-academic appeal. All these efforts to 'give back' were much appreciated.

However, as stated at the beginning of this chapter, appreciation morphed into hostility the moment I went public. Perhaps I was naïve but I was genuinely shocked by the different effects internal and external communication had and the responses to them. Previously, I had never experienced any tension between 'talking back to powerful institutional discourses' and making my study useful to the institution—a tension highlighted by Haugerud (2016). Admittedly, police departments responded differently to my criticism on biocracy, psychological discourses, and the role of psycho-technicians with respect to police discrimination and exclusion—or, for that matter, to the disappearing contours of the police institution at large. However, my insights and arguments had never previously been discredited altogether. That this is exactly what *did* happen after the publicity my work attracted serves as a good reason to look more closely at the word *public* in 'public anthropology'. Like the work of Abu-Lughod on Muslim women's rights, my work was 'caught in cross-publics, in both senses of the word: it crossed different publics and made at least one public very cross. It entered multiple lifeworlds at odds with one another and with anthropology. It was opened up to different criteria of authority and judgment, not to mention rules of civility' (Abu-Lughod 2016, 57) as we will see shortly. Moreover, it is very likely that exactly because my work reached different publics (academics, police officers, politicians, policymakers, mainstream and social media users, human rights activists, etc.) that at least one public became very angry: the NP (as well as their sympathizers, who either agreed with the NP that police discrimination is a marginal phenomenon related to individuals and incidents, or stated that the topic is not worthy of our attention at all, or might even be a good thing, considering the high crime and imprisonment rates of minority groups).

To come to terms on this effect, it is important to clarify what I mean by 'public'. I agree with Fassin (2015) that 'the public' (or better: publics) differs from 'the people' in the sense that the latter exist in a latent, unmediated way, free floating in social space, whereas the former has to be brought into existence. Publics are not pre-existing entities but exist by virtue of being addressed by and concerned with an author's work. So, before I had 'gone public' with my police ethnography, I only had one non-academic public—the police—to which I tried to repay the debts I had incurred during fieldwork. The police had a feeling of ownership towards my research: they controlled what was done with the study. In a way, they lost that control the moment I created other publics in the media, publics which also had an interest in the study, for whatever reason (I already mentioned the group of activists who used my work to protest against the chokehold death of Henriquez). Some of these publics defended the status quo of policing, whereas others could be seen as 'counter publics' who demanded reforms. Considering the antagonistic relationship between these different publics, I found myself in a very difficult position. Like Fassin (2013b), who reflected on the public afterlife of his police ethnography in France (*Enforcing Order* 2013a), I experienced loyalty to different sides, but this loyalty rested on different grounds:

> [M]y loyalty to the police rests on *deontological grounds*, in the sense that it is defined by our everyday interaction in a professional context, whereas my loyalty to their principal public relies on *ethical principles,* in the sense that it is determined by more general concerns about a certain state of the world viewed from the perspective of social justice. (Fassin 2013b, 641, my emphasis)

In my case, things were even more complicated due to the fact that I had worked with many ethnic minority police officers who suffered equally from social injustice.

In sum, in order to increase the profile of public anthropology, it is not enough to simply reach out to audiences beyond the academy and to write with various publics in mind. It is imperative that we also reflect on the reception, discussion, and appropriation/rejection of our work by different publics and analyse this 'public afterlife' of our ethnographies. Understood as such, the (study of the) public afterlife of ethnography is a prolongation of that ethnographic work; it enables us to be engaged with our subject just a little longer, albeit in a different, sometimes more upsetting because more personal way. Reflections on the public afterlife of ethnography can amplify the study and enrich it (Fassin 2015), as I will now show.

In the earlier mentioned press release that was published by my university and which kick-started my study's public afterlife, I emphasized the structural character of police discrimination in The Netherlands. My conclusions were readily accepted by most Dutch newspapers, which printed articles with headings such as 'Discrimination by police is more than just an incident' (*NRC Handelsblad*, 11 June 2015), 'Dutch police discriminate' (*Algemeen Dagblad*, 9 June 2015) or 'Police discrimination also in the Netherlands' (*Trouw*, 9 June 2015). The press release had even travelled to the Dutch Caribbean, where the papers reported: 'Dutch police have wide powers of discretion which has made them vulnerable to discrimination on the grounds of race, said the Tilburg University anthropologist in his Doctor's thesis' (*The Daily Herald*, Saint Martin, 10 June 2015). Immediately after the communication department of my university had published the press release on the university website, the NP responded with its own. While the university's press release was transparent about my employment with the Police Academy, the NP emphasized my affiliation to the university but omitted any mention of my employment contract with the academy. What disconcerted me more, though, was that the Commissioner (Bouman) personally discredited the findings of my study and referred to another study in which the conclusion drawn was that police discrimination was not a structural issue (Van der Leun et al. 2014). This study was often used by the NP whenever public debates on police discrimination flared up. Interestingly, this particular study became a subject of heavy criticism in 2016 after an independent research agency had retrieved information via the Dutch Freedom of Information Act, uncovering an agreement between the responsible researchers and the police in The Hague, where the study had taken place (Buro Jansen en Jansen 2016). Both parties had agreed that observations of police discrimination were to be kept out of publications.

Peculiarly, a few months before, in a personal blog ('the Others') on the police intranet, the Commissioner had written that he considered police discrimination a structural problem. Further, he had done so in much more condemnatory tones than I used, talking about 'the poison of exclusion trickling into our organization' (Bouman 2015). In stark contrast with his 'intramural' performances, however, he stated in his press releases and media appearances that he could not confirm my conclusions and spoke, in contradiction to my dissertation, about incidents as ones caused by human mistakes, invoking the human failure model of rotten apples. As stated earlier, this model was also embraced by the Minister of Security and Justice, who, in his reply to my dissertation, had argued that the pedigree of police diversity training is sufficiently developed to adequately tackle the problem at hand (*Kamerbrief Directoraat-Generaal Polite*, 30 June 2015).

Because I was employed by the Police Academy at that time, I had access to the Commissioner's intranet column, as well as responses to it from police officers. It is telling that within 5 days, the column had elicited more than 200 responses from police officers. The Commissioner had apparently struck a dissonant chord and he had done so in a brave way, proving willing and able to connect police discrimination to other larger issues in the world. His column not only adopted a personal narrative style when addressing police discrimination; he also expressed his worries about the Charlie Hebdo attacks in Paris (which had occurred only weeks before) and the police–minority tensions in Ferguson. With respect to the events in Paris—and terrorism more generally—he defended ethnic minority officers, arguing that he fully understood they had become sick and tired of explaining to their colleagues that they too loathe ISIS and other radical groups.

Although we should take relations of subordination into account, it must be noted that the vast majority of the intranet posts can be read as expressions of appreciation. People articulated their gratitude to the Commissioner for his audacity to touch on this issue. Some posts described how complex the situation is, especially for ethnic minority officers. One of the respondents, who also happened to be a member of our stop forms task force, borrowed an excerpt that circulated widely on social media to express this complexity: 'I am not Charlie … I am Ahmed the dead cop. Charlie disrespected me and ridiculed my faith and culture and I died, defending his right to do so' (this refers to the police officer who was murdered by one of the Charlie Hebdo perpetrators). However, more critical voices could also be heard. One officer posted the following: 'We want to be everyone's police, but does everyone want us to be their police???'—pointing at the increasing problem of legal alienation that was mentioned at the beginning of this book (e.g. Hertogh 2011; Ministerie van

Veiligheid en Justitie 2016; Zouridis 2016). Others connected this issue to 'years of Muslim bashing', which had seriously reduced the 'democratic quality of the police organization'. This 'Muslim bashing' was linked to the deliberate street policy of ethnic profiling, which, some opined, had been responded to by police leaders with 'panic' and 'denial'. Fundamentally, the recurrent point of criticism boiled down to the discrepancy between discourse and action. In the words of one respondent: 'Words have limited value if they aren't followed by deeds … What are your stakes? … Why do we still don't have an independent body to which we can turn [in case of discrimination]?' A small minority of respondents argued that people should stop complaining about discrimination and exclusion, suggesting that people should develop some mental resilience to improve their coping strategies (a position that resonates with the diversity management discourses described in this book).

In line with the predominantly appreciative responses by rank-and-file officers to the acknowledgement of police discrimination as a structural problem, many officers supported my dissertation's findings. This in itself is remarkable, as other police anthropologists have pointed at the silence imposed on lower ranks by those higher up the hierarchy (e.g. Fassin 2013a; Denyer Willis 2015). When my research became public in June 2015, I was e-mailed and telephoned by a number of ethnic minority officers who told me about their grievances. One of them, for example, sent me a passionate message in which he detailed the numerous instances of discrimination which had cost him his hard-won position in the organization—he had even attached the verdicts of the labour inspectorate and the *College voor de Rechten van de Mens* (The Netherlands Institute for Human Rights) which proved him to be right. Similarly, during a closing seminar at the Police Academy (30 June 2015), my conclusions were supported by the audience (about 150 officers). When one of the panel members—a traditional (dare I say 'conservative'?) criminologist—proclaimed that police discrimination was something he never encountered in his academic career, the audience jumped to its feet and one man (from an ethnic minority) yelled at him: 'What world do you live in, for Christ's sake?'

These responses from rank-and-file officers contrasted starkly with those given by the NP. The same day that my university had sent out its press release, a spokesperson of the NP called me from

The Hague, where the NP has its headquarters. He called to share his opinion, one shaped by the institution that employed him, of the dissertation as an exaggerated description of the Dutch police. While some aspects of the police force described in the book rang true, others could be reduced to presuppositions about the world of policing, he argued. Mostly, he nudged me to use a softer, less critical wording in my media appearances in order to stop from blowing things out of proportion. When I asked which specific words he had in mind, two were mentioned: 'road blocks' and 'PsyCops'. Interestingly, these are emic rather than etic terms; that is, they are not analytical terms invented by me to cover certain empirics of policing, they are part of police vernacular, coined and applied by police officers to describe specific practices and policies. The first time I encountered police officers at the police department in Tilburg who talked about 'road blocks', I could not help seeing in my mind's eye the checkpoints and militant groups that have been so vividly described by J.M. Coetzee in *The Life & Times of Michael K*—a book that I happened to be reading at that time. I argued over the phone that I could not be held responsible for their discourse, nor for the fact that these road blocks offered ample opportunities for ethnic profiling, as officers subjected ethnic minorities to more intense scrutiny and more severe sanctions. The NP considered the joint discussion about road blocks and ethnic profiling a serious problem and I remember the pressure I felt during the phone call (and afterwards). I kept arguing, however, that the anthropological method did not allow me to drop emic terms whenever they happened to be politically inconvenient.

My disclosure of Project PSYCOPS to a broader public was even more upsetting to the NP, which had managed to maximize police discretion and kept the project from the public gaze until June 2015 (the final report of over 250 pages (Dijkstra 2014) had not been made public and had to be requested by a journalist on the basis of the Dutch Freedom of Information Act). PSYCOPS became a topic of interest in the media. On 12 June, *Trouw* published an article, quoting experts including Professor Désirée Verweij (a specialist in military ethics), who had stated that PSYCOPS 'is not something you would want from the police, which is supposed to be keeping order'. News about PSYCOPS also aroused widespread indignation on social media platforms such as Twitter and Facebook. People wrote: 'PsyCops, to manipulate the hearts and minds of the plebs'; 'PsyCops, yuck!'; 'Is "Bulletproof" the name of the leader of this project?'; '#PsyCops Amsterdam shows how US situations come to The Netherlands: Militarisation of police force—that's why I follow US police brutality'; 'I want to write something about PsyCops, but this whole operation is so wrong that I barely know where to start.'

A few days after I was telephoned by the spokesperson, I was contacted by a strategic advisor of the NP. He advised me to tone down my public comments. He gave me an off-the-record warning that the local authorities in Amsterdam were about to take me to court for my (allegedly misplaced) critique. This may have been an empty threat or based on hearsay but it is also likely that the public outcry in The Hague that erupted a few days later had changed the political winds and made judicial proceedings untimely. I was never sued. Another crisis had already come to dominate the scene: the chokehold death of Mitch Henriquez.

In the end, the NP did not accept any of my recommendations. In addition to blocking the stop form project, the NP turned down my suggestion to introduce so-called Civilian Complaint Review Boards (CCRBs). CCRBs or other forms of civilian oversight of policing have been implemented in countries including the United States (Bobb 2003), Australia (Prenzler 2000), and the United Kingdom (Savage 2013), and are often vested with investigative subpoena powers to hold police officers accountable for wrongdoing (such as excessive force, abuse of authority, offensive, or discriminatory language). Jurisdictions tend to create such external oversight bodies when internal control mechanisms are not up to standard. Based on my ethnographic work, I suspected lax internal oversight. In fact, as described in the previous chapter, I had spoken with some ethnic minority police officers who had wanted to file official complaints to combat discrimination within the organization, but almost never succeeded in doing so. Often their complaints were not even processed. Instead, conflict mediation or other dialogue techniques were offered. As we saw, such efforts were sometimes experienced by minority officers as attempts to blame the victim. Unfortunately, the chief of the NP stated in a press release on 10 June 2015:

> I have no reason to change the complaint procedure. It is accessible and effective, also when it comes to ethnic profiling and discrimination. Police oversight in the Netherlands is democratic and detailed. Introducing

civilian review boards as a democratic counterforce and monitor of police has, in my view, no added value.

On 1 July 2015, article 68 of the Police Act 2012 (an article that regulates the complaint procedure) was amended. The amendment, which was first announced in the *Staatscourant* (No. 32511) published on 18 November 2014, had indeed made the complaint procedure more democratic, as it guaranteed an independent selection and appointment of the members of the complaint committee. However, in the *Staatscourant* we also read that 'the complaint procedure has been transformed over the years from a formal procedure to a direct personal contact and mediation between complainant and accused. [This trend] has improved contact between the police and the complainant ... and has diminished the legal nature of the procedure and reduced the administrative burden.' While the independent selection of committee members (recruited from outside the police organization) could indeed be considered a step forward, the de-bureaucratization (personal contact instead of formal procedure) could not. A few weeks later, I again emphasized the importance of bureaucratic control of police and I did so together with a fellow police anthropologist who had studied police discrimination in The Netherlands a few years earlier and who had come to similar conclusions (cf. Çankaya 2011, 2012). We published an article in one of the national newspapers in The Netherlands (Çankaya and Mutsaers 2015). Although other newspaper articles appeared in which the need for CCRBs was stressed as well (e.g. Danen 2015); the NP made no further comment.

In a way, going public is a prolongation of fieldwork, as it enables us to stay engaged with our subject matter for longer, albeit in a different, sometimes more upsetting because more personal way. I agree with Fassin (2015), who stated that the public afterlife of ethnography is more than a question of reception; it is also about how public reactions amplify the study and enrich it. The mantra of individualism and individual responsibility that was repeated by the NP in their public appearances amplifies the original study. Whenever suggestions were given to re-bureaucratize the police, the NP stepped up its vigil to make sure that new bureaucratic structures are not introduced. The stop forms project was cancelled in a panic, external oversight initiatives were brushed aside as redundant, and critical perspectives on PSYCOPS and other invasive policing programmes that blur boundaries between the private and the public were dismissed as exaggerations that fail to do justice to the good intentions that led up to these programmes. Each time this topic came up, light was shed on the professionalism and craftsmanship of individual officers and their diversity and awareness trainings. Further, public responses by the NP boiled down to accusations of bias with respect to the nature of police discrimination (is it structural or incidental?). Agreeing with Becker (1967), we can argue that such accusations of bias are more likely to occur when the researcher gives credence to the perspective of a subordinate group in a hierarchical relationship (in my case migrants, both within the police and in neighbourhoods), that is, when someone calls into question the legitimacy of the hierarchy. In such cases, as we saw, the NP are tireless in their attempts to repair the desired 'hierarchy of credibility' (Becker's term) and do not shy away from threatening with litigation.

Reclaiming the Public in Policing II: Public Policing in the Global North and South

These responses to the public afterlife of a police ethnography are certainly not unique. Take, for example, Denyer Willis's *The Killing Consensus* (2015), a product of intense ethnographic labour that took place among the police in Brazil. The author offers us an alternative perspective on the relationship between police and organized crime groups in São Paulo such as the *Primeiro Comando da Capital* (PCC). Rather than conveniently describing them as law enforcers versus lawbreakers, he argues that they are not only both responsible for the routine killings that can turn a favela into a battlefield but they also both act as security-oriented collectives by negotiating periods of peace in which feelings of security among favela residents are elevated. Due to the PCC's clandestine justice systems and the accompanying accoutrements of law (tribunals, security guards, law enforcers, etc.), the police and PCC are not necessarily antagonistic. When Denyer Willis proposed this radically different perspective to a broader public via an op-ed in the *New York Times*, this led to a number of surprisingly positive personal responses of São Paulo's rank-and-file officers. It was felt that the embargo on their opinion was temporarily lifted by the emic stance of the anthropologist, and officers were grateful. However, higher ranking officials refused to respond, at least not until another article appeared on the online news site *Universo On-Line*. A rebuttal of the Public Security Secretariat was published in response, which amounted to character assassination. The author had created 'myths' and had romanticized criminal life, it was claimed. He was mocked, his perspective was ridiculed and doubts were immediately cast on the veracity of his work.

A few years earlier, a similar fate befell Fassin after he had published *Enforcing Order: An Ethnography of Urban Policing* (2013). Fassin had spent fifteen months with an anti-crime squad operating in deprived Parisian suburbs, scrutinizing interactions between the police and, mainly, ethnic minority youth. When he applied to undertake a follow-up project in a different police region, he was confronted with the closed and secretive nature of the French police: 'I came up against a ban on the continuation of my work. A ban couched in "civil" terms, but imposed with a persistence that left little doubt as to the determination to prevent me from completing a study that had been initiated under the best auspices' (Fassin 2013a, 13–14). When his study was published and widely publicized several years later, police comments were embargoed. Those who did respond, the 'top brass', argued that the described practices of racial profiling and discrimination ought to be seen as individual incidents instead of part of a structural problem. We are reminded of Punch's (2003) comments on police misconduct, namely that it is automatically framed by police leadership as a 'rotten apple' problem, prioritizing a human failure model of deviance, even if such deviances are clearly of a systemic and endemic kind—a 'rotten orchard' problem. Such attacks on the work *and* personalities of fellow police ethnographers are a bitter pill to swallow—and other examples can be given as well (such as the trials that Goffman had to go through after she published *On the Run: Fugitive Life in an American City* in 2014; see also Lewis-Kraus 2016). When left undiscussed, they may eventually amount to a sidelining of critical scholars or, worse, the immunity of the police to criticism.

These highly personalized affronts to the quality and credibility of police ethnographers cannot be disconnected, I believe, from the larger issue addressed in this book: the lost art of separating public and private spheres and the non-modularity of present-day policing. It is the same lack of sensitivity to boundaries that mixes the worlds of academia and policing together that also blends the public and private lives of officers and gives non-police institutions a policing responsibility. Let there be no mistake: the whole idea behind a public anthropology of policing is to initiate a rapprochement between police scholarship and practice, not a conflation of them. Critical distance is required at all times to prevent an interweaving of institutions that are better off living apart than as bedfellows who share all their intimacies.

It is to these intimacies and other signs of proximity that I now turn to by way of conclusion. Throughout this book, I have offered case descriptions that in one way or another point to the problematic consequences of state proximity, often manifested in the form of discrimination of and by police officers. Whether it concerns the institutional practice of ethnic profiling, the micro-deportation of migrants, the external integration of community officers, the *gemeinschaftliche* police tweet, the psycho-technical training and management techniques, the autobiographical imperative, the cultural policing, PSYCOPS, or any other example given in the previous chapters; a 'humanization' of police recurs each and every time. Although positive intentions behind this impulse to humanize cannot be dismissed outright, it gives no cause for celebration. In a bid to remain relevant (and wanted) in an increasingly competitive security market (e.g. Van Steden 2002, 2007), and to survive in a time of scarce public resources, the Dutch police force has sought to rid 'obsolete' bureaucratic structures and processes from the organization which are deemed obstacles on the path taken to boost police legitimacy. In their stead came a new, ostensibly more humane form of governance, which we have provisionally called 'biocratic governance' (after Fleming 2014a, 2014b), meant to bring the police closer to 'the people.' Along the way, roles have been replaced by personalities, protocols by discretion, rule-bound behaviour by craftsmanship, law by sentiment, and sincerity by authenticity, and if not altogether replaced, then at least challenged by all these features of the post-bureaucratic organization.

Intuitively, such a development can be easily interpreted as positive and encouraging. As one of the core institutions of the state, a democratic police force must be embedded in society and operate in proximity to and close cooperation with 'the people'. Durkheimian criminology has long emphasized that criminal justice agents have a socially integrative function: they are the glue that holds society together (see the Introduction). But the state in itself is dependent on, even defined by, distance and impartiality. Without these qualities, the *public* governance of society becomes practically impossible. Anthropological studies of police in the Global South, cited throughout this book, have made this very clear. In the words of Beek

> Attesting that public servants collapse the distinction between state and society, public and private, many anthropologists have called into question the adequacy of these categorisations in the everyday realities of non-Western countries ... Blurred boundaries is a key term to describe informal everyday practices of officials, a spatial concept that makes it possible to link everyday practices of officials with theories of the state. (Beek 2012, 552)

In his work, Beek makes two comments on this notion of 'blurred boundaries' that align with the main conclusions that we can draw based on the previous chapters in this book. First, it is important, he says, not to compare an 'idealised image of Western states' with the 'realities of non-Western states' (Beek 2012, 553): 'There may be differences in the scope, frequency and degree of the legal framework applied to regulate the blurring of state-non-state boundaries by public officials, but the blurring itself is inherent in all states and not specific to "African" or "failed" states.' Second, we are advised to comprehend the blurring of boundaries not automatically as a failure of the state but to be open to the possibility that it may well be a means of extending state control. It widens the scope of policing.

Beek's first remark relates closely to the North–South comparisons that have been made throughout this book. In the Introduction, we asked, after Comaroff and Comaroff (2006a), if the world of policing at large is looking ever more post-colonial. Obviously, much more comparative work (that is, more police *anthropology*) is needed to seriously formulate an answer to such a large question, but first indications point at convergence. There are more commonalities between the police 'here' and 'there' than the comfortable separation between North and South has us conveniently believe, and these commonalities all have something to do with blurred boundaries (see also Bierschenk 2017), or what I have called 'non-modularity'. Boundaries between policing and vigilantism, between the internal and external integration of community officers, between legal and illegal police work (such as ethnic profiling or micro-deportations), between state bureaucracy and private value systems, and between police and non-police institutions. Once we dare to suspend exotic views of policing in the Global South as somehow exceptional or 'extreme,' we become open to the empirical fact that many police organizations around the world are similar enough to withstand fruitful comparison (cf. Beek et al. 2017). Then we begin to see that the *jugaad* of police officers in India (Jauregui 2014, 2016) is not so different from the social network policing of community officers in The Netherlands, that the extra-judicial punishment by police officers in Portugal (Zoettl 2017), France (Fassin 2013), or The Netherlands does not differ much from the illegal police violence reported in Taiwan (Martin 2013a) or Mozambique (Kyed 2017), that police vigilantism in The Netherlands, on the one hand, and South Africa or Nigeria (Hornberger 2011, 2013; Owen and Cooper-Knock 2014), on the other, differ only in degree, that invasive policing programmes such as PSYCOPS appear across the globe, and, more generally, that police organizations have a global tendency to become 'total' or 'greedy'.

This brings us to Beek's second remark about the expansion rather than recession of state police. Criticism levelled at the concept and practice of bureaucracy typically assumes that bureaucracy equals state power and that, as a corollary, de-bureaucratization entails a curtailment of state power. However, the empirics of policing discussed in this book shed another light on this matter. The de-bureaucratization—and thus the loss of boundaries—of the Dutch police has potentially deleterious results, precisely because it stretches the outer bounds of police power. It enables an inward and outward invasion, of the private lives of police *and* policed, who are no longer merely treated as employees or citizens but also on the basis of their authenticity or ethnicity. Following Walzer (1983, 1984), I believe that we must become aware of the dangerous effects of such a *Gleichschaltung*, or systematic coordination of different social spheres of life. It seems counterintuitive but good fences, as Walzer said, make just societies.

Unchallenged, such developments may result in an 'unlimited' police force that is no longer constrained by the public contours that normally delineate a legal bureaucracy. Those who take Western police forces as their vantage point may brush this statement aside as radical or defeatist, but I believe that the power of anthropology is to make comparisons and actually do something with them. We should take lessons from policing in countries in the Global South where the form of social organization that we know as bureaucracy has traditionally been weak (Bierschenk 2017). Stories abound of the privatization of public police, of blatant forms of police racism, corruption, and other illegal police practices. I believe it is time that we appreciate bureaucracy for its virtues. It may be the last straw in reclaiming the public in policing.

Appendix: A Note on Methodology

If this were a standard account of how I went about collecting and analysing my data I would say that I conducted eighty-two interviews with police officers and relevant others, scattered across the country (I visited eighteen police teams); that eighteen diaries were kept by police officers for a week each, in which they reported on daily events related to diversity issues; and that I 'shadowed' individual police officers for a total of twelve months in the cities of Amsterdam (four months), Tilburg (five months), and Bergen op Zoom (three months). I would then continue making some formal statements about the interview schedule, the diary format, and common themes that emerged in my fieldnotes. I would conclude with some compulsory remarks on transcription work, coding, interrater reliability, and perhaps even say a thing or two about the software used to analyse my data.

Such accounts rarely exert a gravitational pull on readers and I, for one, am glad that I do not feel the need to write such an account. The fact that I have placed my notes on methodology to the very end of this book should not be read as a depreciation of them. On the contrary, I consider them valuable and believe that some time must be dedicated to an academic discussion on ethnographic methods—especially now that the dominant position of the technician, as described in Chapter 4, makes it appear ever more obsolete to go beyond positivistic endeavours to improve the technology of measurement. To give some counterweight to the hegemony of the technician, I will turn to old discussions on ethnography and apply these to my own case study of the Dutch police. As I go about doing this, I shall deal with some familiar issues such as the intersubjectivity, bias, layered analysis, representativeness, the nature of interviews, self-reflexivity, complicity, context, the importance of anecdotes, shadowing, and distance/presence. I will follow the chronology of my fieldwork while dealing with all this to make the point that conducting ethnography is also a learning process.

2008–2009: Learning How to Ask

Whenever friends or colleagues jokingly ask me why a Dutch anthropologist is so obsessed with cops—their prosody often gives away their expectation that cannabis has something to do with it—I always answer in jest that there is little difference between the two, anthropologists and the police. First, both have occupational contact with the widest spectrum of human beings and behaviour. If cops work with crack dealers, so do anthropologists (Bourgeois 2002; Karandinos et al. 2014). If cops work with 'unauthorized' migrants, so do anthropologists (Blommaert 2009; Peutz 2006). Cops work on white-collar crime and anthropologists do so too (Ho 2009). Cops and anthropologists alike pay attention to loitering youths (Fassin 2013a). If cops work on the trafficking of human bodies and organs so do anthropologists (Scheper-Hughes 2004). Second, I tell them that the anthropological equivalent of undercover police operations is the idea of 'going native', blending in, immersing oneself. I say so tongue in cheek, of course, because where undercover cops always try to keep their identities concealed, anthropologists are—especially these days—ethically obliged to play by the book and reveal their true identities and purposes at all times. However, both work in a bottom-up fashion and 'from within' when gathering intelligence/information. Both conduct intensive fieldwork, are physically close to the people they scrutinize, and have accepted interviewing/interrogating as a powerful technique in modern society that is at their disposal. Third, because they operate not in laboratories or other more or less controlled settings but in real-life situations, the work of both cops and anthropologists is fundamentally unpredictable and subjective in nature. Their investigations are almost never replicable, the circumstances never identical. These comparisons normally arouse laughter and although they are meant to tease, they can nonetheless be put to good use.

When I started my fieldwork at the police in 2008 as a young researcher, I was no card-carrying ethnographer. I had taken—with much interest I may add—several ethnography courses as an undergraduate student in cultural anthropology and I had conducted fieldwork in Guatemala for several months, but that was about it. So, when I first set foot in a police station in the spring of 2008, I barely knew what to ask and, more importantly, how to ask. Had I read Briggs' *Learning How to Ask* (1986), I would have realized that interviewing police officers comes with a specific set of skills and insights that, when absent, inevitably lead to communication blunders. And I blundered! I believe this had to do with the communication routines and norms that worked their way into the interview situation and my failure to see the extent to which an organizational community like the police is used to very different communicative routines than the anthropologist (cf. Cicourel 1968). So, for example, when I first arrived at the police station to interview rank-and-file officers I thought I came as a trained anthropologist, prepared to embrace emic perspectives and local forms of knowledge (Geertz 1983). So, I mainly asked open questions and barely used an interviewing schedule. To my disappointment, the answers were short and formal, they were very opposite of the narrative material I had hoped to collect. It took me quite a while to realize that this mismatch of expectations may have had to do with the fact that rank-and-file officers often play the role of interviewer as well. And when they do, for instance in stop-and-search encounters or interrogations, the interview either has a formal Q&A structure or is full of tactics, ploys, stratagems, and manoeuvres. I am not saying that my 'informants' (a term that emphasizes the role confusion) could not distinguish interviews in the sphere of criminal justice from academic interviews, but the fact is that people have communication routines that stick to them. (Conversely, I would make a bad police officer, trying to get a life narrative out of every stop-and-search encounter.) In this respect, I had to depart from Briggs' point of view that the 'very success of [an] interview depends ... on the researcher's capacity for allowing native communicative routines to work their way into the interview situation' (Briggs 1986, 28). Had I done so, my interview transcripts would have remained disturbingly short throughout my study.[1]

Furthermore, the communication routines of police officers make it difficult for them to talk about themselves as perpetrators or victims, concepts that are central in discourses about discrimination and racism. In the most stereotypical sense, police officers catch perpetrators and assist victims; they belong to neither of these categories. One can image the difficulties that arise when officers are invited to talk about specific instances of discrimination *within* the police station (remember that my initial focus was on inter-ethnic labour relations). Although I was primarily interested in police discrimination as a systemic problem, understood as a public issue rather than an issue of troubled individual minds, it struck me that native Dutch police officers, mainly at the beginning of my study, appeared to deploy defence strategies to exonerate themselves from blame. In particular, they seemed to use what we can call 'single-out strategies' ('it happens, but I try to stay far away from it'). I found these interviews very difficult, and it sometimes felt as if the interviewees thought that I—a white, middle-class researcher—betrayed them. As I will describe shortly, such difficulties gradually disappeared when my study became more ethnographic; that is, when I moved beyond the use of interviews only and improved my contact with officers. It was also only then that I realized that in many cases, native Dutch officers were perhaps not using defence strategies at all but were simply stating the truth: police discrimination is a systemic problem in which they are often implicated against their will.

Talking about victimhood was often equally difficult in the beginning. Like anthropologists, police officers are used to talking *with* victims but not *as* victims. Had I limited my data gathering endeavours to the first round of interviews, I would have probably concluded that all was well and that we could skip merrily off into the sunset. Moreover, it was only

[1] However, I did indeed benefit form allowing 'native communicative routines' to work their way into the interview situation later on, when I saw the importance of canteen talk and anecdotes for police officers, to which I will return later.

much later that I came to realize that the silencing of victims of discrimination within the organization was part and parcel of police discrimination as a systemic problem. Not only were minority officers not used to talking about themselves as victims; whenever they tried, they were either confronted with psychological discourses on mental resilience, empowerment, self-assertion, and the like—which reframed victims as losers—or they faced a similar neoliberal logic centred on confessions and techniques of the self that gave their superiors more insight into their inner life, insights that were often used against them. In any case, talk of victimhood was either off limits or a risky endeavour.

Initially, it did not dawn on me that the interviews I conducted with them could also be interpreted by officers as an improper probing into their inner life (their experiences, feelings, and emotions, attitudes, opinions, complaints, etc.), very much like the psycho-techniques that some of them lamented. Was I complicit in the neoliberal logic of confessions and the self as the only basis of human agency? This is a question I have been preoccupied with for a very long time and with which I was confronted most directly when a Moroccan-Dutch community officer said to me: 'I hope you're not one of those people who takes everything I said with him only to advance his own career.'

I cannot deny that I was a little hurt by his remark—more so because I aspired to be an engaged anthropologist from the first day of my study—but I understood his concern. After all, on the surface, my interviews resembled the psycho-techniques he objected to (he explicitly mentioned the work of various psycho-technicians as examples). First, I too posed questions of a very personal nature—in my interviews but also in the diaries that eighteen officers kept for a week and in which they were invited to report on specific instances of discrimination and how they experienced these.[2] In a way, my research could also be seen as an act of 'humanization'. Second, many technicians worked in a hit-and-run

[2] The eighteen officers in question had completed a digital diary, which they gave to me prior to the interview. I used what Zimmerman and Wieder dubbed the 'diary–diary–interview' method (Zimmerman and Wieder 1977). I commissioned people to keep an annotated and chronologically organized diary for a week according to a set of instructions. These instructions turned the diarist into a 'surrogate observer' who kept an eye on ethnicity-related or diversity-related events at work. The diarist was questioned about an event according to a who/what/when/where/how formula, providing information regarding the actual event, time, location, people involved, context, etc. I urged diarists to make entries daily. Both ethnic minority (seven) and majority (eleven) officers kept a diary. During the interviews, diarists were prompted to elaborate on their writing and to use it as a springboard to explore other, related events. Whenever possible there was a time span of several weeks between the last day of the diary and the interview, in order to allow for reflection on short-term consequences of reported events.

fashion, as described in Chapter 4, and were completely disconnected from the local contexts in which they worked. Similarly, my interviews were 'constrained encounters' (Briggs 1986) as well. For the first round of interviews, I often made appointments with individual officers, conducted the interviews, and disappeared again—at least for a while. 'Feeding back' to the police departments, as described in Chapter 5, was taken very seriously but did not always involve all interviewees of a particular department. This may have left some of them with negative feelings (for which I apologize). Finally, psycho-technicians focused purely on individuals, without concern for relationships, structure, or context. Although I always used my interviews to study individual experiences as indicative of patterns and developments of wider scope and significance (Blommaert and Dong 2010; more following), I can also understand that interviewees interpreted the fact that I interviewed them individually and separately as an act of individualization in itself.

These, I suppose, are some of the limitations a researcher is confronted with when (s)he exclusively relies on interviewing to gather data and barely knows how to ask (and how to reflect on the answers). Blommaert and Dong (2010) write that there is no such thing as a bad interview because every interview yields something, a discourse organized between two parties (interviewer and interviewee). I agree, but some interviews are simply better than others and, certainly, we ought to take more from the field than interview materials only (Blommaert and Dong agree with both qualifications). Fortunately, the work of Briggs (1986) and others like him came as a timely intervention.

2011–2013: Doing Fieldwork

Things improved substantially once I had decided (and was given permission) to 'shadow' officers in addition to interviewing them. Shadowing is a good substitute for participant observation when the latter is not possible. Since I was not trained as a police officer and thus had to take a non-executive oath at the Police Academy, full-blown participant observation was not an option. The downside of it was that complete immersion in the field was never possible. I was employed by the Police Academy (from January 2011) and most of the time was accepted as a colleague by officers in the field, but at the same time I was continually identified as non-executive and thus not considered a 'real' cop.[3] However, shadowing also comes with several advantages (Czarniawska 2007).

[3] Czarniawska (2007) mentioned the need to negotiate continuously one's access to the field as another downside of shadowing. Due to my employment at the Police Academy, I experienced no difficulties getting access to police teams. Gaining permission from individual police officers to shadow them was relatively

One of the main advantages of shadowing over stationary observation is its mobility. This makes it particularly suitable for police ethnography, since police officers, except when they are doing administrative work, are constantly on the move. I shadowed individual police officers, each time over the course of several weeks. I joined them everywhere: in the office, during car, bicycle, or foot patrols, at community meetings, on house searches, at social gatherings such as after-work drinks or farewell parties, for house visits, during interrogations, etc. Being 'in the shadow' of officers was almost never an issue. To my surprise, I could usually follow them everywhere and only once did I remain in the office at a police officer's urging (this happened when he was about to engage in a very personal conversation with a station chief). The only practical issue was note-taking. Notes were taken relatively inconspicuously during shifts whenever I had the time (often in the back of the car or in a corner of the police station), or immediately after a shift ended, when I arrived home, or at my university office.

Spending so much time together—and in so many different situations—considerably improved my relationships with those officers I shadowed, as well as their companions.[4] After only a short period of time, officers no longer saw me as a 'jet plane ethnographer' (Bate 1997) who only paid them short visits for interviews and quick observations. Prolonged

unproblematic as well. Only once an officer told me that he would not feel comfortable if I shadowed him because he was reintegrating after a period of absence. After some weeks, I shadowed one of his colleagues with whom he often joined a beat (I did not know this beforehand) and we built up a very pleasant working relationship, which ended up with my shadowing him after all.

[4] I joined officers of different kinds of police teams: in Bergen op Zoom I observed detectives (*recherche* in Dutch); in Tilburg I worked with officers of a community policing team (*wijkteam* in Dutch); and in Amsterdam I joined officers of a community policing team as well as a rapid response unit (*noodhulp* in Dutch). Most of these officers almost never worked alone. The detectives I worked with spent most of their time at the station, where they worked together in groups of different sizes (I did not count, but I guess that office spaces had room for four to ten persons). The officers working for the rapid response unit in Amsterdam shared one big office space, which, at first sight, was very chaotic. Chitchat, jokes, tough talk, as well as work-related communication about specific cases, neighbourhoods, and persons of interest went on and on, often all at once. However, when an emergency call came in it was often only a matter of seconds before designated officers were on their way to the scene. They never went alone. The community policing team was in the open office space (in the back of the building, right after the—also open—canteen). Community officers and constables could be found clustered around several workstations. The only ones who occasionally undertook a beat alone were the community officers (sergeants); constables always went in pairs. In Tilburg, people worked in offices that had space for four to six persons.

contacts were visibly appreciated and as a result, some of the communication problems described in the previous section began to disappear. Native Dutch police officers no longer automatically interpreted questions about police discrimination as a reproach. Time afforded us to talk about context, about structure, and about the wider web of human relations that was spun by police practices and policies. These became the focus of the interviews and 'on the beat' conversations. Similarly, those officers who had fallen victim to discrimination or other practices of exclusion began to see that I was not there to simply 'measure their minds' or judge their shortcomings (in terms of mental resilience, multicultural personality, or whatever). Once they realized this, they not only found the courage to talk about *themselves* as victims of discrimination but also about neighbourhood residents and their experiences of exclusion. This, by the way, was also true for some ethnic majority officers.

While shadowing officers I spent dozens of hours with them, roaming around in a police car, watching them writing reports, standing post at the front door during a house search. This gave me plenty of opportunity to appreciate the importance of anecdotes. Before, while using formal interviews and diaries only, I made my best effort to reconstruct real-life events. But due to the Q&A style of questioning that officers used, this turned out to be very difficult. Now, however, I could capitalize on car and canteen talk, allowing another—far more productive—sort of 'native communication routine' to work its way into our conversations. Anecdotes, I believe, are the 'raw diamonds' in fieldwork conversations; they are our best and most valued 'facts' as it is through anecdotes that we find out how our questions resonate in officers' own lifeworlds (Blommaert and Dong 2010, 52). When officers embarked on an anecdote, I never interrupted, not even when they told stories that were not even remotely connected to my area of interest. I learned that sometimes, more can be found out by *not* asking questions (see Blommaert and Dong 2010).

Following officers not only physically but also in their narrative worlds is one of the best ways, I think, to depart from pre-set lines of inquiry and pre-established truths. Paying close attention to anecdotes makes ethnography what Hymes calls more 'democratic': 'a mutual relation of interaction and adaptation' between ethnographers and the people they study (Blommaert and Dong 2010, 12; Hymes 1996, 4). Whenever officers shared an anecdote, either in a private dialogue with me or in the company of other officers, I always attempted to figure out how the police officers in question related to the knowledge they shared through their storytelling. In line with sociolinguistic approaches, I looked at anecdotes (and at conversations and interviews more generally) as communicative events that involve both referential and indexical modes of signification. The *referential* function of language 'lies in its ability to point to persons, objects, events, and processes' (Briggs 1986, 42), and I focused on it to get a grip on the correspondence between the 'content' of an officer's expressions and some state of affairs in 'the real world'. Whenever possible, I triangulated different accounts of the same event. I did so not under the presumption that this could give us the 'objective truth' but because I believe that human intersubjectivity lies at the foundation of anthropological investigations (cf. Bunzl 2002). As such, the production of a certain 'truth' about something becomes an intersubjective enterprise, which is neither completely objective nor completely subjective but dependent upon a mutual understanding of the world by different and collaborating or conflicting subjects—including the ethnographer (Ong 1987).

In addition to the referential function of language, I also addressed its *indexical* function in my analysis, as the referential function is only one part of language use. Acts of communication also 'produce *indexical* meaning: social meaning, interpretive leads between what is said and the social occasion in which it is being produced' (Blommaert 2005, 11). Through an indexical analysis we learn about the context in which certain expressions are uttered (the social situation) as well as about social roles and interaction goals. I was particularly interested in anecdotes that were told by officers in the presence of others (interlocutors but also eavesdroppers and overhearers), because these provided an extra opportunity to study social relationships. For example, in Chapter 2 (in the section The Everydayness of Migrant-Hostile Policing) I recounted the thoughts and feelings of officers about 'road blocks' and 'target groups'. The officers present on that occasion shared some anecdotes about this topic—first in the car on our way to the gas station where the traffic control took place, and later during the traffic control. Mehmet, a Turkish-Dutch senior constable, actively participated in this storytelling and voiced his thoughts aggressively about why certain minority groups deserved it to be severely scrutinized by police. He was clearly trying to impress his colleagues with his tough stance towards minorities (something that was rather quaint considering his own ethnic background), but something was not quite right about it. Between this event and my (scheduled) interview with Mehmet, it slowly dawned on me that Mehmet's behaviour was a 'public performance', which, as we know from Scott, often takes place to appeal to the expectations of the more powerful; 'out of prudence, fear or the desire to curry favour' (Scott 1990, 2). Scott uses the term 'public transcripts' to describe the 'open interaction' between people; these transcripts, where they are not 'positively misleading', are 'unlikely to tell the whole story about power relations'. Indeed, during our interview—and thus in a completely different setting—Mehmet talked in a totally different way about these issues: he empathized with ethnic minority youth (who, he said, must surely grow tired from being stopped and frisked ten times a day), and argued for the need of a 'professional' police (meaning 'neutral' and 'fair' officers). None of this is to argue that either backstage or onstage performances ought to be given priority in our search for 'the truth'. Rather, the differences, contradictions, and tensions between different (forms of) talk in different contexts make it interesting to take the referential and indexical functions of language under scrutiny.

A focus on anecdotes transformed my ethnography into a mutual relation of interaction and adaptation between me, as the ethnographer, and the officers involved in my study. In addition to officers feeding me with anecdotes, I also often provided them with the same sort of materials. More specifically, I shared (anonymized) anecdotes with other officers, which I had collected at other police departments while having informal talks or formal interviews. I did this for both practical and analytical reasons. Sometimes, it was necessary to get a conversation started. Not everyone is equally talkative and occasionally offering officers an anecdote to reflect on proved fruitful. At the same time, transporting anecdotes across local policing contexts was another heuristic to lift instances to a level of relevance higher than just the event and to interpret part–whole relationships (Blommaert and Dong 2010). As I began to lift anecdotes out of their context and started to discuss them with officers employed by various departments, particular cases became 'cases of something', part of a larger class, category, social development, etc. These generalizations allowed me to develop a theoretical apparatus that I could subsequently bring to bear on new data. In this way, I developed my theories on biocracy/bureaucracy, state proximity/externality, and the like.

As briefly described in Chapter 4, this procedure helped me to understand uniquely situated events as crystallizations of various layers of context; both micro-contexts that are more changeable, accidental, and unpredictable, as well as macro-contexts such as policies, politics, organizational structures, etc. (Blommaert and Dong 2010). By looking for the larger issues in smaller places and events, to borrow from Eriksen (1995), I was able to develop the sort of sociological imagination needed to counter neoliberalism and its dogmatic focus on individuals and introspections. Scaling up and down in my analysis, I created an interplay between my empirical data and theoretical apparatus—'a dialectic between reflection and immediacy' (Rabinow 1977, 38)—that enabled me to question the official stance of the NP with respect to police discrimination (i.e. that it can be relegated to the level of incidents and individuals). Herein lies the subversive power, the counter-hegemonic potential, of ethnography: by constantly paying attention to text *and* context, ideas that give primacy to the individual and the incidental can be put into perspective, questioned, or dwarfed by juxtaposing them with alternatives and dissident perspectives. As Marcus (1998) reminds us, this helps us rethink and destabilize established orders. It is important to state that I did not simply consider something a higher-order phenomenon (i.e. a structural thing) when it occurred frequently and regularly. I did not simply add up events and then claim I had found 'structures', 'systems', 'practices', etc. Rather, I always tried to identify text trajectories that could help me connect lower-order to higher-order phenomena (cf. Blommaert 2001). Thus, for instance, I explored textual links between micro-deportations and migration policies and found them in talk about 'zones'; I looked for intertextualities connecting everyday stop-and-search encounters and predictive policing strategies and found them in talk about 'target groups';[5] I was interested in the relationship between the work of psycho-technicians and the career inequalities between officers with various ethnic backgrounds and found it in discourses of authenticity and craftsmanship.

In this way I began to see how small things became meaningful in relation to bigger things and how these bigger things had their grounding in small things.[6] Moreover, I also shared my analyses with officers in the field. This greatly enhanced the intersubjective character of my study. On the one hand, this process led to a host of insightful suggestions, criticisms, and corrections of issues that I had missed. Feeding back my findings and analyses to officers helped me to commit to a fair construction of knowledge that balances and checks different perspectives and interpretations (Mutsaers et al. 2015; Van der Aa 2012). For example, it was not until very late in my fieldwork that I began to understand—as a result of officers' corrections—that police racism does not lead to the total submission of ethnic minority youth. Whenever I shadowed officers who were busy with stop-and-search activities, all I could see was a total subordination of juveniles vis-á-vis police. When I shared my observations with officers, they brought to my attention that this was only part of the story. What I did not see—they argued—were the more imperceptible types of resistance used by juveniles to question police authority: false compliance, slander, mocking, sabotage, collective theatre, playing innocent, disguised aggression, etc., the low-profile forms of resistance described by Scott in *Weapons of the Weak* (1985) and *Domination and the Arts of Resistance* (1990). Such corrections greatly advanced my understanding of police power.

Feeding back my findings and analyses also helped officers to understand their own daily habits, customs, or struggles through the analytical frames that I offered them. This too was part of the sort of 'epistemic solidarity' (Van der Aa 2012, 98) that I attempted to have with officers.

[5] As I write the final pages of this book, in July 2017, news has emerged that The Netherlands is going to be the first country in the world that will use 'big data' for predictive policing on a national level (in countries such as the United Kingdom and the United States it is only used in local contexts). The NP intends to implement the so-called Crime Anticipation System nationwide in 2017.

[6] By 'small' I do not mean inconsequential or unimportant.

Such solidarity is driven by praxis and takes 'knowledge as a crucial instrument for social change. In order for this knowledge to really address the problems at hand, it needs to be shared and cooperative' (Van der Aa 2012, 98). This includes knowledge-based collaboration with police (despite its many challenges, which we encountered some in the previous chapter). For example, one day in 2013, I had a conversation with a young Turkish-Dutch senior constable, Serkan, whom I had come to know very well over the years. He said that for some time, he felt that he was pretending to be someone else, someone he did not want to be. He had adopted certain personality features he felt were not of his own making or desire. He talked about how he interchangeably experienced his 'real me' and 'fake me'. As he told me this, I remembered a discussion we had in 2008, in which he already mentioned these 'two Serkans' that alternately popped up at work. I suggested that this was a long-lasting problem and he agreed; it was taxing and very hard to come to grips with, he said. His employer offered him psychological help and shortly thereafter, Serkan had accepted the sort of psychologism that is centred on mental instability, identity conflicts, and so on, as *the* explanation of all his problems. When I had listened to him for a while, I decided to suggest an alternative approach. Perhaps his problem was not principally of a psychological but of a sociological nature. I reminded Serkan of something *he* had told *me* before, that he felt confronted with a form of identity regulation at work, which constantly drove him to behave in a different way than he normally behaved. Over time, these interventions turned him into a different person. I also told him that he was not the only one who had been subjected to such forms of labour control. We talked at length about the popularity of biocratic management at the police and about its negative effects. In the end, Serkan became a staunch defender of bureaucratic structures and checks and balances and one of the key figures in the stop forms task force described in the previous chapter.

Thus far I have largely dealt with how I collected, processed, and analysed discursive materials (anecdotes, conversations, interviews, and other forms of text, talk, or speech) that tell us something about how officers talk about (and reflect on) what they do and say. As noted earlier, however, these are not the only sort of materials one brings from the field. One of the great advantages of shadowing over more traditional methods such as participant observation is that the former does not require a simultaneous action and observation (Czarniawska 2007). This improves the chance to observe what people do and say, in addition to studying how they talk about the things they do and say. In light of this distinction, Van Maanen discriminates 'operational data' from 'presentational data':

Field data represent primarily the ethnographer's recording of first-order concepts as they arise from the observed talk and action of participants

> in the studied scene. This information is of two generic but distinct types. First, there is the 'operational data' which document the running stream of spontaneous conversations and activities engaged in and observed by the ethnographer while in the field. These data surface in known and describable contexts and pertain to the everyday problematics of informants going about their affairs. Second, there are the 'presentational data' which concern those appearances that informants strive to maintain (or enhance) in the eyes of the fieldworker, outsiders and strangers in general, work colleagues, close and intimate associates, and to varying degrees, themselves ... In short, operational data deal with observed activity (behaviour per se) and presentational data with the appearances put forth by informants as these activities are talked about and otherwise symbolically projected within the research setting. (Van Maanen 1979, 542)

The primacy of observations is one of the methodological advantages of shadowing and permits the ethnographer to also preserve an outsider's stance in addition to the proximity to his or her subject that allows him or her to build trust and reciprocity (Czarniawska 2007). In a similar vein, Fassin writes about the combination of 'presence' and 'distance' (Fassin 2013). 'With presence, comes a reciprocal acquaintance between the observer and observed: a form of mutual trust progressively develops, which makes possible an access to the everyday and the common sense of those under study' (Fassin 2013, xi–xii). Distance, however, means stepping aside and taking the perspective of an outsider. This combination of presence and distance—contact and critique, familiarity and estrangement, insider and outsider positions—allows the ethnographer to collect both presentational and operational data.

Allow me to offer an example. One of the police departments where I had worked for some months was managed by a station chief who appeared to be a forerunner in combating illicit profiling and other forms of police racism. In his conversations with officers and with me, he seized every opportunity to make clear that he condemned such practices. He was also the one who called together the district management team to talk about ethnic profiling, described in Chapter 2. Under his leadership, police racism became a subject of lively interest. Extrapolating from these presentational data, he was a 'good cop'. The operational data that I gathered on this station chief, however, pointed in a different direction. His actual behaviour turned out to be rather migrant-hostile. After I had turned off the recorder after one of our interviews, he started talking about the integrity of Turkish-Dutch officers in the district and asked me to keep my eyes open for corruption. After all, it was among Turkish-Dutch officers that corruption cases most often came to light, he said. At these critical moments, I could keep my distance and acted as an outsider. I never paid heed to his demand.

Let there be no mistake about it: this is not to argue that operational data are essentially better or more trustworthy than presentational data. The various cases discussed in this book tell us this much. Both Karin and Harry talked about how they were forced to discriminate against other ethnic groups (see Chapter 2). Had I only looked at the operational data—the running stream of activities—I would have come to very different conclusions. Both officers did indeed discriminate against individuals from ethnic minorities, but not because they wanted to: they would have been sanctioned by their superiors if they had done otherwise. The representational data that I retrieved from my conversations with them, gave me a more 'objective' perspective on everyday police activities such as proactive controls, if by 'objectivity' we mean that many objects and perspectives were used to gather information (Czarniawska 2007). Objectivity, as defined in opposition to subjectivity, is never possible in anthropological investigations that, as I wrote before, are intersubjective to their very core. Subjects have feelings, sentiments, emotions, and so on. I do too. I never made it a secret that a commitment to justice and equality has galvanized this book. Then again, I agree with Geertz who once wrote that he has 'never been impressed by the argument that, as complete objectivity is impossible … one might as well let one's sentiments run loose … That is like saying that as a perfectly aseptic environment is impossible, one might as well conduct surgery in a sewer' (Geertz 1973, 30). Throughout my ethnographic project I have given my best efforts to come as close to reality as possible, by combining operational and presentational data, distance and presence, local knowledge and abstraction. Indeed, very much like cops do.

References

Aas, K.F. 2011. '"Crimmigrant" bodies and bona fide travellers: Surveillance, citizenship and global governance'. *Theoretical Criminology 15* (3): 331-46.

Abu-Lughod, L. 2016. 'The cross-publics of ethnography: The case of "the Muslim woman"'. *American Ethnologist 43* (4): 595-608.

Adang, O., H. Quint, and R. van der Wal. 2010. *Zijn Wij Anders? Waarom Nederland Geen Grootschalige Etnische Rellen Heeft.* Apeldoorn: Politieacademie.

Albrecht, H-J. 2007. 'Legitimacy and criminal justice: Inequality and discrimination in the German criminal-justice system'. In *Legitimacy and Criminal Justice: International Perspectives*, edited by T. Tyler, 302-32. New York, NY: Russell Sage Foundation.

Algemeen Dagblad. 2015. 'Nederlandse politie discrimineert'. 9 June, <https://www.ad.nl/binnenland/nederlandse-politie-discrimineert~a8346f08/>.

Aliverti, A. 2012. 'Making people criminal: The role of the criminal law in immigration enforcement'. *Theoretical Criminology 16* (4): 417-34.

Aliverti, A. 2017. 'The wrongs of unlawful immigration'. *Criminal Law and Philosophy 11* (2): 375-91.

Alvesson, M. and H. Willmott. 2002. 'Identity regulation as organizational control: Producing the appropriate individual'. *Journal of Management Studies 39* (5): 619-44.

Amar, P. 2010. 'Introduction. New racial missions of policing: Comparative studies of state authority, urban governance, and security technology in the twenty-first century'. *Ethnic and Racial Studies 33* (4): 575-92.

Amnesty International. 2013. *Proactief politieoptreden vormt risico voor mensen-rechten. Etnisch profileren onderkennen en aanpakken.* Viewed 29 November 2013, <http://www.amnesty.nl>.

Anderson, B. 2011. 'Facing the future enemy: US counterinsurgency doctrine and the pre-insurgent'. *Theory, Culture & Society 28* (7–8): 216-40.

Andersson, R. 2014. *Illegality, Inc.: Clandestine Migration and the Business of Bordering Europe.* Oakland, CA: University of California Press.

Andrijasevic, R. 2010. 'From exception to excess: Detention and deportation across the Mediterranean space'. In *The Deportation Regime. Sovereignty, Space, and the Freedom of Movement*, edited by N. De Genova and N. Peutz, 147-65. Durham, NC: Duke University Press.

Anthony, P.D. 1977. *The Ideology of Work.* Abingdon: Routledge.

Arendt, H. 1961. *Between Past and Future.* New York, NY: Penguin Books.

Baritz, L. 1960. *The Servants of Power. A History of the Use of Social Science in American Industry*. New York, NY: John Wiley.
Barry, A., T. Osborne, and N. Rose. eds. 1996. *Foucault and Political Reason*. New York, NY: Routledge.
Barth, F. ed. 1969. *Ethnic Groups and Boundaries. The Social Organization of Cultural Difference*. Long Grove, IL: Waveland Press, Inc.
Bate, S.P. 1997. 'Whatever happened to organizational anthropology? A review of the field of organizational ethnography and anthropological studies'. *Human Relations 50* (9): 1147-75.
Bauman, Z. 1989. *Modernity and the Holocaust*. London: Polity Press.
Bauman, Z. 1998. *Globalization. The Human Consequences*. Cambridge: Polity Press.
Bauman, Z. 2000a. 'Social issues of law and order'. *The British Journal of Criminology 40* (2): 205-21.
Bauman, Z. 2000b. *Liquid Modernity*. Cambridge: Polity Press.
Bayley, D. and C.D. Shearing. 1996. 'The future of policing'. *Law & Society Review 30* (3): 585-606.
Becker, H. 1967. 'Whose side are we on?' *Social Problems 14* (3): 239-47.
Beek, J. 2012. '"There should be no open doors in the police": Criminal investigations in northern Ghana as boundary work'. *Journal of Modern African Studies 50* (4): 551-72.
Beek, J. and M. Göpfert. 2012. 'Police violence in West Africa: Perpetrators' and ethnographers' dilemmas'. *Ethnography 14* (4): 477-500.
Beek, J., M. Göpfert, O. Owen, and J. Steinberg. 2017. 'Introduction: Policing in Africa reconsidered'. In *Police in Africa*, edited by J. Beek, M. Göpfert, O. Owen, and J. Steinberg, 1-18. London: Hurst & Company.
Beeman, W.O. 1987. 'Anthropology and the print media'. *Anthropology Today 3* (3): 2-4.
Bell, V. 1996. 'The promise of liberalism and the performance of freedom'. In *Foucault and Political Reason*, edited by A. Barry, T. Osborne, and N. Rose, 81-97. New York, NY: Routledge.
Benedict, R. 1934. *Patterns of Culture*. Boston, MA: Houghton Mifflin Company.
Berger, B.M. 1985. 'Foreword'. In *Frame Analysis. An Essay on the Organization of Experience*, edited by E. Goffman, xi-xviii. Boston, MA: Northeastern University Press, original work published 1974.
Berger, P. 1973. '"Sincerity" and "authenticity" in modern society'. *The Public Interest 31*: 81-90.
Bielby, W.T. 2008. 'Promoting racial diversity at work: Challenges and solutions'. In *Diversity at Work*, edited by A.P. Brief, 53-86. Cambridge: Cambridge University Press.
Bierschenk, T. 2017. 'Who are the police in Africa?' In *Police in Africa*, edited by J. Beek, M. Göpfert, O. Owen, and J. Steinberg, 103-20. London: Hurst & Company.
Bigo, D. 2006. 'Internal and external aspects of security'. *European Security 15* (4): 385-404.

Binkley, S. 2011. 'Psychological life as enterprise: Social practice and government of neo-liberal interiority'. *History of the Human Sciences 24* (3): 83-102.

Bittner, E. 1970. *The Functions of the Police in Modern Society. A Review of Background Factors, Current Practices, and Possible Role Models*. Chevy Chase, MD: National Institute of Mental Health Centre for Studies of Crime and Delinquency.

Blommaert, J. 2001. 'Context is/as critique'. *Critique of Anthropology 21* (1): 13-32.

Blommaert, J. 2005. *Discourse*. Cambridge: Cambridge University Press.

Blommaert, J. 2007. 'Sociolinguistic scales'. *Intercultural Pragmatics 4* (1): 1-19.

Blommaert, J. 2009. 'Language, asylum and the national order'. *Current Anthropology 50* (4): 415-41.

Blommaert, J. 2013a. *Ethnography, Superdiversity and Linguistic Landscapes. Chronicles of Complexity*. Bristol: Multilingual Matters.

Blommaert, J. 2013b. 'Review article. Policy, policing and the ecology of social norms: Ethnographic monitoring revisited'. *International Journal of Sociology of Language 219*: 123-40.

Blommaert, J. and J. Dong. 2010. *Ethnographic Fieldwork. A Beginner's Guide*. Bristol: Multilingual Matters.

Blommaert, J., P. Mutsaers, and H. Siebers. 2012. *De 360° Werknemer. De Nieuwe Arbeidscultuur en de Eindeloze Concurrentie*. Berchem: EPO.

Bobb, M. 2003. 'Civilian oversight of the police in the United States'. *Saint Louis University Public Law Review* 22: 151-66.

Body-Gendrot, S. 2010. 'Police marginality, racial logics and discrimination in the banlieues of France'. *Ethnic and Racial Studies 33* (4): 656-74.

Bonilla, Y. and J. Rosa. 2015. '#Ferguson: Digital protest, hashtag ethnography, and the racial politics of social media in the United States'. *American Ethnologist 42* (1): 4-17.

Bonjour, S. 2010. 'Between integration provision and selection mechanisms. Party politics, judicial constraints, and the making of French and Dutch policies of civic integration abroad'. *European Journal of Migration and Law 12* (3): 299-318.

Bonnet, F. and C. Caillault. 2015. 'The invader, the enemy within and they-who-must-not-be-named: How police talk about minorities in Italy, the Netherlands and France'. *Ethnic and Racial Studies 38* (7): 1185-201.

Boogaard, B. and C. Roggeband. 2010. 'Paradoxes of intersectionality. Theorizing inequality in the Dutch police force through structure and agency'. *Organization 17* (1): 53-75.

Bosworth, M. and M. Guild. 2008. 'Governing through migration control. Security and citizenship in Britain'. *British Journal of Criminology 48* (6): 703-19.

Bouman, G. 2013. *Zonder onderscheid het verschil zien*. Viewed 5 May 2014, <http://www.politie.nl>.

Bouman, G. 2015. 'De anderen'. Intranet National Police of the Netherlands.

Bourgeois, P. 2002. 'Understanding inner-city poverty: Resistance and self-destruction under U.S. apartheid'. In *Exotic No More. Anthropology on the Front Lines*, edited by J. MacClancy, 15-32. Chicago, IL: University of Chicago Press.

Bowling, B. and J. Sheptycki. 2012. *Global Policing*. London: Sage.

Bradley, D. and C. Nixon. 2009. 'Ending the "dialogue of the deaf": Evidence and policing policies and practices. An Australian case study'. *Police Practice & Research. An International Journal 10* (5): 423-35.

Braverman, H. 1974. *Labor and Monopoly Capital. The Degradation of Work in the Twentieth Century*. New York, NY: Monthly Review Press.

Briggs, C.L. 1986. *Learning How to Ask: A Sociolinguistic Appraisal of the Role of the Interview in Social Science Research*. Cambridge: Cambridge University Press.

Broeders, D. 2010. 'Return to sender? Administrative detention of irregular migrants in Germany and the Netherlands'. *Punishment & Society 12* (2): 169-86.

Brondo, K.V. 2010. 'Practicing anthropology in a time of crisis: 2009 Year in review'. *American Anthropologist 112* (2): 208-18.

Brown, G.R. 2016. 'The blue line on thin ice: Police use of force modifications in the era of cameraphones and *Youtube*'. *The British Journal of Criminology 56* (2): 293-312.

Brubaker, R. 2002. 'Ethnicity without groups'. *Archives Européenes de Sociologie 43*: 163-89.

Bunzl, M. 2002. 'Foreword to Johannes Fabian's *Time and the Other: Syntheses of a Critical Anthropology*'. New York, NY: Columbia University Press.

Burawoy, M. 2005. '2004 Presidential Address: For Public Sociology'. *American Sociological Review 70*: 4–28.

Buro Jansen & Jansen. 2016. *Wetenschappers in Dienst van de Overheid: Het Onderzoek van de Universiteit van Leiden naar Etnisch Profileren in Den Haag. Een Reconstructie*. Viewed 20 December 2016, <http://www.burojansen.nl>.

Buur, L. 2006. 'Reordering society: Vigilantism and expressions of sovereignty in Port Elizabeth's Townships'. *Development and Change 37* (4): 735-57.

Cabot, H. 2018. 'The good police officer: Ambivalent intimacies with the state in the Greek asylum procedure'. In *The Anthropology of Police*, edited by K. Karpiak and W. Garriott. 209–29. London: Routledge.

Caldeira, T.P.R. 2002. 'The paradox of police violence in democratic Brazil'. *Ethnography* 3 (3): 235-63.

Cameron, D. 2000. *Good to Talk?* Los Angeles, CA: Sage.

Campbell, A. 1996. 'Tricky tropes: Styles of the popular and the pompous'. In *Popularizing Anthropology*, edited by J. MacClancy and C. McDonaugh, 58-82. New York, NY: Routledge.

Campbell, S. and C. Roberts. 2007. 'Migration, ethnicity and competing discourses in the job interview: Synthesizing the institutional and personal'. *Discourse & Society 18* (3): 242-71.

Çankaya, S. 2008. *Welkom in Politië*. Amsterdam: Drukkerij Elco b.v.

Çankaya, S. 2011. *Buiten Veiliger dan Binnen. In- en Uitsluiting van Etnische Minderheden binnen de Politieorganisatie*. Delft: Eburon.

Çankaya, S. 2012. *De Controle van Marsmannetjes en Ander Schorriemorrie. Het Beslissingsproces tijdens Proactief Politiewerk*. Den Haag: Boom Lemma.

Çankaya, S. and P. Mutsaers. 2015. Minder bureaucratie betekent bij politie meer discriminatie. *NRC Handelsblad*, 13 July, <https://www.nrc.nl/nieuws/2015/07/13/minder-bureaucratie-betekent-bij-politie-meer-disc-1514609-a939424>.

Carter, J. 2000. 'New public management and equal opportunities in the NHS'. *Critical Social Policy 20* (1): 61-83.

Choongh, S. 1998. 'Policing the dross: A social disciplinary model of policing'. *The British Journal of Criminology 38* (4): 623-34.

Chrifi, A. 2010. *De Regisseur van je Eigen Leven*. Groningen: Uitgever PAMAC.

Cicourel, A. 1968. *The Social Organization of Juvenile Justice*. New Brunswick, NJ: Transaction Publishers.

Comaroff, J.L. and J. Comaroff. 2004. 'Policing culture, cultural policing: Law and social order in postcolonial South Africa'. *Law and Social Inquiry 29* (3): 513-45.

Comaroff, J.L. and J. Comaroff. 2006a. 'Preface. In *Law and Disorder in the Postcolony*, edited by J. Comaroff and J.L. Comaroff, vii-x. Chicago, IL: University of Chicago Press.

Comaroff, J.L. and J. Comaroff. 2006b. 'Law and disorder in the postcolony: An introduction'. In *Law and Disorder in the Postcolony*, edited by J. Comaroff and J.L. Comaroff, 1-56. Chicago, IL: University of Chicago Press.

Comaroff, J.L. and J. Comaroff. 2007. 'Law and disorder in the postcolony'. *Social Anthropology 15* (2): 133-52.

Comaroff, J. 2013. 'Foreword'. In *Policing and Contemporary Governance. The Anthropology of Police in Practice*, edited by W. Garriott, xi-xxi. New York, NY: Palgrave MacMillan.

Coser, L.A. 1974. *Greedy Institutions. Patterns of Undivided Commitment*. New York, NY: The Free Press.

Costea, B., N. Crump, and K. Amiridis. 2008. 'Managerialism, the therapeutic habitus and the self in contemporary organizing'. *Human Relations 61* (5): 661-85.

Coutin, S.B. 2011. 'The rights of noncitizens in the United States'. *The Annual Review of Law and Social Science* 7: 289-308.

Coutin, S.B. and E. Vogel. 2016. 'Migrant narratives and ethnographic tropes: Navigating tragedy, creating possibilities'. *Journal of Contemporary Ethnography 46* (6): 631-44.

Covaleski, M.A., M.W. Dirsmith, J.B. Heian, and S. Samuel. 1998. 'The calculated and the avowed: Techniques of discipline and struggles over identity in big six public accounting firms'. *Administrative Science Quarterly 43* (2): 293-327.

Coxe, W.W. 1940. 'Professional problems of applied psychology'. *Journal of Consulting Psychology 4* (3): 96-103.

Coupland, D. and M. Reed. 2004. 'Introduction: Bureaucracy in the age of enterprise'. *Organization 11* (1): 5-12.

Crouch, D. 2016. Danish children's rights activist fined for people trafficking. *The Guardian*, 11 March.

Cruikshank, B. 1996. 'Revolutions within: Self-government and self-esteem'. In *Foucault and Political Reason*, edited by A. Barry, T. Osborne, and N. Rose, 231-52. New York, NY: Routledge.

Czarniawska, B. 2007. *Shadowing and Other Techniques for Doing Fieldwork in Modern Societies*. Herndon: Copenhagen Business School Press.

Da Silva, G.M.D. and I. Cano. 2007. 'Between damage reduction and community policing: The case of Pavão-Pavãozinho-Cantagalo in Rio de Janeiro's favelas'. In *Legitimacy and Criminal Justice: International Perspectives*, edited by T. Tyler, 186-214. New York, NY: Russell Sage Foundation.

Danen, R. 2015. Doorbreek het zwijgen over racistisch gedrag van politie. *Trouw*, 18 July.

De Genova, N.P. 2002. 'Migrant "illegality" and deportability in everyday life'. *Annual Review of Anthropology 31*: 419-47.

De Jong, M. and C. van der Veen. 2011. *Qatgebruik onder Somaliërs in Nederland*. Viewed 7 March 2014, <http://www.rijksoverheid.nl>.

De Koning, A. 2017. '"Handled with care". Diffuse policing and the production of inequality in Amsterdam'. *Ethnography 18* (4):535–55.

De Leeuw, M. and S. van Wichelen. 2012. 'Civilizing migrants: Integration, culture and citizenship'. *European Journal of Cultural Studies 15* (2): 195-210.

De Vries, S. 2010. *Diversiteit: Hoofd, Hart en Buik. De Inclusieve Aanpak*. Assen: Koninklijke Van Gorcum BV.

Denyer Willis, G. 2015. *The Killing Consensus. Police, Organized Crime, and the Regulation of Life and Death in Urban Brazil*. Oakland, CA: University of California Press.

Denyer Willis, G. 2016. *Policing, ethnography and abandonment in Latin America*. Viewed 20 September 2017, <http://www.law.ox.ac.uk>.

DiFruscia, K.T. 2012. 'Work rage: The invention of a human resource management anti-conflictual fable'. *Anthropology of Work Review 33* (2): 89-100.

Dijkstra, C. 2014. *Anders Kijken. Van Probleemgericht Sturen naar Contextgericht Beïnvloeden*. Houten: Badoux.

Diphoorn, T. and E. Grassiani. 2016. 'Securitizing capital: A processual-relational approach to pluralized security'. *Theoretical Criminology 20* (4): 430-55.

Donovan, J.M. 2008. *Legal Anthropology. An Introduction*. Lanham, MD: AltaMira Press.

Douglas, M. 1987. *How Institutions Think*. Abingdon and New York, NY: Routledge.

Douglas, M. 1992. *Risk and Blame. Essays in Cultural Theory*. New York, NY: Routledge.

Douglas, M. and A. Wildavsky. 1983. *Risk and Culture. An Essay on the Selection of Technological and Environmental Dangers*. Berkeley, CA: University of California Press.

Du Gay, P. 1994. 'Making up manager: Bureaucracy, enterprise, and the liberal art of separation'. *The British Journal of Sociology 45* (4): 655-74.

Du Gay, P. 1999. 'Is Bauman's bureau Weber's bureau?: A comment'. *The British Journal of Sociology 50* (4): 575-87.

Du Gay, P. 2005. 'The values of bureaucracy: An introduction'. In *The Values of Bureaucracy*, edited by P. Du Gay, 1-16. Oxford: Oxford University Press.

Durkheim, E. 1997. *The Division of Labor in Society*. New York, NY: The Free Press.

Eakin, H. 2016. 'Liberal, harsh Denmark'. *The New York Review of Books LXIII* (4): 34-6.

Epp, C.R., S. Maynard-Moody, and D. Haider-Markel. 2014. *Pulled Over. How Police Stops Define Race and Citizenship*. Chicago, IL: University of Chicago Press.

Eriksen, T.H. 1995. *Small Places, Large Issues. An Introduction to Social and Cultural Anthropology (3rd Edition)*. London: Pluto Press.

Eriksen, T.H. 2006. *Engaging Anthropology. The Case for a Public Presence*. London: Bloomsbury.

Evans-Prichard, E.E. 1946. 'Applied anthropology'. *Africa XVI*: 92-101.

Fairclough, N. 1992. *Discourse and Social Change*. Cambridge: Polity Press.

Fassin, D. 2013a. *Enforcing Order. An Ethnography of Urban Policing*. Cambridge: Polity Press.

Fassin, D. 2013b. 'Why ethnography matters: On anthropology and its publics'. *Cultural Anthropology 28* (4): 621-46.

Fassin, D. 2014. 'Petty states of exception: The contemporary policing of the urban poor'. In *The Anthropology of Security: Perspectives from the Frontline of Policing, Counter-terrorism and Border Control*, edited by M. Maguire, C. Frois, and N. Zurawski, 104-17. London: Pluto Press.

Fassin, D. 2015. 'The public afterlife of ethnography'. *American Ethnologist* 42 (4): 592-609.

Fassin, D. 2018. 'A moral interpretation of police deviance'. In *The Anthropology of Police*, edited by K. Karpiak and W. Garriott, 175–87. London: Routledge.

Fekete, L. 2005. 'The deportation machine: Europe, asylum and human rights'. *Race & Class 47* (1): 64-91.

Fekete, L. 2011. 'Accelerated removals: The human costs of EU deportation policies'. *Race & Class 52* (4): 89-97.

Ferguson, J. 2012. 'Structures of responsibility'. *Ethnography 13* (4): 558-62.

Fleming, P. 2014a. *Resisting Work. The Corporatization of Life and Its Discontents*. Philadelphia, PA: Temple University Press.

Fleming, P. 2014b. 'Review article: When "life itself" goes to work: Reviewing shifts in organizational life through the lens of biopower'. *Human Relations 67* (7): 875-901.

Flentrop, L. and S. De Vries. 2011. *Vakmanschap met een Plus*. Den Haag: OBT.

Foucault, M. 1972. *Power/Knowledge. Selected Interviews and Other Writings 1972–1977*. New York, NY: Pantheon Books.

Foucault, M. 2008. *The Birth of Biopolitics: Lectures at the Collège de France, 1978–1979*. London: Palgrave.

Garriott, W. 2013. 'Introduction. Police in practice: Policing and the project of contemporary governance'. In *Policing and Contemporary Governance. The Anthropology of Police in Practice*, edited by W. Garriott, 1-30. New York, NY: Palgrave MacMillan.

Geertz, C. 1973. *The Interpretation of Cultures*. New York, NY: Perseus Books Group.

Geertz, C. 1983. *Local Knowledge*. London: Fontana Press.

Geertz, C. 2004. 'What is a state if it is not a sovereign? Reflections on politics in complicated places'. *Current Anthropology 45* (5): 577-93.

Gellner, E. 1994. *Conditions of Liberty*. London: Penguin Press.

Gershon, I. 2011. 'Neoliberal agency'. *Current Anthropology 52* (4): 537-55.

Gibney, M.J. 2008. 'Asylum and the expansion of deportation in the United Kingdom'. *Government and Opposition 43* (2): 146-67.

Giddens, A. 1990. *The Consequences of Modernity*. Cambridge: Polity Press.

Goffman, A. 2014. *On the Run. Fugitive Life in an American City*. Chicago, IL: The University of Chicago Press.

Goffman, E. 1961. *Asylums. Essays on the Social Situation of Mental Patients and Other Inmates*. London: Penguin Books.

Goffman, E. 1974. *Frame Analysis. An Essay on the Organization of Experience*. Boston, MA: Northeastern University Press.

Goldstein, D. 2003. '"In our own hands": Lynching, justice and the law in Bolivia'. *American Ethnologist 30* (1): 22-43.

Goldstein, D. 2010. 'Toward a critical anthropology of security'. *Current Anthropology 51* (4): 487-517.

Goldstein, J. 1960. 'Police discretion not to invoke the criminal process: Low-visibility decisions in the administration of justice'. *The Yale Law Journal 69* (4): 543-94.

Gomberg-Muñoz, R. 2013. '2012 Public anthropology year in review: Actually, Rick, Florida could use a few more anthropologists'. *American Anthropologist 115* (2): 286-96.

Gonzales, R.G. and L.R. Chavez. 2012. '"Awakening to a nightmare": Abjectivity and illegality in the lives of undocumented 1.5-generation Latino immigrants in the United States'. *Current Anthropology 53* (3): 255-81.

Goodey, J. 2006. 'Ethnic profiling, criminal (in)justice and minority populations'. *Critical Criminology 14* (3): 207-12.

Göpfer

Gordon, C. 1991. 'Governmental rationality: An introduction'. In *The Foucault Effect. Studies in Governmentality*, edited by G. Burchell, C. Gordon, and P. Miller, 1-52. Chicago, IL: The University of Chicago Press.

Gore, C. and D. Pratten. 2003. 'The politics of plunder: The rhetorics of order and disorder in southern Nigeria'. *African Affairs 102* (407): 211-40.

Göpfert, M. 2016. 'Repairing the law: The search for justice in the Nigerien gendarmerie'. *Theoretical Criminology 20* (4): 446-61.

Gowricharn, R. and S. Çankaya. 2017. 'Policing the nation: Acculturation and street-level bureaucrats in professional life'. *Sociology 51* (5): 1101–17.

Grey, C. and H. Willmott. eds. 2005. *Critical Management Studies. A Reader*. Oxford: Oxford University Press.

Grillo, R.D. 2003. 'Cultural essentialism and cultural anxiety'. *Anthropological Theory 3* (2): 157-73.

Groenendijk, K. 2011. 'Pre-departure integration strategies in the European Union: Integration or immigration policy?' *European Journal of Migration and Law 13*: 1-30.

Groeneveld, S. 2015. 'Explaining diversity management outcomes: What can be learned from quantitative survey research?' In *The Oxford Handbook of Diversity in Organizations*, edited by R. Bendl, I. Bleijenbergh, E. Henttonen, and A. Mills, 281-97. Oxford: Oxford University Press.

Hall, S., C. Critcher, T. Jefferson, J. Clarke, and B. Roberts. 1978. *Policing the Crisis. Mugging, the State and Law & Order*. London: Palgrave MacMillan.

Hall, S. 2002. 'Race, articulation, and societies structured in dominance'. In *Race Critical Theories*, edited by P. Essed and D.T. Goldberg, 38-68. Oxford: Blackwell Publishers.

Hallsworth, S. 2006. 'Racial targeting and social control: Looking behind the police'. *Critical Criminology 14* (3): 293-311.

Hannerz, U. 1999. 'Reflections on varieties of culturespeak'. *European Journal of Cultural Studies 2* (3): 393-407.

Hannerz, U. 2010. 'Diversity is our business'. *American Anthropologist 112* (4): 539-51.

Hansen, B. 2006. 'Performers of sovereignty: On the privatization of security in urban South Africa'. *Critique of Anthropology 26* (3): 279-95.

Harcourt, B. 2007. *Against Prediction: Profiling, Policing, and Punishment in the Actuarial Age*. Chicago, IL: University of Chicago Press.

Harkin, D.M. 2015. 'The police and punishment: Understanding the pains of policing'. *Theoretical Criminology 19* (1): 43-58.

Harris, D.A. 2006. 'U.S. experiences with racial and ethnic profiling: History, current issues, and the future'. *Critical Criminology 14*: 213-39.

Haugerud, A. 2016. 'Public anthropology in 2015: *Charlie Hebdo*, Black lives matter, migrants, and more'. *American Anthropologist 118* (3): 585-601.

Heijink, K., H. Andersson, J.T.A.M. Berkhout, E.E. Nordholt, P.C. Peters, M.A. Straver, and J. Wiarda. 1977. *Politie in Verandering*. Viewed 8 September 2017, <http://www.politieacademie.nl>.

Herbert, S. 2006. *Citizens, Cops, and Power. Recognizing the Limits of Community*. Chicago, IL: University of Chicago Press.

Hertogh, M. 2011. 'Loyalists, Cynics, and Outsiders: Who are the critics of the criminal justice system in the UK and the Netherlands?' *International Journal of Law in Context 7* (1): 31-46.

Hertogh, M. 2014. '"No justice, no peace!" Conceptualizing legal alienation in the aftermath of the Trayvon Martin case'. In *Law, Society and Community: Socio-Legal Essays in Honour of Roger Cotterrell*, edited by R. Nobles and D. Schiff, 187-206. Aldershot: Ashgate Publishing.

Herzfeld, M. 1992. *The Social Production of Indifference. Exploring the Symbolic Roots of Western Bureaucracy*. Chicago, IL: University of Chicago Press.

Ho, K. 2009. *Liquidated. An Ethnography of Wall Street*. Durham, NC: Duke University Press.

Hoebel, E.A. 1954. *The Law of Primitive Man. A Study in Comparative Legal Dynamics*. Cambridge, MA: Harvard University Press.

Höpfl, H.M. 2006. 'Post-bureaucracy and Weber's "modern" bureaucrat'. *Journal of Organizational Change Management 19* (1): 8-21.

Hornberger, J. 2004. '"My police—your police": The informal privatization of the police in the inner city of Johannesburg'. *African Studies 63* (2): 213-30.

Hornberger, J. 2011. *Policing and Human Rights: The Meaning of Violence and Justice in the Everyday Policing of Johannesburg*. Abingdon: Routledge.

Hornberger, J. 2013. 'From General to Commissioner to General: On the popular state of policing in South Africa'. *Law & Social Inquiry 38* (3): 598-614.

Huey, L. 2007. *Negotiating Demands: The Politics of Skid Row Policing in Edinburgh, San Francisco, and Vancouver.* Toronto: University of Toronto Press.

Hughes, E. 1984. *The Sociological Eye. Selected Papers.* New Brunswick: Transaction Publishers, original work published 1971.

Hymes, D. 1996. *Ethnography, Linguistics, Narrative Inequality: Toward an Understanding of Voice.* London: Taylor & Francis.

Jaffe, R. 2013. 'The hybrid state: Crime and citizenship in urban Jamaica'. *American Ethnologist 40* (4): 734-48.

Jaffe, R. 2015. 'From Maroons to dons: Sovereignty, violence and law in Jamaica'. *Critique of Anthropology 35* (1): 47-63.

Jauregui, B. 2013. 'Dirty anthropology: Epistemologies of violence and ethnical entanglements in police ethnography'. In *Policing and Contemporary Governance. The Anthropology of Police in Practice,* edited by W. Garriot, 125-53. New York, NY: Palgrave MacMillan.

Jauregui, B. 2014. 'Provisional agency in India: *Jugaad* and legitimation of corruption'. *American Ethnologist 41* (1): 76-91.

Jauregui, B. 2016. *Provisional Authority: Police, Order, and Security in India.* Chicago, IL: University of Chicago Press.

Jencks, C. 2014. 'On America's front lines'. *The New York Review of Books LXI* (15): 34-6.

Johansen, M-L. 2017. 'Policing radicalization: The reconfiguration of dangerous hotspots in the city'. Paper presented at the workshop *Urban Policing and Practices of B/Ordering,* Copenhagen, 22-3 June.

Johnson, J.L. 2007. 'When the poor police themselves: Public insecurity and extralegal criminal-justice administration in Mexico'. In *Legitimacy and Criminal Justice: International Perspectives,* edited by T. Tyler, 167-85. New York, NY: Russell Sage Foundation.

Jones, T., R. Van Steden, and H. Boutellier. 2009. 'Pluralisation of policing in England & Wales and the Netherlands: Exploring similarity and difference'. *Policing & Society 19* (3): 282-99.

Júnior, D.P. and J. Muniz. 2006. '"Stop or I'll call the police!" The idea of police, or the effects of police encounters over time'. *British Journal of Criminology 46*: 234-57.

Kallinikos, J. 2003. 'Work, human agency and organizational forms: An anatomy of fragmentation'. *Organization Studies 24* (4): 595-618.

Kallinikos, J. 2004. 'The social foundation of the bureaucratic order'. *Organization 11* (1): 13-36.

Kallinikos, J. 2007. 'The institution of bureaucracy: Administration, pluralism, democracy'. *Economy and Society 35* (4): 611-27.

Kamerbrief Directoraat-Generaal Politie. 2015. *Reactie op het Rapport 'A Public Anthropology of Policing-Law Enforcement and Migrants in the Netherlands'.* Viewed 8 September 2017, <http://www.rijksoverheid.nl>.

Karandinos, G., L.K. Hart, F.M. Castrillo, and P. Bourgois. 2014. 'The moral economy of violence in the US inner city'. *Current Anthropology 55* (1): 1-22.

Karpiak, K. 2016a. 'No longer merely "good to think": The new anthropology of police as a mode of critical thought'. *Theoretical Criminology 20* (4): 419-29.

Karpiak, K. 2016b. 'The anthropology of police'. In *The Sage Handbook of Global Policing*, edited by B. Bradford, B. Jauregui, I. Loader, and J. Steinberg, 102-21. London: Sage.

Karpiak, K. and W. Garriott. 2018. 'Introduction: Disciplines, fields, and problems'. In *The Anthropology of Police*, edited by K. Karpiak and W. Garriott, 1–20. London: Routledge.

King, W.R. and T.H. Dunn. 2006. 'Dumping: Police-initiated transjurisdictional transport of troublesome persons'. In *The Police and Society. Touchstone Readings*, edited by V.E. Kappeler, 385-402. Long Grove, IL: Waveland Press.

Kyed, H.M. 2017. 'Inside the police stations in Maputo City: Between legality and legitimacy'. In *Police in Africa*, edited by J. Beek, M. Göpfert, O. Owen, and J. Steinberg, 213-30. London: Hurst & Company.

Lamphere, L. 2003. 'The perils and prospects for an engaged anthropology. A view from the United States'. *Social Anthropology 11* (2): 153-68.

Lane, C.M. 2009. 'Man enough to let my wife support me. How changing models of career and gender are reshaping the experiences of unemployment'. *American Ethnologist 36* (4): 681-92.

Lane, C.M. 2011. *A Company of One. Insecurity, Independence, and the New World of White-Collar Unemployment*. Ithaca, NY: Cornell University Press.

Larrabee, J.A. 1997. '"DWB (Driving While Black)" and equal protection: The realities of an unconstitutional police practice'. *Journal of Law and Policy 6* (1): 291-329.

Lassiter, L.E. 2005. 'Collaborative ethnography and public anthropology'. *Current Anthropology 46* (1): 83-106.

LECD. 2006. *Jaarverslag 2006. Het Jaar van de Bewustwording*. Apeldoorn: Politieacademie.

Leerkes, A., G. Engbersen, and J. van der Leun. 2012a. 'Crime among irregular immigrants and the influence of internal border control'. *Crime, Law and Social Change 58*: 15-38.

Leerkes, A., M. Varsanyi, and G. Engbersen. 2012b. 'Local limits to migration control: Practices of selective migration policing in a restrictive national policy context'. *Police Quarterly 15* (4): 446-75.

Legge, K. 1995. *Human Resource Management: Rhetorics and Realities*. London: MacMillan Press.

Lévi-Strauss, C. 1955. *Tristes Tropiques*. London: Penguin Books.

Lewis-Kraus, G. 2016. The trials of Alice Goffman. *The New York Times Magazine*, 12 January.

Lipsky, M. 2010. *Street-Level Bureaucracy. Dilemmas of the Individual in Public Services. 30th Anniversary Expanded Edition*. New York, NY: Russell Sage Foundation, original work published 1980.

Loftus, B. 2009. *Police Culture in a Changing World*. Oxford: Oxford University Press.

Loftus, B. 2010. 'Police occupational culture: Classic themes, altered times'. *Policing and Society 20* (1): 1-20.

Loftus, B. 2013. 'Border regimes and the sociology of policing', *Policing and Society 25* (1): 115-25.

Low, S.M. and S.E. Merry. 2010. 'Engaged anthropology: Diversity and dilemmas: An introduction to Supplement 2'. *Current Anthropology 51* (S2): 203-26.

MacClancy, J. 1996. 'Popularizing anthropology'. In *Popularizing Anthropology*, edited by J. MacClancy, and C. McDonaugh, 1-57. New York NY: Routledge.

MacClancy, J. ed. 2002a. *Exotic No More. Anthropology on the Front Lines*. Chicago, IL: University of Chicago Press.

MacClancy, J. 2002b. 'Introduction: Taking people seriously'. In *Exotic No More. Anthropology on the Front Lines*, edited by J. MacClancy, 1-14. Chicago, IL: University of Chicago Press.

MacClancy, J. 2017. 'Transcending the academic/public divide in the transmission of theory: Raglan, diffusionism, and mid-century anthropology'. *History and Anthropology 28* (2): 235-53.

Maguire, M., C. Frois, and N. Zurawski. 2014. 'Introduction. The anthropology of security: Prospects, retrospects and aims'. In *The Anthropology of Security. Perspectives from the Frontline of Policing, Counter-Terrorism and Border Control*, edited by M. Maguire, C. Frois, and N. Zurawski, 1-24. London: Pluto Press.

Manning, P.K. 2010. *Democratic Policing in a Changing World*. Boulder, CO: Paradigm Publishers.

Malinowski, B. 1926. *Crime and Custom in Savage Society*. London: Transaction Publishers.

Maravelias, C. 2007. 'Freedom at work in the age of post-bureaucratic organization'. *Ephemera. Theory & Politics in Organization* 7 (4): 555-74.

Marcus, G.E. 1998. *Ethnography through Thick and Thin*. Princeton, NJ: Princeton University Press.

Martin, J.T. 2007. 'A reasonable balance of law and sentiment: Social order in democratic Taiwan from the policeman's point of view'. *Law & Society Review 41* (3): 665-97.

Martin, J.T. 2013a. 'Legitimate force in a particularistic democracy: Street police and outlaw legislators in the Republic of China on Taiwan'. *Law & Social Inquiry 38* (3): 615-42.

Martin, J.T. 2013b. 'Police as linking principle: Rethinking police culture in contemporary Taiwan'. In *Policing and Contemporary*

Governance: The Anthropology of Police in Practice, edited by W. Garriott, 157-80. New York, NY: Palgrave Macmillan.
Martin, J.T. 2016. 'Calling the police, more or less democratically'. *Theoretical Criminology 20* (4): 462-81.
Martin, J.T. 2018. 'Police culture: What it is, what it does, and what we should do with it'. In *The Anthropology of Police*, edited by K. Karpiak and W. Garriott, 34–53. London: Routledge.
Maryns, K. and J. Blommaert. 2002. 'Pretextuality and pretextual gaps: On de/refining linguistic inequality'. *Pragmatics 12* (1): 11-30.
Merry, S.E. 2000. *Colonizing Hawai'i: The cultural power of law*. Princeton, NJ: Princeton University Press.
Merry, S.E. 2010. 'What is legal culture? An anthropological perspective'. *The Journal of Comparative Law 5*(2): 40-58.
Miller, J. 2010. 'Stop and search in England. A reformed tactic or business as usual?' *British Journal of Criminology 50* (4): 954-74.
Miller, P. and N. Rose. 1988. 'The Tavistock Programme. The government of subjectivity and social life'. *Sociology 22* (2): 171-92.
Miller, P. and N. Rose. 1994. 'On therapeutic authority: Psychoanalytical expertise under advanced liberalism'. *History of the Human Sciences 7* (3): 29-64.
Mills, C.W. 1951. *White Collar. The American Middle Classes*. Oxford: Oxford University Press.
Mills, C.W. 1959. *The Sociological Imagination*. Oxford: Oxford University Press.
Ministerie van Binnenlandse Zaken en Koninkrijksrelaties. 1996. *Politie en diversiteit 1996–2000*. Den Haag: Ministerie van Binnenlandse Zaken en Koninkrijksrelaties.
Ministerie van Veiligheid en Justitie. 2016. *Recht en veiligheid in de 21e Eeuw: Discussiestuk over de strategische uitdagingen voor het Ministerie van Veiligheid en Justitie*. Viewed 8 September 2017, <http://www.rijksoverheid.nl>.
Moss, P. and C. Tilly. 1996. '"Soft" skills and race: An investigation of black men's employment problems'. *Work and Occupation 23* (3): 252-76.
Mutsaers, P. 2012. *Aanpak bureaucratie bij politie is gevaarlijk*. Viewed 9 September 2014, <http://www.socialevraagstukken.nl>.
Mutsaers, P., H.G. Siebers, A. de Ruijter, and T. Jochoms. 2012. 'Nationalisering van de Nederlandse Politie'. *Openbaar Bestuur 22* (4): 2-6.
Mutsaers, P. 2013. *Mediation dreigt werknemersrechten te ondergraven*. Viewed 9 September 2014, <http://www.socialevraagstukken.nl>.
Mutsaers, P. and H. Siebers. 2013. 'Low intensity ethnic cleansing in the Netherlands'. *Tilburg Papers in Culture Studies 38*: 1-25.
Mutsaers, P. 2014a. 'An ethnographic study of the policing of internal borders in the Netherlands: Synergies between criminology and anthropology'. *British Journal of Criminology 54* (5): 831-48.

Mutsaers, P. 2014b. '"All of me". Psychologizing Turkish-Dutch police officers in the Netherlands'. *Anthropology of Work Review 35* (2): 72-83.

Mutsaers, P. 2014c. *Ethnic profiling as a societal institution in the Netherlands*. Viewed 24 January 2015, <http://www.anthropoliteia.net>.

Mutsaers, P. 2014d. *Psychological operations and the policing of migrants in the Netherlands*. Viewed 24 January 2015, <http://bordercriminologies.law.ox.ac.uk>.

Mutsaers, P., H. Siebers, and A. De Ruijter. 2014. 'Becoming a minority: Ethno-manufacturing in the Netherlands'. In *Becoming Minority: How Discourses and Policies Produce Minorities in Europe and India*, edited by J. Tripathy and S. Padmanabhan, 174-95. New Delhi: Sage.

Mutsaers, P. 2015a. *A Public Anthropology of Policing: Law Enforcement and Migrants in the Netherlands*. Tilburg: Tilburg University.

Mutsaers, P. 2015b. *Charlie Hebdo, purity, danger and taboo: Lessons from Mary Douglas*. Viewed 24 January 2015, <http://www.anthropoliteia.net>.

Mutsaers, P. 2015c. 'Van ethnic profiling naar thickening borderlands'. *Cahiers Politiestudies 35* (2): 75-92.

Mutsaers, P., J. Simpson, and K. Karpiak. 2015. 'The anthropology of police as public anthropology'. *American Anthropologist. 117* (4): 786-9.

Mutsaers, P. and M.-L. Trux. 2015. 'In search of "the real". The subversive potential of ethnography in the field of diversity management'. In *The Oxford Handbook of Diversity in Organizations*, edited by R. Bendl, I. Bleijenbergh, E. Henttonen, and A. Mills, 317-36. Oxford: Oxford University Press.

Mutsaers, P. 2016a. 'Review of The Anthropology of Security: Perspectives from the Frontline of Policing, Counter-Terrorism and Border Control, edited by M. Maguire, C. Frois and N. Zurawski (London: Pluto Press)'. *Theoretical Criminology 20* (4): 523-24.

Mutsaers, P. 2016b. 'Contributions to an anthropology of work. On the role of psycho-technicians in the management of freedom within the Dutch police'. *Critique of Anthropology 36* (2): 122-44.

Mutsaers, P. 2016c. 'Rechtscultuur en rechtsvervreemding in Nederland'. *Beleid en Maatschappij 43* (4): 169-72.

Mutsaers, P. 2016d. *The police anthropologist an a**hole?* Viewed 8 September 2017, <http://www.law.ox.ac.uk>.

Mutsaers, P. and T. Van Nuenen. 2018. 'Protesting police'. In *The Anthropology of Police*, edited by K. Karpiak and W. Garriott, 153–71. London: Routledge.

Mutsaers, P. 2019. '#BlackLivesMatter: Understanding anti-police protest as a cultural practice'. In *Cultural Practices of Victimhood*, edited by M. Hoondert, P. Mutsaers, and W. Arfman, 167–92. London: Routledge.

Mutsaers, P. forthcoming. 'Changing Chrontopes of Policing: TimeSpace, Race and Juvenile Justice in Amsterdam'. *Environment and Planning D: Society & Space*.

Noon, M. 2007. 'The fatal flaws of diversity and the business case for ethnic minorities'. *Work, Employment & Society 21* (4): 773-84.

NRC Handelsblad. 2015. Discriminatie door de politie is dus meer dan alleen incident. 11 June.

Nuhrat, Y. 2018. 'Policed bodies and subjectivities: Football fans at the Gezi uprising in Turkey'. In *The Anthropology of Police*, edited by K. Karpiak and W. Garriott. London: Routledge.

Ombudsman. 2012. *Vreemdelingenbewaring: Strafregime of maatregel om uit te zetten?* Viewed 5 October 2013, <http://www.nationaleombudsman.nl>.

O'Neill, M. and B. Loftus. 2013. 'Policing and surveillance of the marginal: Everyday contexts of social control'. *Theoretical Criminology 17* (4): 437-54.

Ong, A. 1987. *Spirits of Resistance and Capitalist Discipline. Factory Women in Malaysia*. Albany, NY: State University of New York Press.

Ong, S.J. and A. Collier. 2005. 'Global assemblages, anthropological problems'. In *Global Assemblages: Technology, Politics, and Ethics as Anthropological Problems*, edited by A. Ong and S.J. Collier, 3-21. Malden: Blackwell Publishing.

Open Society Justice Initiative. 2012. *Reducing Ethnic Profiling in the European Union. A Handbook of Good Practices*. New York, NY: Open Society Foundations.

Opstelten, I. 2012. 'Minder regels, meer op straat: Aanval op de bureaucratie en versterking van vakmanschap in de basispolitiezorg en recherche'. Viewed 12 September 2017, <http://www.rijksoverheid.nl>.

Orr, J. 2004. 'The militarization of inner space'. *Critical Sociology 30* (2): 451-81.

Osterweil, M. 2013. 'Rethinking public anthropology through epistemic politics and theoretical practice'. *Cultural Anthropology 28* (4): 598-620.

Owen, O. 2016. 'Government properties: The Nigeria police force as total institution?' *Africa 86* (1): 37-58.

Owen, O. and S.J. Cooper-Knock. 2014. 'Between vigilantism and bureaucracy: Improving our understanding of police work in Nigeria and South Africa'. *Theoretical Criminology 19* (3): 355-75.

Pauschinger, D. 2017. '*Drying ice* and the loss of control to gain control: Understanding Rio's police and their everyday borders'. Paper presented at the workshop *Urban Policing and Practices of B/Ordering*, Copenhagen, 22–23 June.

Peacock, J.L. 1997. 'The future of anthropology'. *American Anthropologist 99* (1): 9-29.

Penglase, B. 2013. 'Invading the *favela:* Echoes of police practices among Brazil's urban poor'. In *Policing and Contemporary Governance: The Anthropology of Police in Practice*, edited by W. Garriott, 31-52. New York, NY: Palgrave MacMillan.

Peutz, N. 2006. 'Embarking on an anthropology of removal'. *Current Anthropology 47* (2): 217-41.

Poelert, B. 2006. 'Van diversiteit als social issue naar multiculturele competenties'. *Het Tijdschrift voor de Politie 68* (10): 25-9.

Pratten, D. 2008. 'Introduction. The politics of protection: Perspectives on vigilantism in Nigeria'. *Africa 78* (1): 1-15.

Prenzler, T. 2000. 'Civilian oversight of police: A test of capture theory'. *British Journal of Criminology 40*: 659-74.

Punch, M. 2003. 'Rotten orchards: "Pestilence," police misconduct and system failure'. *Policing & Society 13* (2): 171-96.

Punch, M., K. van der Vijver, O. Zoomer. 2002. 'Dutch "COP". Developing community policing in the Netherlands'. *Policing: An International Journal of Police Strategies & Management 25* (1): 60-79.

Raaijmakers, M. 2008. *Authentiek Verbinden. Diversiteits-management vanuit een Veranderkundig Perspectief.* PhD Thesis, Groningen: Rijksuniversiteit Groningen.

Rabinow, P. 1977. *Reflections on Fieldwork in Morocco*. Berkeley, CA: University of California Press.

Radcliffe-Brown, A.R. 1940. 'On joking relationships'. *Africa 13* (3): 195-210.

Rebhun, L.A. 1999. *The Heart is Unknown Country. Love in the Changing Economy of Northeast Brazil*. Stanford. CA: Stanford University Press.

Reub, T. 2016. Verdachte agenten met steun van de baas. *NRC Handelsblad*, 6 October.

Reuss-Ianni, E. 1983. *Two Cultures of Policing. Street Cops and Management Cops*. New Brunswick: Transaction Publishers.

Robb Larkins, E. 2013. *The Spectacular Favela: Violence in Modern Brazil*. Oakland, CA: University of California.

Robb Larkins, E. 2015. *The Spectacular Favela: Violence in Modern Brazil*. Oakland, CA: University of California Press.

Rodgers, D. and B. O'Neill. 2012. 'Infrastructural violence: Introduction to a special issue'. *Ethnography 13*: 401-12.

Rodrigues, P. and M.A.H. van der Woude. 2016. 'Proactieve politiecontrole en onderscheid naar etniciteit of nationaliteit'. *Nederlands Juristenblad 32*: 2294-302.

Roitman, J. 2006. 'The ethics of illegality in the Chad Basin'. In *Law and Disorder in the Postcolony*, edited by J. and J.L. Comaroff, 247-72. Chicago, IL: University of Chicago Press.

Rosas, G. 2006. 'The thickening borderlands. Diffused exceptionality and "immigrant" social struggles during the "War on Terror"'. *Cultural Dynamics 18* (3): 335-49.

Rosas, G. 2012. *Barrio Libre. Criminalizing States and Delinquent Refusals of the New Frontier*. Durham, NC: Duke University Press.

Rose, N. 1989. *Governing the Soul. The Shaping of the Private Self.* London: Free Association Books.

Rose, N. 1996. 'Governing "advanced" liberal democracies'. In *Foucault and Political Reason*, edited by A. Barry, T. Osborne, and N. Rose, 37-64. New York, NY: Routledge.

Rosen, L. 2006. *Law as Culture: An Invitation*. Princeton, NJ: Princeton University Press.

Rumford, C. 2012. 'Towards a multiperspectival study of borders'. *Geopolitics 17* (4): 887-902.

Sabloff, J.A. 2011. 'Where have you gone, Margaret Mead? Anthropology and public intellectuals'. *American Anthropology 113* (3): 408-16.

Sausdal, D. 2018. 'Pleasures of policing: An additional analysis of xenophobia'. *Theoretical Criminology 22* (2): 226–42..

Savage, S.P. 2013. 'Seeking "civilianess": Police complaints and the civilian control model of oversight'. *British Journal of Criminology 53*: 886-904.

Scheper-Hughes, N. 2004. 'Parts unknown. Undercover ethnography of the organs-trafficking underworld'. *Ethnography 5* (1): 29-73.

Scheper-Hughes, N. 2006. 'Death squads and democracy in Northeast Brazil'. In *Law and Disorder in the Postcolony*, edited by J. Comaroff and J.L. Comaroff, 150-87. Chicago, IL: University of Chicago Press.

Scheper-Hughes, N. 2009. 'Making anthropology public'. *Anthropology Today 25* (4): 1-3

Scholten, S. and P. Minderhoud. 2008. 'Regulating immigration control: Carrier sanctions in the Netherlands'. *European Journal of Migration and Law 10* (2): 123-47.

Scott, J. 1985. *Weapons of the Weak: Everyday Forms of Peasant Resistance*. New Haven, CT: Yale University Press.

Scott, J. 1990. *Domination and the Arts of Resistance: Hidden Transcripts*. New Haven, CT: Yale University Press.

Sennett, R. 1974. *The Fall of Public Man*. Cambridge: Cambridge University Press.

Sennett, R. 2008. *The Craftsman*. London: Penguin Books.

Sharma, A. and A. Gupta. eds. 2006. *The Anthropology of the State. A Reader*. Malden: Blackwell Publishing.

Shearing, C.D. and P.S. Stenning. 1983. 'Private security: Implications for social control'. *Social Problems 30* (5): 493-506.

Shields, J. and D. Grant. 2010. 'Psychologising the subject: HRM, commodification, and the objectification of labour'. *The Economic and Labour Relations Review 20* (2): 61-76.

Shore, C. and S. Wright. 2000. 'Coercive accountability: The rise of audit culture in higher education'. In *Audit Cultures. Anthropological Studies in Accountability, Ethics and the Academy*, edited by M. Strathern, 57-89. New York, NY: Routledge.

Shostak, M. 1981. *Nisa. The Life and Words of a !Kung Woman.* Cambridge, MA: Harvard University Press.

Siebers, H. 2009a. '(Post)bureaucratic organizational practices and the production of racioethnic inequality at work'. *Journal of Management and Organization 15* (1): 62-81.

Siebers, H. 2009b. 'Struggles for recognition. The politics of racioethnic identity among Dutch national tax administrators'. *Scandinavian Journal of Management 25* (1): 73-84.

Siebers, H. 2009c. 'Discrimination and cultural closure at work: Evidence from two Dutch organizations'. In *Paradoxes of Cultural Recognition: Perspectives from Norway and the Netherlands*, edited by S. Alghasi, Th. Eriksen, and H. Ghorashi, 91-109. Hampshire: Ashgate.

Siebers, H. 2010a. 'The impact of migrant-hostile discourses in media and politics on racioethnic closure in career development in the Netherlands'. *International Sociology 25* (4): 475-500.

Siebers, H. 2010b. 'Organisatiecultuur en verhulde discriminatie: Over het onthullen van discriminatie in hedendaagse organisaties'. In *Gelijke Behandeling: Oordelen en Commentaar 2009*, edited by C.J. Forder, 237-54. Nijmegen: Wolf Legal Publishers.

Siebers, H. 2017. 'What turns migrants into ethnic minorities at work? Factors erecting ethnic boundaries among Dutch police officers'. *Sociology 51* (3): 608-25.

Siebers, H. and M.H.J. Dennissen. 2015. 'Is it cultural racism? Discursive oppression and exclusion of migrants in the Netherlands'. *Current Sociology 63* (3): 470-89.

Siebers, H. and J. Van Gastel. 2015. 'Why migrants earn less: In search of the factors producing the ethno-migrant pay gap in a Dutch public organization'. *Work, Employment and Society 29* (3): 371-91.

Silverstein, M. 2005. 'Axes of evals: Token versus type interdiscursivity'. *Journal of Linguistic Anthropology 15* (1): 6-22.

Skolnick, J.H. 1966. *Justice without Trial: Law Enforcement in Democratic Society*. New Orleans, LO: Quid Pro Books.

Smith, D.J. 2004. 'The Bakassi boys: Vigilantism, violence, and political imagination in Nigeria'. *Cultural Anthropology 19* (3): 429-55.

Smith, D.J. 2007. 'The foundations of legitimacy'. In *Legitimacy and Criminal Justice: International Perspectives*, edited by T. Tyler, 30-58. New York, NY: Russell Sage Foundation.

Steinberg, J. 2012. 'Security and disappointment: Policing, freedom, and xenophobia in South Africa'. *British Journal of Criminology 52*: 345-60.

Stinchcombe, J.B. 1980. 'Beyond bureaucracy: A reconsideration of the "professional" police'. *Police Studies: The International Review of Police Development 3*: 49-60.

Thompson, P. 2011. 'The trouble with HRM'. *Human Resource Management Journal 21* (4): 355-67.

Tomaskovic-Devey, D., M. Mason, and M. Zingraff. 2004. 'Looking for the driving while black phenomenon: Conceptualizing racial bias processes and their associated distributions'. *Police Quarterly* 7 (1): 3-29.

Tomaskovic-Devey, D., C.P. Wright, R. Czaja, and K. Miller. 2006. 'Self-report of police speeding report stops by race: Results from the North Carolina Reserve Record Check Survey'. *Journal of Quantitative Criminology* 22: 279-97.

Townley, B. 1993. 'Foucault, power/knowledge, and its relevance for human resource management'. *The Academy of Management Review 18* (3): 518-45.

Tucker, J. 1999. *The Therapeutic Corporation*. Oxford: Oxford University Press.

Tyler, T. 2006. *Why People Obey the Law*. Oxford: Princeton University Press.

Urciuoli, B. 2008. 'Skills and selves in the new workplace'. *American Ethnologist 35* (2): 211-28.

Urciuoli, B. 2010. 'Entextualizing diversity: Semiotic incoherence in institutional discourse'. *Language & Communication 30* (1): 48-57.

Van der Vijver, K. and O. Zoomer. 2004. 'Evaluating community policing in the Netherlands'. *European Journal of Crime, Criminal Law, and Criminal Justice* 12 (3): 251-67.

Van der Aa, J. 2012. 'Helping adolescents and their families in Antwerp'. *Dante Magazine* 6 (1): 20-2.

Van der Leun, J.P. and M.A.H. van der Woude. 2011. 'Ethnic profiling in the Netherlands? A reflection on expanding preventive powers, ethnic profiling and a changing social and political context'. *Policing & Society: An International Journal of Research and Policy 21* (4): 444-55.

Van der Leun, J.P., M.A.H. van der Woude, R.D. Vijverberg, R.P.M. Vrijhoef, and A.J. Leupen. 2014. *Etnisch Profileren in Den Haag? Een Verkennend Onderzoek naar Beslissingen en Opvattingen op Straat*. Den Haag: Boom Lemma.

Van der Sluis, A., P. Marks, and V. Bekker, 2011. 'Nodal policing in the Netherlands: Strategic and normative considerations on an evolving practice'. *Policing* 5(4): 365-71.

Van der Woude, M.A.H., J.P. van der Leun, and J-A.A. Nijland. 2014. 'Crimmigration in the Netherlands'. *Law & Social Inquiry 39* (3): 560-79.

Van der Zee, K.I. and J.P. van Oudenhoven. 2001. 'The multicultural personality questionnaire: Reliability and validity of self- and other ratings of multicultural effectiveness'. *Journal of Research in Personality 35* (3): 278-88.

Van Liempt, I. 2011. '"And then one day they *All* moved to Leicester": The relocation of Somalis from the Netherlands to the UK explained'. *Population, Space and Place* 17 (3): 254-66.

Van Maanen, J. 1978. 'The asshole'. In *Policing: A View from the Street*, edited by P.K. Manning and J. Van Maanen, 221-38. Santa Monica, CA: Goodyear Publishing Company.

Van Maanen, J. 1979. 'The fact of fiction in organizational ethnography'. *Administrative Science Quarterly 24* (4): 539-50.

Van Maanen, J. 1988. *Tales of the Field. On Writing Ethnography.* Chicago, IL: University of Chicago Press.

Van Maanen, J. 2010. 'Ethnography as work: Some rules of engagement'. *Journal of Management Studies 48* (1): 218-34.

Van Steden, R. 2002. 'Politiefunctie in private handen: De ontwikkeling van commerciele beveiliging en opsporing in Nederland'. *Tijdschrift voor Veiligheid en Veiligheidszorg 1* (3): 3-11.

Van Steden, R. 2007. *Privatizing Policing: Describing and Explaining the Growth of Private Security.* Den Haag: Boom Juridische Uitgevers.

Van Veelen, A. 2016. De politie moet geen jachttrofeeën twitteren. *NRC Handelsblad*, 4 November.

Verdery, K. 1996. *What Was Socialism, and What Comes Next?* Princeton, NJ: Princeton University Press.

Verdery, K. 1999. *The Political Lives of Dead Bodies: Reburial and Postsocialist Change.* New York, NY: Columbia University Press.

Verdery, K. 2018. '"The boys with blue eyes": An anthropology of a secret police'. In *The Anthropology of Police*, edited by K. Karpiak and W. Garriott, 101–18. London: Routledge.

Vine, D. 2011. '"Public anthropology" in its second decade: Robert Borofsky's Center for a public anthropology'. *American Anthropologist 113* (2): 336-49.

Vriesema, J. and G. Kruyt. 1987. *Binnen komen, binnen blijven. Verslag van een onderzoek naar beleid en uitvoering van instroom, opleiding en integratie van allochtone agenten in de korpsen Gemeentepolitie Amsterdam, Den Haag en Rotterdam.* Den Haag: Ministerie van Sociale Zaken en Werkgelegenheid.

Wacquant, L. 2009. *Punishing the Poor: The Neoliberal Government of Social Insecurity.* Durham, NC: Duke University Press.

Walters, W. 2002. 'Deportation, expulsion and the international police of aliens'. *Citizenship Studies 6* (3): 265-92.

Walzer, M. 1983. *Spheres of Justice. A Defense of Pluralism and Equality.* New York, NY: Basic Books.

Walzer, M. 1984. 'Liberalism and the art of separation'. *Political Theory 12* (3): 315-30.

Watson, T.J. 2004. 'HRM and critical social science analysis'. *Journal of Management Studies* 42 (3): 447-67.

Watson, T.J. 2010. 'Critical social science, pragmatism and the realities of HRM'. *The International Journal of Human Resource Management 21* (6): 915-31.

Weber, M. 1978. *Economy and Society*. Berkeley, CA: University of California Press.

Weber, L. 2002. 'The detention of asylum seekers: 20 reasons why criminologists should care'. *Current Issues in Criminal Justice 14*: 9-30.

Weber, L. 2011. '"It sounds like they shouldn't be here": Immigration checks on the streets of Sydney'. *Policing & Society: An International Journal of Research and Policy 21* (4): 456-67.

Weber, L. and B. Bowling. 2004. 'Policing migration. A framework for investigating the regulation of global mobility'. *Policing & Society: An International Journal of Research and Policy 14* (3): 195-212.

Weber, L. and B. Bowling. 2008. 'Valiant beggars and global vagabonds: Select, eject, immobilize'. *Theoretical Criminology 12* (3): 8-36.

Werkgeversvisie Politie. 2008. *Een Inspirerend Fundament*. De Bilt: Landelijk Programma HRM Politie.

Westley, W.A. 1953. 'Violence and the police'. *American Journal of Sociology 59* (1): 34-41.

Whyte, W.H. 1956. *The Organization Man*. Philadelphia, PA: University of Pennsylvania Press.

Willen, S.S. 2007. 'Toward a critical phenomenology of "illegality": State power, criminalization, and abjectivity among undocumented migrant workers in Tel Aviv, Israel'. *International Migration 45* (3): 8-36.

Wilkins, V.M. and B.N. Williams. 2008. 'Black or blue: Racial profiling and representative bureaucracy'. *Public Administration Review July/August:* 654-64.

Wilkins, V.M. and B.N. Williams. 2009. 'Representing blue: Representative bureaucracy and racial profiling in the Latino community'. *Administration & Society 40* (8): 775-98.

Wilson, J.Q. 1968. *Varieties of Police Behavior. The Management of Law & Order in Eight Communities*. Cambridge, MA: Harvard University Press.

Winthagen, T. and S. De Vries. 2011. *Leren van experts: Een zoektocht naar een groter leereffect van de inzet van de expertgroep diversiteit.* Den Haag: OBT.

Zedner, L. 2004. *Criminal Justice*. Oxford: Oxford University Press.

Zedner, L. 2010. 'Security, the State, and the citizen: The changing architecture of crime control'. *New Criminal Law Review 13*: 379-403.

Zimmerman, D.H. and D.L. Wieder. 1977. 'The diary. Diary-interview method'. *Urban Life 5* (4): 479-98.

Zoettl, P.A. 2017. 'Minor narratives: Extrajudicial punishment of youth offenders by police officers in Portugal'. *International Journal of Law, Crime and Justice 48*: 27-39.

Zouridis, S. 2016. 'Eerherstel voor de technocratie … Maar wel waarmaken, alstublieft'. In *Onder de Motorkap van de Modernisering. Essays voor Gabriël van den Brink*, edited by M. Van Hulst and T. Jansen, 131-40. Den Haag: Boom.

Index